I0024515

THE ECOSYSTEM OF EXILE POLITICS

THE ECOSYSTEM OF EXILE POLITICS

Why Proximity and Precarity Matter for Bhutan's Homeland Activists

Susan Banki

CORNELL UNIVERSITY PRESS ITHACA AND LONDON

Dedicated with the greatest of love to my family

Copyright © 2024 by Cornell University

All rights reserved. Except for brief quotations in a review, this book, or parts thereof, must not be reproduced in any form without permission in writing from the publisher. For information, address Cornell University Press, Sage House, 512 East State Street, Ithaca, New York 14850. Visit our website at cornellpress.cornell.edu.

First published 2024 by Cornell University Press

Library of Congress Cataloging-in-Publication Data

Names: Banki, Susan, 1969– author.
Title: The ecosystem of exile politics : why proximity and precarity matter for Bhutan's homeland activists / Susan Banki.
Description: Ithaca : Cornell University Press, 2024. | Includes bibliographical references and index.
Identifiers: LCCN 2024018163 (print) | LCCN 2024018164 (ebook) | ISBN 9781501778193 (hardcover) | ISBN 9781501778209 (paperback) | ISBN 9781501778216 (epub) | ISBN 9781501778223 (pdf)
Subjects: LCSH: Transnationalism—Political aspects—Bhutan. | Refugees—Political activity—Bhutan. | Political refugees—Bhutan.
Classification: LCC JV8752.8 .B36 2024 (print) | LCC JV8752.8 (ebook) | DDC 325/.21095498—dc23/eng/20240617
LC record available at https://lccn.loc.gov/2024018163
LC ebook record available at https://lccn.loc.gov/2024018164

Contents

Acknowledgments   vii

Abbreviations   ix

A Note on Terminology and Place Names   x

Maps   xi

1. Introduction   1

2. The Bhutan Back Story   17

3. The Passage of Protest   33

4. The Power of Proximity   53

5. Precarity in Exile   72

6. Expansion of the Ecosystem   92

7. Conclusion   114

Notes   125

Bibliography   149

Index   163

Acknowledgments

After sixteen years in the making, I now face the daunting task of acknowledging everyone who has had a hand in helping this book come to fruition. I came to understand the complex nature of Bhutan's refugee issues thanks to the openness of many Bhutanese Nepali refugees. Deserving special mention are I. P. Adhikari, Bhakti Bhandari, Ganga Dhungel, Om Dhungel, Y. P. Dhungel, Ratan Gazmere, Bhakta Ghimire, Ram Karki, Hari Khanal, Narayan Sharma, and R. P. Subba. Thank you for your trust. D. N. S. Dhakal was kind enough to host me at the Bhutanese Refugee Cultural Complex. I remember with great fondness the late Bhampa Rai. I recall the late Govinda Rizal, gone far too soon.

I am indebted to early workshops with generous and like-minded scholars: one was on Bhutanese refugees at the School of Oriental and African Studies, organized by Michael Hutt; another was at the University of Sydney, sponsored by the Sydney Social Sciences and Humanities Advanced Research Centre, where Nicholas Van Hear read an early version of the book and discussed it with me in depth. An Ultimate Peer Review was made somewhat less terrifying by the engaged participation of Alex Lefebvre, Caroline Lenette, Dinesh Wadiwel, Elisabeth Valiente-Riedl, Fiona Gill, Jacqui Clark, Jennifer Wilkinson, Michael Humphrey, Michelle Peterie, Phil Orchard, and Simon Rice. Colleagues at the Sydney Southeast Asia Centre—Michele Ford, Natali Pearson, Kristy Ward, and Lis Kramer—provided equal parts incisive editing and inspiration.

Many read sections of early drafts and offered generous comments, among them Alexander Betts, Anita Fabos, David Scott FitzGerald, Hannah Lewis, Jeannette Money, John Krinsky, Jonathan Gold, Martin Jones, Salo Coslovsky, Shanthi Robertson, and Susan Park. Roger Haydon and Jim Lance at Cornell University Press went beyond the call of publishing duty to help shape this book as it is today. Danielle Celermajer provided consistent and consistently helpful mentorship, especially when I just could not get past the conclusion. I am deeply saddened that the late Stephen Castles never got to see the book in print and am ever grateful for our friendship.

I thank a wonderful set of supporters who helped with parts of research along the way, from translating assorted articles, to sending long-forgotten video clips, to providing background material, to research assistance: Alison Francis, Amanda Burrell, Ben Goldsmith, Charles Simpson, Chris Marcatili, Ellen Field, Gina Hawkes, Gopal Gartoula, Grishma Rimal, John Zeleznak, Kamal Sigdel,

Mom Bishwakarma, Nicole Phillips, Peter Frey, and Priyanka Pokhrel. Stuart Rollo, in particular deserves a thousand thanks for wonderful work, especially at the last hour.

A community of friends held me close at exceedingly tough times: Cindi, Gary, Susan, John, Slav, Sophy, Dave, Lee, Gill, Ivor, Emma, Laura, and, of course, the Faffers' swimming club.

To my family I owe the greatest thanks of all, because they sacrificed the most while I was writing and offered the sweetest support nevertheless. My children Pepper and Ziggy lost out on my presence at soccer games and martial arts but kept the cuddles coming. My husband Josh has run the family activities far more effectively than I might have and has been my steadfast cheerleader and tech support, never losing hope in the face of all of life's challenges. My mother, Judy Banki, endured my quick temper while I was under pressure and kept reading and revising, even in her mid-nineties. She and my late father, Paul Banki, are the source of my passion for social justice, and to them, and my entire family, I give my most affectionate gratitude and love.

Abbreviations

AHURA	Association of Human Rights Activists
AMCC	Appeal Movement Coordinating Council
BNDP	Bhutan National Democratic Party
BPP	Bhutan People's Party
BRAVVE	Bhutanese Refugees Aiding the Victims of Violence
BRRRC	Bhutanese Refugee Representative Repatriation Committee
BSC	Bhutan State Congress
BWYEP	Bhutanese Women and Youth Empowerment Program
CDO	Chief District Officer
COHRE	Centre for Housing Rights and Evictions
DNC	Druk National Congress
DNC-D	Druk National Congress-Democratic
FCB	Food Corporation of Bhutan
GCRPPB	Global Campaign for the Release of Political Prisoners in Bhutan
GNLF	Gorkhaland National Liberation Front
HUROB	Human Rights Organization of Bhutan
IOM	International Organization for Migration
JMC	Joint Ministerial Committee
JVT	Joint Verification Team
NCSCP	National Council for Social and Cultural Promotion
NIE	National Institute of Education
NUCRA	National Refugee Coordination Unit
PFHR	People's Forum on Human Rights
RBA	Royal Bhutan Army
SAARC	South Asian Association for Regional Cooperation
SI	Socialist International
SUB	Students Union of Bhutan
UDHR	Universal Declaration of Human Rights
UFD	United Front for Democracy
UNHCR	United Nations High Commissioner for Refugees
VMF	Voluntary Migration Form

A Note on Terminology and Place Names

Ethnic Nepalis in Bhutan nearly all come from the southern districts of Bhutan and, as such, within Bhutan are called the Lhotshampa, which is the word for "Southerner" in Dzongkha, Bhutan's national language. While some researchers (including this author, in the past) have used the term Lhotshampa, it has more recently been eschewed by those who have left the country, who reject being labeled by a country that they claim has excluded them in a language that few of them speak. After consultation with several members of the population, young and old, both those who remain in Nepal and those who have resettled overseas, both political and nonpolitical, I have elected to use the term "Bhutanese Nepali," which acknowledges the homeland and also notes the ethnicity that was at least one of the causes of departure. I have also chosen not to use a hyphen between "Bhutanese" and "Nepali" in deference to an excellent discussion that suggests that the hyphen itself may be a way of reinforcing contemporary forms of (American) racialization: Andrew Nelson and Kathryn Stam, "Bhutanese or Nepali? The Politics of Ethnonym Ambiguity," *South Asia: Journal of South Asian Studies* 44, no. 4 (2021): 772–89.

For the purposes of consistency and clarity, I have adopted the most contemporary forms of many place names in this book, such as Samtse. This choice may sit at odds with some of the names used by Bhutanese refugees, who remember these places by their old names, such as Samchi. I am mindful that renaming places can have highly political overtones and that my choice to align with the current Bhutanese government may feel like a slight for those who are concerned that their histories are being erased. I hope this book, overall, does the opposite.

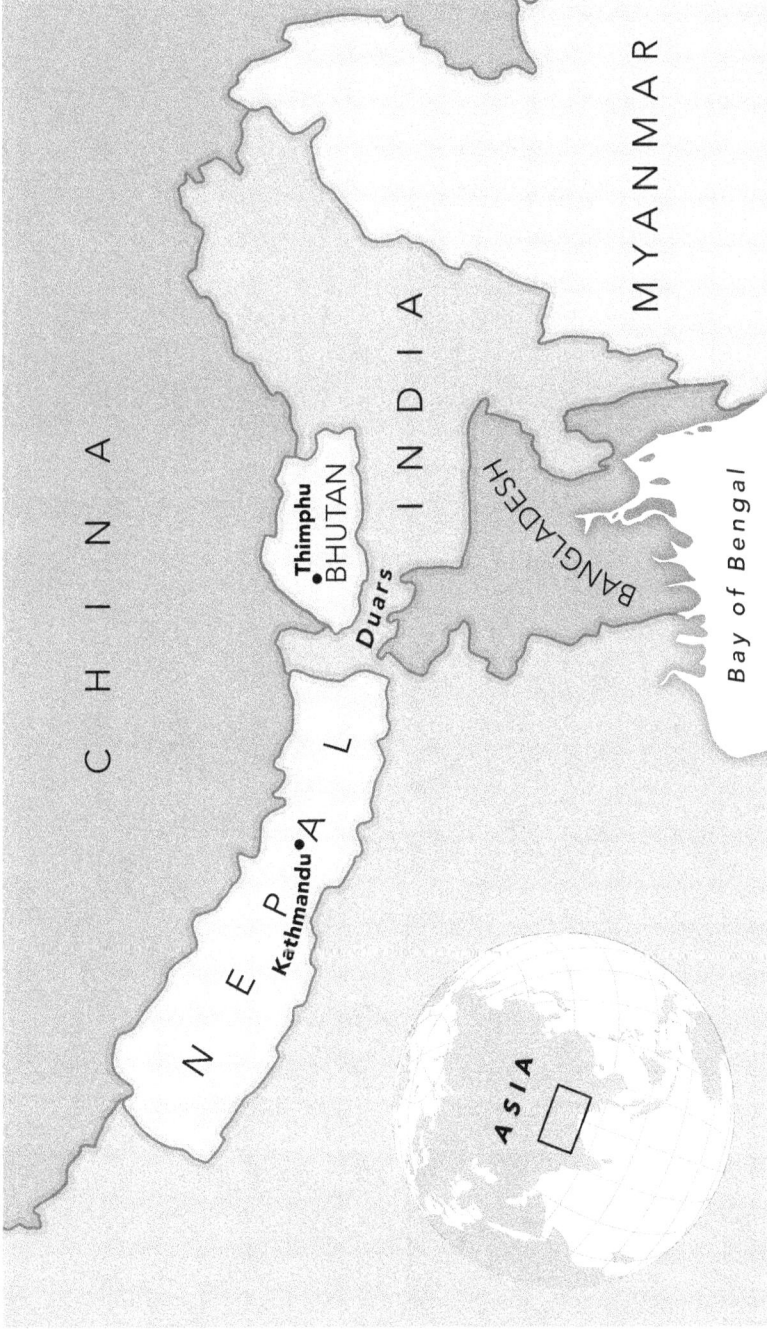

MAP 1. Regional map of Bhutan and surrounding countries

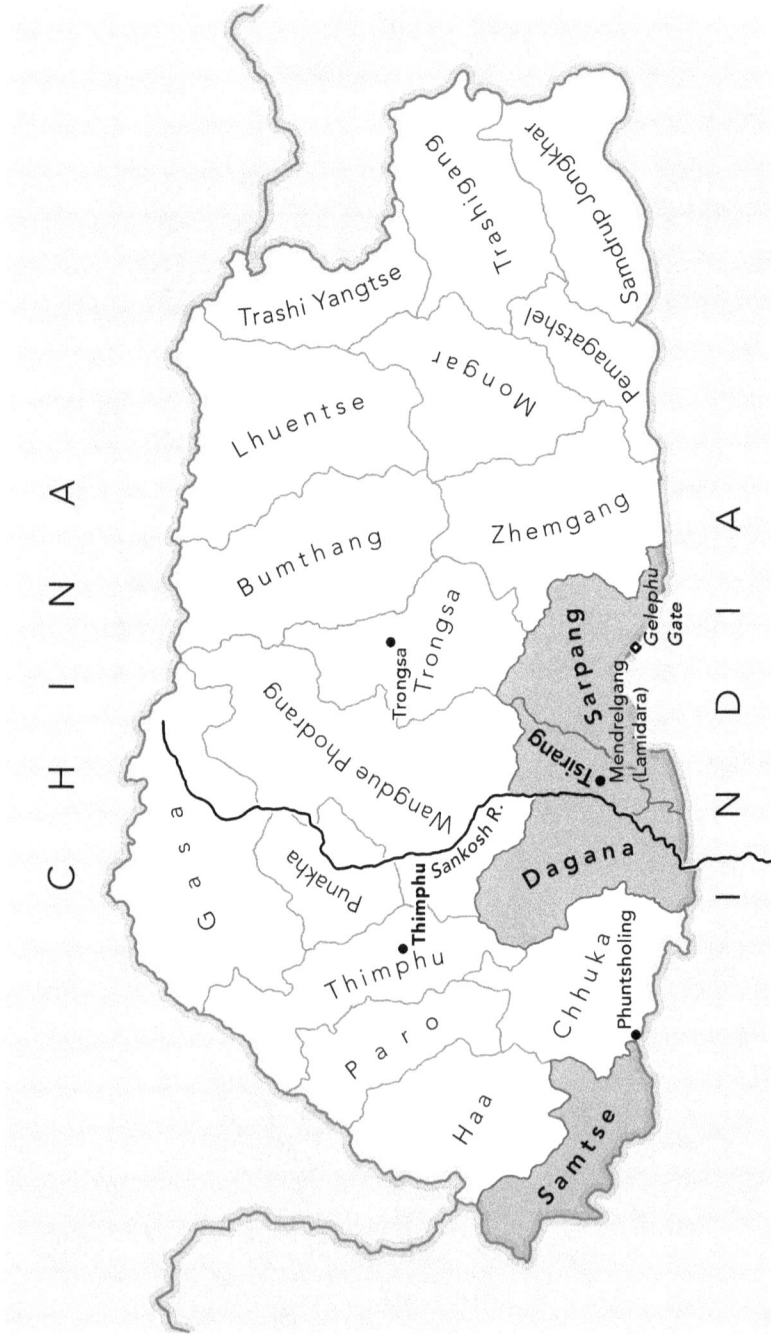

MAP 2. District map of Bhutan

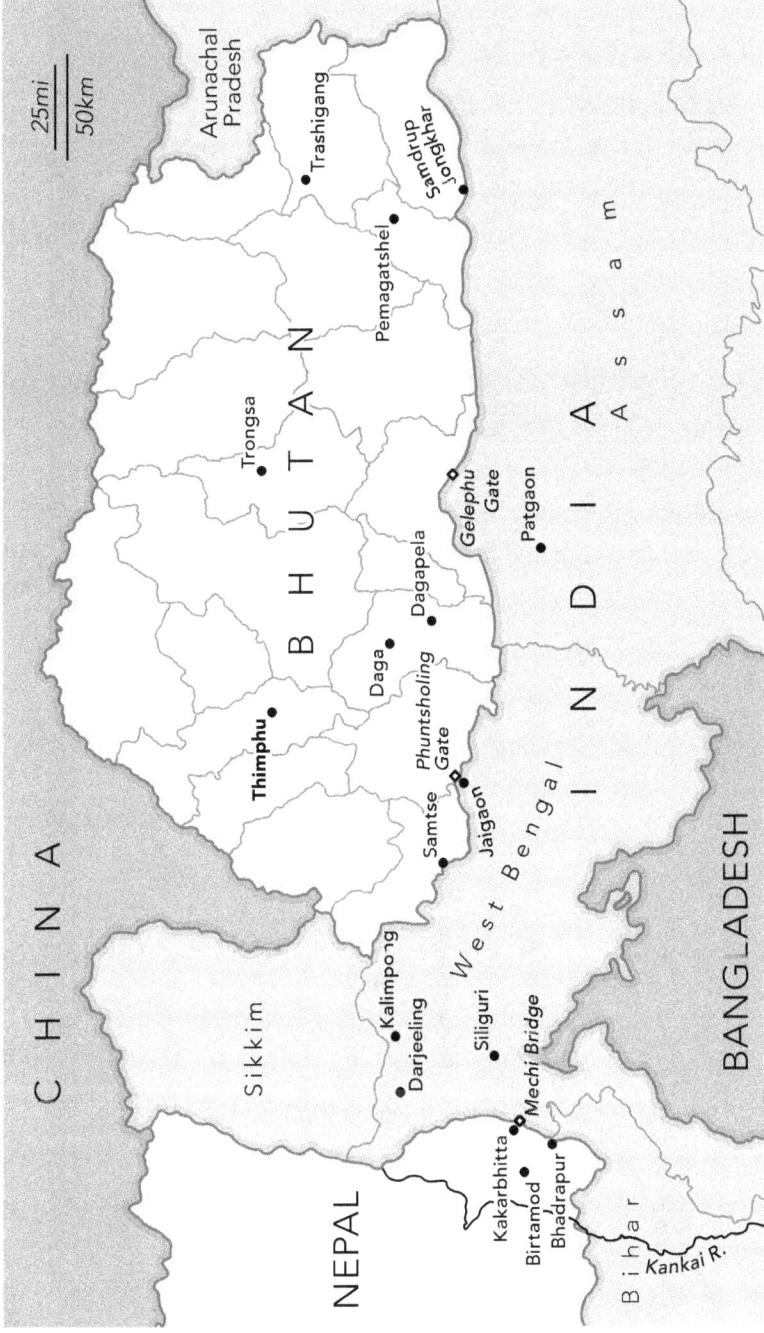

MAP 3. Sites of proximate homeland activism

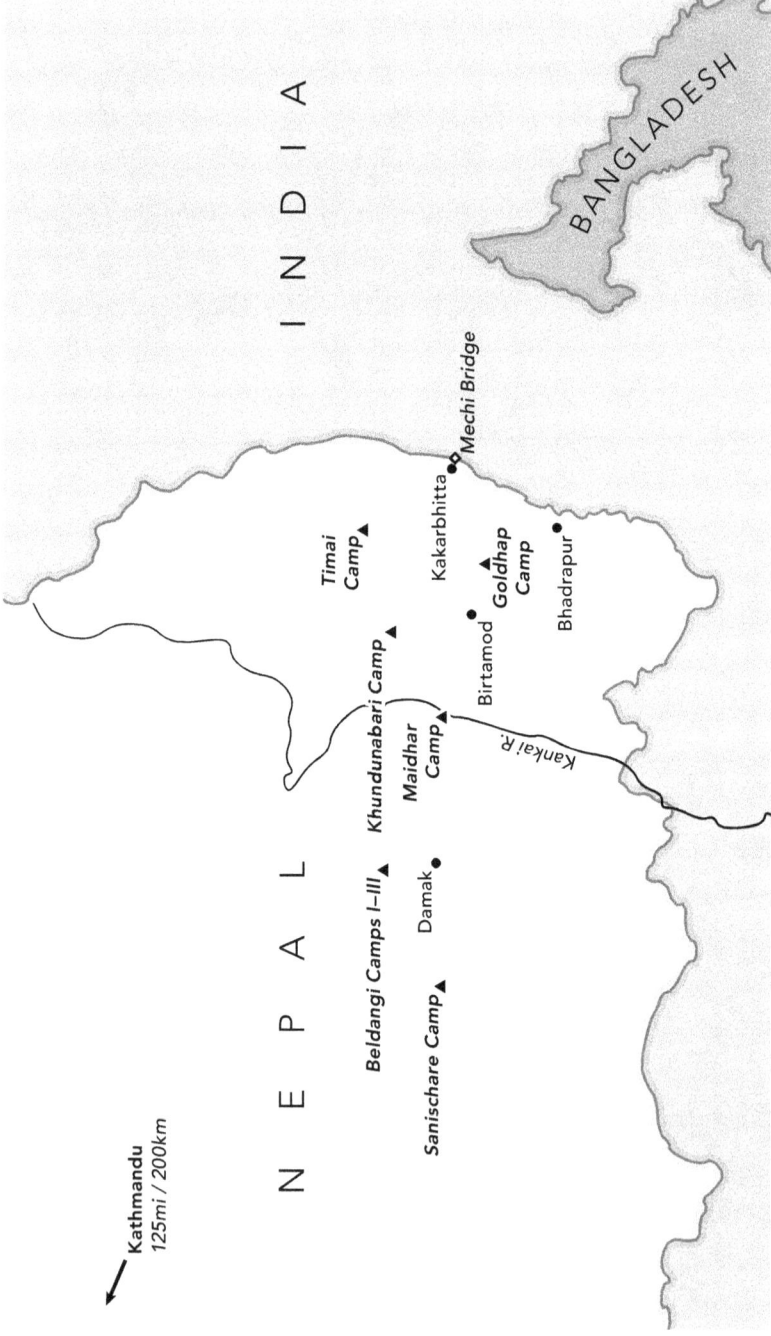

MAP 4. Bhutanese refugee camps in eastern Nepal

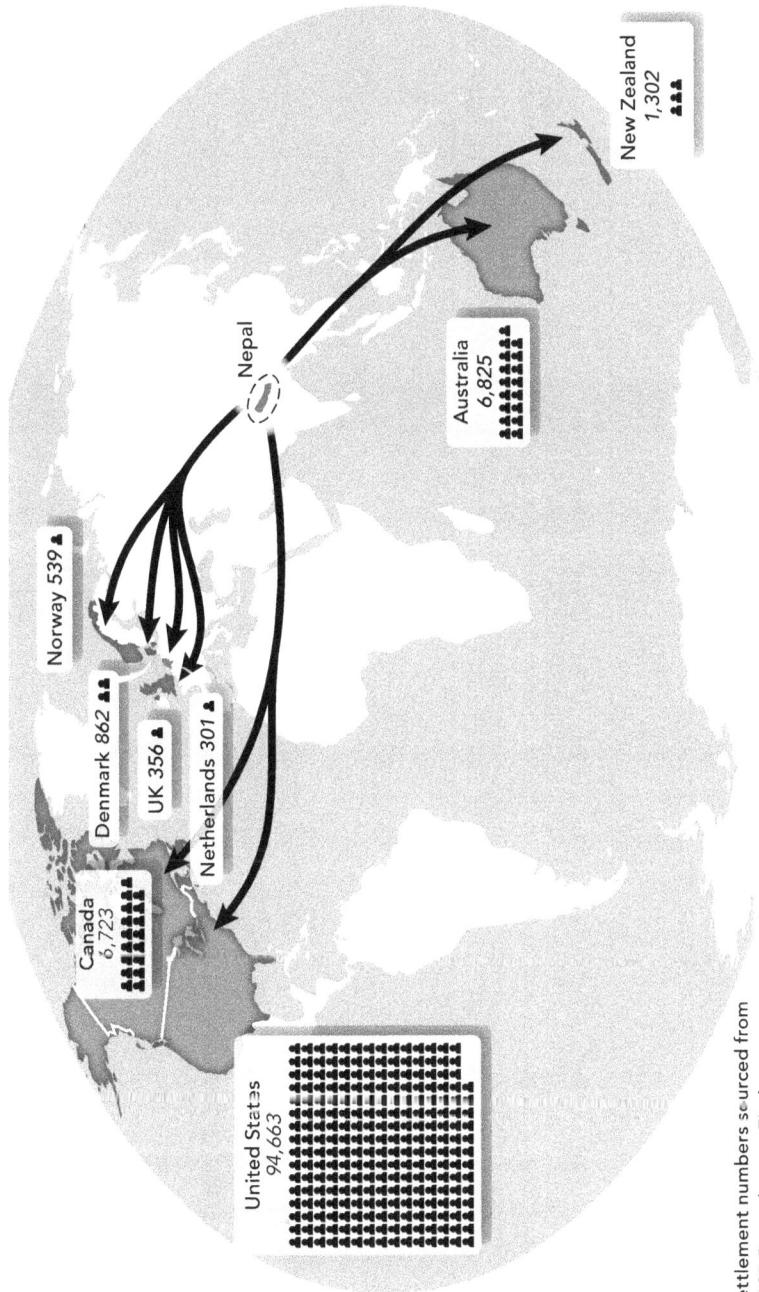

Resettlement numbers sourced from
UNHCR Resettlement Finder

MAP 5. Countries of resettlement for Bhutanese refugees

INTRODUCTION

> **Today you have here a country saying that for whatever reasons it has decided it does not want a certain section of its people. . . . Today it is Bhutan doing it, what if tomorrow Bangladesh decides to say of all those below the poverty line, "we have no obligation, if we do not want them we will simply kick them out." We are asking for major problems, because nations are not made by boundaries, they are made by people.**
>
> —Bhim Subba

Ratan Gazmere left Bhutan after his release from prison, where he had been held because he penned pamphlets criticizing the government. He crossed into Nepal, where he joined more than 80,000 Bhutanese Nepalis who had fled Bhutan's southern regions in the early 1990s and who now resided in one of seven refugee camps in Nepal that housed Bhutanese refugees. To contest the Bhutanese government's claim that those who left were never Bhutanese citizens to begin with, Ratan Gazmere got creative. Armed with a scanner, an old computer, and a small amount of funding, he and his organization, the Association of Human Rights Activists (AHURA), developed a sophisticated digital database that had the capacity to track every single Bhutanese refugee, which town and district they came from, the leader of their home village, and when they left Bhutan and under what circumstances.

Within a year, AHURA had collected and scanned critical documentation from nearly 50,000 refugees, including passports, land receipts, and income statements. A user had only to click on one name to see many connective relationships—refugees from the same district, refugees who left in the same month, refugees with similar documentation—which showed the impressive extent to which this population could substantiate claims to citizenship. Collecting this data required AHURA members to go regularly to all seven refugee camps in Nepal, interview refugees in their huts, collect their documents, return to AHURA's local office outside the camp, scan the documents, and return to the camps to give back each refugee's documents. AHURA's efforts to collect this wealth of information were necessarily based in Nepal, where the vast majority of Bhutan's refugees were located at the time.

Bhakta Ghimire was working in a cement factory in Samtse in southern Bhutan when he heard rumors that Bhutanese Nepalis were being evicted from their homes following a national census exercise. He paid for a taxi to drive the seven hours to his parents' village to check on them and discovered an empty house. His family was gone. He crossed into India to find them, expecting to return soon. But after a week, it was clear that Bhutanese Nepalis were moving in only one direction: leaving Bhutan and not returning. Bhakta Ghimire himself never returned to his job at the cement factory. After five years of exile, he and other activists organized a series of refugee marches to highlight the peaceful desires of the refugees to return to their land in Bhutan. "The main focus of the march was to appeal [to] the King of Bhutan. There were some rumors that the real situation in southern Bhutan was not known by the King. So . . . we wanted to make the King know."[1]

The plan was to leave Nepal, walk through India—a journey of a few days on foot—then cross into Bhutan and, from there, travel north to the capital, Thimphu, to personally deliver a request to the king to recognize and reinstate the citizenship of the refugees and to release political prisoners. On crossing into India from Nepal, the first marchers were arrested and imprisoned in India. A few days later, another wave came, and they, too, were soon arrested and imprisoned. More waves of marchers, more arrests, more imprisonments. In the end, seventeen waves of marchers, totaling thousands, crossed into India over the course of several months. While nearly all were imprisoned, Bhakta Ghimire was in one of two groups that made it all the way into Bhutan. The images and stories of quiet and orderly masses walking through the streets, and their subsequent arrests and imprisonment, were critical to garnering public attention. India served as the main stage for these symbolic protests.

Mangala Sharma had a well-connected job working for the United Nations Development Programme in Thimphu when she spoke out about her government's repression. Subsequently, she and her young family were served eviction papers from their home and threatened by former neighbors. She realized that even a UN job would not protect her: her husband's family's house was burned down, her older brother was imprisoned, and she witnessed firsthand the destruction of the village in the south where she had grown up. She left Bhutan in the middle of the night with her family, crossed through India, and traveled to Nepal, a country that she had never even visited. "I remember, before we left, I was telling my husband, will we get milk there? Will we be able to buy yogurt for the girls?"[2]

Young, articulate, and English-speaking, Mangala Sharma was an effective spokesperson for those who had left Bhutan. Groups with whom she came into contact in Nepal funded her international travel. In Australia, she did numerous television interviews. In New York, she talked about her experiences at Freedom

House. In Geneva, she spoke at several meetings of the United Nations High Commissioner for Refugees (UNHCR). In 1995, while still breastfeeding her younger child, she led a delegation of Bhutanese refugee women to the Fourth World Conference on Women in Beijing. There, for the first time since her exile, she encountered women from northern Bhutan. The Bhutanese delegation ignored her, but Mangala Sharma had the chance to tell all the participants in the room about the women she had interviewed in the refugee camps in Nepal who had survived rape or the torture or death of loved ones. It was in the neutral territory of the international arena that she was able to hold the floor, not only in front of the Bhutanese but in front of women from all over the world.

Ratan Gazmere, Bhakta Ghimire, and Mangala Sharma exemplify the phenomenon of exile politics. Each expressed opposition to their homeland government by working from the outside. But where is the outside, precisely? As these examples show, activists mobilize from multiple sites of activism, both near the home country and further afield. This is so even in a situation like this one, where nearly all of Bhutan's refugees lived initially in one nearby country, Nepal. While the spotlight is often reserved for those activities that play out in the international arena—dissidents making speeches at the United Nations Human Rights Council, for example—the case of Bhutan's homeland activists demonstrates that other sites of activism are equally, if not more, important in furthering the cause of those who seek reform. These sites are most often in interaction with one another; Ratan Gazmere passed on a CD-ROM of the digital database to other activists lobbying Indian and Nepali government officials at a regional meeting, and Mangala Sharma relied on information her organization collected from refugee camp residents in Nepal when she spoke in distant locations.

These dynamic sites of exile can be viewed as elements of an ecosystem, in which the hubs in different physical places interact with one another toward a common purpose of placing pressure on the home country. At the same time, these hubs, like the organisms in an ecosystem, possess their own strategies for survival, or repertoires of activism. Parts of the ecosystem are producers, creating the resources to keep activism afloat. Other parts are consumers, who rely on those resources for sustenance. The hubs of the ecosystem sometimes trade protection for nourishment, just as organisms do. Drawing on the experiences of Bhutan's homeland activists over place and time, this book demonstrates in detail how physical sites are differentiated by what activists do, given their position relative to the homeland. Physical proximity, this book shows, offers sites through which the power to mobilize and engage in struggle against the state becomes more pronounced and visceral. At the same time, sites proximate to the homeland are spaces of risk and disempowerment, where homeland activists are rarely able to obtain secure legal and social protection. In other words, in an ecosystem of exile politics, there are circulating and dynamic expressions of power, expressions that emanate both from the state and from resisters to that state power. Power, in all its forms, is mediated through physical proximity to the homeland and its uncomfortably conjoined twin, precarity. In an ecosystem of exile politics, physical proximity is both a boon and a bane.

Examining Bhutanese Exile Politics

Why examine the exile politics of Bhutan? The country is better known for its benevolent king, stunning mountain scenery, enviro-friendly agricultural policies, and a thoughtful approach to development through Gross National Happiness than for a contested history with an ethnic minority population. Yet a closer read of Bhutan's history over the past century reveals dramatic power struggles characterized by mysterious deaths, assassinations, palace intrigue, and, most recently, a massive refugee exodus. A country in which "the spectrum of political organization was essentially 'frozen'"[3] lends itself well to the study of exile politics, as internal political challenges were not welcome and people opposing government policies therefore fled.

However, it would be neither helpful nor accurate to paint Bhutan as a totalitarian regime. Bhutanese powerholders made attempts to integrate the ethnic minority population before fear took over. The country's transition to democracy, while imperfect, has not witnessed the same kind of democratic backsliding that has characterized, for example, many countries of Southeast Asia.[4] Studying Bhutanese exile politics illuminates the important point that such activism is not limited to countries that are traditionally considered highly authoritarian, and it allows us to ask questions about the role of outside pressure when the inside resembles not a dictatorship but a hybrid regime or an illiberal democracy.[5]

As a topic of study, exile politics sits at the intersection of the literatures of diasporas, migration, and social movements. While both political scientists and sociologists have written extensively about the phenomenon, very few have highlighted the critical role of physical space. This book extends our understanding of exile politics by illustrating that the multiple physical nodes of a diaspora movement play specific roles. It identifies proximate activists and proximate activism as key elements in the exile politics ecosystem, and it locates this proximity in a broader social and political field.

This book also contributes to an increasing recognition within the forced-migration literature that refugee populations are agents in their own right rather than only recipients of aid.[6] It offers empirical research that details creative and innovative activism ignited by refugees themselves, such as the database described earlier, or the researching, writing, and distribution of an informative, sometimes irreverent, and always piercingly critical newsletter about Bhutan. I further build on the work of scholars who caution against focusing solely on the most powerful players and thus understanding only "the last stage of a complicated process" and "reducing the role of challengers, painting them as secondary figures in the formation of their own international networks."[7] Instead, this book explains transnational processes by animating the activities and motivations of refugees-cum-activists and activists-cum-refugees.

Labeling the Phenomenon

The literature on exile politics is abundant and goes by several names.[8] In this book, I use the terms "exile politics," "diaspora mobilization," and "homeland activism" interchangeably to describe *oppositional activism targeted toward the home country by those outside of that country*. While politicians and activists very often play different roles in domestic politics, in situations of exile the very same actors often serve all these roles, lessening the need for differentiating language. In the case of Bhutan's homeland activists, sometimes they act like politicians, working within a power system even while outside of their national polity, and sometimes they act like activists, organizing marches and documenting harms done to their compatriots. That the roles of the politician and the advocate bleed into one another is not unheard of, but it is perhaps more common in exile, where migrants and refugees frequently have their social positions upended rather quickly and may take on new roles.

It should never be far from our thinking that these actors are people who have crossed borders and are therefore migrants (who left willingly) or refugees (who left because they were forced). Whether we call them the former or the latter has less to do with the truth of their situation and more to do with the institutional bodies that find it expedient for them to be one thing or the other. These are ambivalent and fluid categories.[9] I show my cards from the outset because I call them refugees. Many of them were unwilling departees, although the narrative of coercion is contested by the government of Bhutan. I cover more of these specifics in the coming chapters.

Explaining the Ecosystem

Exile politics function very much like a physical ecosystem. With their differentiated abilities for producing, consuming, and decomposing resources, parts of an ecosystem interact in order to transfer nutrients between themselves. In the same way, the hubs of an ecosystem of exile politics—the physical sites where sustained or momentary acts of homeland activism are carried out—are differently able to collect, publish, and redeploy the element that represents the "carbon" of activism: information about events in the homeland. As in the natural world, some of these interactions are visible, as when demonstrators march with slogans and aim to garner media attention for their cause back home. Others are clandestine, like the hushed crossborder work of gathering information about problems at home, which mimics the literal underground interactions between fungi and trees.

In a natural ecosystem, an organism's physical location—its position relative to sun, water, or shelter, for example—helps explain why it behaves and grows as it does. Similarly, in exile politics, physical location matters. By demonstrating that physical proximity benefited Bhutan's early exile activists, the research here illuminates and modifies what we understand about notions of spatial politics. While scholars, most famously Doreen Massey, Henri Lefebvre, and Edward Soja, have long linked social space and political power, examining an ecosystem of exile politics shows us that physical place is politically marked as well.[10] In the context of technologies that survey, monitor, measure, register, count, territorialize, colonize, and claim virtually all physical places on the globe, this "first space"—the physical—remains the central stage on which everyday actions take place, including the nuts and bolts of power jostling, or politics.[11]

My claim that exile politics functions like an ecosystem with differentiated physical hubs has a few important progenitors. Fiona Adamson's examination of the spatial dimensions of power—highlighting the "spatial turn" in political geography—is foundational for this book, as it elevates the role of physical spaces and the interconnections between them; part of her analysis centers on homeland activism in the "global peripheries" and calls for more work that does the same.[12] Adamson showcases examples of diaspora populations whose position in the core or periphery inform their actions, much as this book does. Yet Adamson's association of the periphery as resource-poor and weakly institutionalized, compared with a distant diaspora that is understood to be rich and heavily institutionalized, requires nuance. For homeland activists, proximate locations are often the primary hubs of mobilization, facilitating core activities that rely on rich resources, while distant dispersed locations might be considered peripheral. A consideration of the risks of mobilizing in near and far countries has been overlooked in this analysis, something I cover below.

The relevance of distance to transnational politics is also extant in the work of Lyons and Mandaville, who have highlighted how globalization and the spread of information technologies have transformed the relationship between physical distance and diaspora politics.[13] Their scholarship points to a dynamic between local specificity of politics, place, and community, and the formation of transnational networks and institutions in the struggle to deploy resources, assert claims, and achieve political outcomes in exile politics. The structurally reordering effects of globalization have, largely through the amplification of networks, increased the action potential of the frequently diffuse elements of the diaspora community, which can go on to effect wider systemic political change and impact political and social alignments in the homeland itself.

Alexander Betts and Will Jones, while not overly focused on physical space, have likewise pointed to institutions and resources as a key factor in strengthening and weakening diaspora political movements.[14] They offer a capacious empirical study of the Zimbabwean and Rwandan refugee diasporas and theorize a diaspora life cycle in which two main factors contribute to continuing meaningful political mobilization: (1) the presence of, and funding from, internal animators—those who are members of the diaspora community of activists, rather than external ones, whose interests may wane; and (2) movements that rely on institutional animators rather than on individual animators. This is a critical contribution to the literature on homeland activism, as it demonstrates the possibilities for institutional strength in nearby locales, a phenomenon supported by my research. However, I offer an alternative to their conceptualizations of "diaspora death" and "diaspora afterlife," suggesting instead that while the structural problems in the home country remain unaddressed, homeland activism may wax and wane but remains very much alive.

Maria Koinova, in a growing body of work on the political mobilization of conflict-generated diasporas, illuminates the causes, processes, and effects of homeland activism in empirically rich and detailed comparative research.[15] Foregrounding the importance of physical space in different locales, both further away and nearby, Koinova notes that manifestations of diaspora/transnational political action are dependent on their relative position to one another, both in terms of the strength of social networks and the physical location of the diaspora group. This "sociospatial positionality" aligns with the assertions I offer, highlighting that physical proximity to the home country is an important component of diaspora engagement.[16] In incorporating power, fluidity, and perceptions into this relational arrangement, Koinova hints at the ways that homeland activism is shaped by forces that are linked to, and sometimes in tension with, physical space: power and precarity.

In her 2021 book *Diaspora Entrepreneurs and Contested States*, Koinova offers a more formal, structured typology of diaspora politics.[17] She articulates a complex political dynamic between "diaspora entrepreneurs" and their home states, which takes different forms depending on the characteristics of the entrepreneurs themselves and the interplay between familiar sociospatial variables like proximity, as well as critical events, global influences, host state foreign policy, and the behaviors and interests of home state government and civil society. Here Koinova makes an important intervention by bridging traditional agent/structure debates on the drivers of political formation and action by articulating a method for understanding socio-spatial positionality and the complex linkages of diaspora entrepreneurs in their global context, an enterprise that builds on earlier mentioned observations of the impact of globalization on exile politics. While I have not adopted Koinova's exact typology of diaspora entrepreneurs in this book, my interviews with specific actors affirm Koinova's "mobilisation trajectory"[18] by demonstrating that relationships (local, regional, global), informed by proximity and distance, play a critical role in shaping the work of homeland activists.

Power and Precarity in Exile

At its core, activism is a quest for the redistribution of power, whether the power sought is about wanting a voice in government, trying to shift public attitudes, or asserting social and symbolic identities. In the case of homeland activism, those who contest current power structures are not just outside of the physical country but outside the traditional structures that permit such contestation. Here, physical displacement highlights and reinforces the lack of power at home, with consequences for the routes that activists take when they leave home and the precarious situations in which they find themselves once they depart. Therefore, theorizing power and precarity are helpful to guide our understanding of an exile politics ecosystem.

An ecosystem of exile politics functions as a response to state power, which itself is fueled by practices of membership that seek to include some and exclude others. Roberto Esposito argues that the power of communities derives from their fear of external threats. Likening the powerholder to a biological body, Esposito argues that the "immunitary dispositif" creates a pressing need to eject any foreign substance.[19] The modern state is today's most visible powerholder, and the "indelible imprint of conflict and violence"[20] characteristic of modernity suggests that nation-states will transfer that violence into immunitary acts to maintain power, viewing challengers as viruses and seeking to expel them. This expulsion is the precursor to the ecosystem that subsequently develops.

Following expulsion, protest by definition becomes transnational as it crosses and operates "over and beyond" state borders, challenging states from the outside in.[21] An entire subgenre of beyond/without/contesting borders literature is built upon this.[22] Implied in this literature, but rarely explicit, is the importance of focusing on the transnational *routes* undertaken by those expelled or otherwise migrating. By examining the paths taken by homeland activists moving through "Northern South Asia,"[23] this book reinforces the notion that routes are not only reflections of the current geopolitical landscape, but, as Noelle Brigden points out, fixtures in reordering it. Brigden's Central American routes and my routes similarly reveal "incomplete sovereignty at borders, call[ing] forth a spectacle of violence to project state power."[24]

What follows in this transnational space is an iterative arrangement between activism and "bordering practices," that is, state actions that serve to change the porosity of the border based on who is crossing.[25] Suzan Ilcan points out that these bordering practices, such as militarized border crossings, localized border policies, and the formation of special police and agencies to enforce them, in fact ignite transnational movements for migrant justice. But this relationship moves in both directions. Building on Esposito, I assert that states preempt the power of transnational movements and, therefore, construct contexts of fear. This is particularly the case in regions with porous borders, who feel the breath of the borderlands down their necks. Northern South Asia is one region uniquely placed for political and physical conditions of porosity, thereby experiencing what Willem Van Schendel has called "apprehensive territoriality."[26] This is indeed an apt description of the reactions of the Bhutanese government to calls for change that were perceived to be transnational.

So far, I have stitched together a theoretical narrative in which power, protest, and bordering practices bump up against each other in iterative and nonsequential ways. The resulting expulsion into a new physical space (across the borders) opens the door for an ecosystem of exile politics. What is missing from this analysis thus far, however, is the ways that power is exerted in these new physical spaces, and how homeland activism is rendered risky in new ways as a result. In other words, when we think about those who cross borders, we must consider their precarity.

Guy Standing's work on precarity initially focused on the ways that workers of all sectors were made vulnerable by market forces,[27] but both Standing and many others who followed quickly incorporated labor migration into the equation.[28] People who leave their countries to pursue needed work opportunities are most often in a legal limbo that opens the door for severe exploitation and lures migrants into the "hyper-precarity trap."[29] Similarly, the "ambiguous architecture of precarity" experienced by Syrian refugees in Turkey extends the familiar application of precarity as a concept purely about the workplace to the wider refugee context.[30] A tangled suite of policies, directives, and norms, emanating from local, national, and international institutions, creates precarity in refugee lives. This is manifested administratively through their sociolegal status, as well as physically through the precarious experiences and everyday living situation of refugees and the control over the spaces in which they live, work, and transit.[31] The experience of "precarity of place" suggests not that migrants' choices and behaviors will necessarily be colored by the *fact* of exploitation, detention, or deportation, but the *risk* thereof.[32]

Precarity has also increasingly come to be understood as a concept linked to the potential for political action. Precarity is not just a set of conditions but a starting point for mobilization that responds to those conditions, with the migrant singled out to play a role in upending current neoliberal power structures that have rendered her precarious in the first place.[33] But if the precarious migrant has the "subversive potential" to rise above exploitation,[34] then it follows rather logically that refugees have similar potential to mobilize against the thing that has rendered them precarious to begin with: the home state. These precarities—identified in this book as legal (the absence of documentation permitting residence), political (the risks associated with challenging power as a foreigner), and social (the social fragmentation and disunity that come from vulnerability and insecurity)—are not just conditions experienced by refugees, but the points through which they come to engage in activism.

Researching Bhutan from the Outside In

Bhutan's relationship with its exiled population has produced fraught and contested narratives. On the one side, we hear about a country genuinely fearful of losing its identity to violent outsiders and, on the other side, we learn about a devoted minority population that loved its king and the land and was forcibly expelled simply for asking for recognition. Research that addresses the claims of these conflicting parties must make its methods transparent. This is particularly important because even the best-known scholars in the field, who have made strenuous efforts to be objective, have been rebuked by both sides. Ever since publishing the widely acclaimed *Unbecoming Citizens*, which detailed the faults of both the Bhutanese government and its opponents, the author Michael Hutt has been the object of such criticism within Bhutan that he has stopped even trying to enter the country.[35]

Bhutan's highly restrictive visa regime—which requires all tourists outside of the region to come on an organized tour and keeps other visitors to a minimum—ensures that those writing about Bhutan have a choice to make: they can write critically, and likely suffer the consequence of being denied access into the country, in which case their research will necessarily lack firsthand government narratives, or they can toe the line and gain or maintain access to the country and its representatives. How very ironic that a desire to enter Bhutan—one of the key issues for homeland activists—influences the way that scholars write about the fabled country!

Two social scientists who conduct research in Bhutan privately admitted to me that they frame their research questions such that delicate topics never arise, and a third said he needed to wait—perhaps years—to publish his controversial findings if he wanted to continue his research. As for me, I recognized years ago that by writing critically about the government, I risked not being able to enter the country. I have not done so since commencing my research. The absence of pro-government interviews in my book is therefore hardly surprising. Though I have read academic books that are sympathetic to the claims of the Bhutanese government,[36] my entry point has been almost entirely through what we might call the "dissident discourse," that is, through the voices, texts, and images of those who have worked to challenge government narratives. I am mindful that in this way, I mirror the homeland activists I research: I focus on the country from the outside in. I describe this approach in detail below.

Hanging Out and Reading Up and Down

Understanding the fine-grained work of activists, particularly their less visible tactics, calls for research that simply cannot be carried out merely by examining publicly available information, such as doing protest event analysis or reviewing the websites of activists' groups. Nor can one determine the extent of discouraged or prohibited activities through quick and impersonal surveys.

To tell the story of Bhutan's homeland activists and their origins, my book draws on research conducted over sixteen years, from 2007 to 2023. Interviews in Nepal, India, Australia, Europe, and the United States with ninety-seven people offer an incisive and nuanced view of refugee flight, exile, and political opposition. This includes interviews with nearly all of the country's most prominent homeland activists, as well as focus group discussions with other members of the refugee population. A full count of Bhutanese homeland exile groups over time would number close to fifty, but many of these were defunct by the time I started my research, or their members had switched affiliations, or their advocacy activities were minimal. I am confident that I have gained the views from members of every long-standing homeland organization, something no other researcher from the Global North has done. I have also interviewed humanitarian aid workers (including local field workers, whose perspectives are often neglected), US, Australian and Nepali government officials, UN agency representatives, and regional journalists. Where necessary, I have employed the assistance of Nepali interpreters, although I am mindful of the limitations of mediated conversations.[37] I therefore offer an in-depth examination of exile politics that lies outside the realm of visible political channels. In most instances, the people I interviewed were happy to have their full names used. Where they were not, I have deidentified them.

Apart from formal interviews, I also spent time with Bhutanese activists and refugees in a variety of political, social, and cultural contexts. I traced their journeys from their refugee camp huts in Nepal's east to the International Organization for Migration (IOM) resettlement center in Kathmandu to their citizenship ceremonies in the distant diaspora. I attended cultural festivals and political rallies. I have been painted with the traditional red *tika* during the Hindu festival of Dashain, and I have listened while opinionated, strong-willed, and deeply committed activists argued about important historical key moments in their struggle. I have taken out my pen and paper and complied when an elderly refugee turned to me, eyes burning, and said, "Write down these names. These are the ones who died."[38] I have shared laughter with those who marveled at their prior bravado in prison, refusing the orders of the guards, and I have shared sadness with those who mourned relatives they have not seen again.

I follow Graeme Rodgers in his assessment that, when done properly, "hanging out" allows researchers to bridge refugees' quotidian experiences with the global systems that rendered them refugees to begin with.[39] Through this kind of research, I developed a strong sense of who the Bhutanese refugee activists are. It should be said here that my intent is not to idealize them as perfect champions of their causes. Scholars do refugees (and, in this case, activists) a disservice if we write about them as unflawed figures, sacrificing everything in pursuit of just goals.[40] Instead, I suggest that the activists I came to know display the complexity of human characteristics: often courageous, sometimes frightened, inclined toward both reflection and vindication. Clear-eyed, practical, and imaginative. Angry, resentful, and suspicious. Often, they vied for public recognition or international legitimacy. They competed for funding. The movement—chaotic, fragmented, only partially effective—reflected humanity as a whole.

There is another value to hanging out with a community, quite specific to refugee activists. Society's tendency to turn certain refugees into celebrities might suggest that homeland activism is a task carried out only by "emigrandezza"— high-profile émigrés who become the darlings of the human rights community.[41] Indeed, the recent emphasis on human rights defenders, including those in exile, tends to individualize the work of dissent and protect human rights defenders as such.[42] But while the best-known activists may enjoy the limelight in secure locations, Ratan Gazmere, Bhakta Ghimire, Mangala Sharma, and many others relied on numerous people in the background who advanced the cause of home-land activism both through quiet, less visible activities and through highly public contentious acts. Further, it is often the lesser-known figures who are at greater risk. Spending time in these communities has allowed me to meet and write about both the public figures and those less visible.

To be sure, there are reasonable concerns about the reliability of informa-tion that comes from refugee self-representation—either through hanging out with them or through oral histories. I address these concerns in expected and tra-ditional ways, through trying to understand the issues from many sides, which I refer to as "reading up and down," by which I mean using source material from the international level (UN reports, for example) all the way "down" to the mi-crolocal level (notes written from one refugee to another, for example). In be-tween, I examined regional sources, like the approximately forty pieces authored by Dr. S Chandrasekharan available through the South Asia Analysis Group, and refugee sources, like the annual reports of community-based organizations that worked in the camps, refugee anthologies (in my possession), several online web publications by refugees and their supporters, most notably *Bhutan News Service*, and the monthly publications of the Human Rights Organization of Bhutan (HUROB) from 1993 to 1996, helpfully published in their entirety on Digital Hi-malaya. On these multiple levels, materials produced by refugees, activists, and other relevant stakeholders gave me a multidimensional perspective of a con-flict that many see as one-sided.

Positionality

While we are "hanging out" with refugees, we are expected to remain objective enough to see clearly the nuances of the stories they tell. Not every refugee story reveals a single bright truth that shines over other less true narratives. Just as migrants' journeys are performed and, thereby, "become a resource for mobil-ity," refugee narratives about their activism become resources for further activ-ism.[43] It is the researcher's job to interpret that narrative, not to accept it as true. Part of doing that is identifying and acknowledging our biases in order to over-come them—what we call positionality.

Much has been written on positionality and transnational research,[44] and po-sitionality and refugee research.[45] Many researchers acknowledge their posi-tionality, and I am no different. I am white. I am privileged, relative to the pop-ulations of refugees I have interviewed. I am a woman. But there is something more, something that I myself hadn't considered until a meeting with Balaram

Poudel, the founder and leader of one of the first Bhutanese exile organizations, the Bhutan People's Party (BPP).

I first heard of Balaram Poudel early on when I began my research in 2007. In Nepal, people mentioned him with some trepidation, and warned me to be careful if I met him because the BPP was believed to be behind some recent violence. I was told that he didn't speak English anyway and that an interpreter would not be objective. I followed Balaram Poudel in the news for the next twelve years and tried several times to meet him during my trips to Nepal. He was difficult to contact, and the timing never worked out. In March 2019, however, we were both in Kathmandu at the same time and I had a trusted interpreter. Finally, I had my chance to meet this grizzled refugee, potentially a dangerous revolutionary.

We met in a public space, in the garden of my hotel. Balaram Poudel looked, physically, exactly as I had seen in many photographs: wizened features, a prominent nose, and his signature gray hat. But there were some surprises. He spoke English quite well, and we relied only occasionally on my interpreter. He spoke quietly, in heavily accented English, with no revolutionary bravado. He was thoughtful and curious and, to my mind, seemed void of a personal agenda. We spoke for over two hours. He was candid about the BPP's problems but did not think these defined all that the organization had done. He asked my opinions. He drank the sweet Nepali tea that came to our table, but quietly refused any other food.

When it was time to conclude, we stood up and I thanked him for his time. He turned to me, took my hands, and put them on his head. This is different from the usual gesture one might expect in the region, where the elder will place his hands on the head of a younger person as a blessing. By placing my hands on *his* head, he sought *my* blessings. His hands shook a bit as he asked me to do good work that would help his people. I thanked him again and walked away.

I did not let Balaram Poudel see the tears that I had shed. With his gentle demeanor, his stooped shoulders, and his thick accent, Balaram Poudel reminded me of my own refugee father, a survivor of the Holocaust and my most ardent supporter until his death in 2006, just one year before I met my first refugee from Bhutan. While I had expected the assumptions that might come with being a white woman of relative privilege, and had also considered my positionality as a researcher whose view was skewed by spending time with my informants, I had not considered two of the forces that shaped my thinking the most: being the only child of a refugee, and being the Jewish child of a Holocaust survivor.

I tell this story not to draw links between Bhutan and Germany, nor to forgive any violence on the part of exile organizations that may have propagated it, but simply to reinforce the notion that researchers are as susceptible as their interviewees to interpretations and constructions of history that foreground one telling of truth over others.

Outline

In this chapter, I have introduced several homeland activists from Bhutan. I have reviewed the concepts and fields of study on which I rely to help understand an ecosystem of exile politics. I have discussed my methods and reflected on my positionality. I have dipped into contrasting narratives about the country of Bhutan.

I tell the remainder of the story of Bhutan's homeland activists, and the ecosystem that developed around them, in five chapters. In chapter 2, I examine the back story of Bhutan, where the seeds of a future exile politics ecosystem were planted, through the lens of *power*. After a brief review of the premodern era and a necessary discussion of the country's demographics, I contextualize the country's lesser-known early incidences of exile politics. With geopolitical changes afoot, I chronicle homeland activism's emergence in the 1950s and the immunitary response of Bhutan's powerholders. The chapter concludes on the precipice of significant changes for Bhutan's ethnic Nepalis.

Chapter 3 takes a hard, objective look at the years leading up to exile through to the refugees' expulsion, when internal activism transformed into homeland activism through the *passage of protest*. I present government perspectives and motivations, along with the experiences of several refugees, demonstrating that actions of good faith and ill intent were committed on all sides. I examine the relationship between transnational action and the fear it engendered in Bhutan, where the very porous borders that permitted activists to cross easily also led to Bhutan's "apprehensive territoriality."[46] In this phase, the ecosystem took root, with a small number of proximate hubs sprouting.

In chapter 4, I demonstrate how homeland activists were constituted and defined by their *proximity* to Bhutan. These activists deconstructed and reinterpreted Bhutan's Shangri-La image and utilized sophisticated research and presentation technologies to communicate their grievances to outside audiences. For those involved in promoting democracy, raising awareness, and reversing exile, proximate places provided fertile ground for activism. Human rights documentation was aided by a significant volume of people who could substantiate stories of abuse and expulsion. Lobbying was possible because of previously established networks borne of proximate relationships. Marches back to Bhutan that showed just how close the refugees were to their homeland possessed tremendous symbolic currency, capturing the attention of local and international media.

Chapter 5 flips the proximity coin over and finds *precarity* on the other side. I show how proximity and precarity were interlinked and in tension for Bhutanese refugees in both Nepal and India. While both countries allowed a modicum of mobilization at some points, the legal status of refugees remained uncertain, their homeland activism increasingly risky, and their social connections frayed. Further, I demonstrate that these consequences were not just coincidental occurrences for Bhutanese refugees, but tied to their proximity to Bhutan. With legal, political, and social precarity taking a toll on the refugee population, the ecosystem began to weaken.

Chapter 6 examines the *paradox* of refugee resettlement for the ecosystem of exile politics. I turn to the post-2008 era, where, in the context of resettlement and a democratic transition in Bhutan, homeland activism has undergone tectonic shifts. New sites of activism have emerged in the distant diaspora as nearly 100,000 Bhutanese refugees have resettled to countries of the Global North. This expansion of the ecosystem has led to an erosion of old forms of activism and an introduction of new and adaptive forms. The centrality and urgency of exile politics in the lives of resettled refugees has diminished. The chapter highlights several paradoxes, but the most striking is that while distant diasporas may eliminate political precarity, they render homeland activists unable to tap into the advantages of proximity.

Chapter 7 emphasizes the book's major contributions: the construct of exile politics as an ecosystem, the centrality of physical space as a consideration in homeland activism, the power of physical proximity for homeland activists, and the precarity engendered by proximity. Ending on a note of hopeful speculation, it concludes by suggesting that the Bhutanese ecosystem of exile politics may have a new role to play in reconciling a decades-old diaspora to its homeland.

Bhutan remains a mythical place for even well-traveled tourists and, after nearly thirty years of exile, it is becoming a mythical place for the country's exiled population, who have never been able to return. So many of them—not only activists like Ratan Gazmere, Bhakta Ghimire, and Mangala Sharma, but all refugees of every age—have expressed the desire to return, if only to visit the land from which they and their parents and grandparents came. I believe that return to Bhutan of some kind or another is still possible, as is a form of reconciliation that would grant some closure to the multiplicity of actors who remain invested in Bhutan's future. Perhaps naïvely, I hope that an honest look at the historical and political forces that launched homeland activism may help to facilitate that process. An illumination of this sort would, perhaps, temper the need for an oppositional form of exile politics.

THE BHUTAN BACK STORY

Since our society is a small one, anybody going against the government gets easily branded as an anti-element. . . . There are no . . . platforms where one can freely deliberate and develop political consciousness.

—Thinley Penjore

The Himalayan country of Bhutan is known for its promotion of Gross National Happiness and more recently as a peaceful Shangri-La–like monarchy that willingly transitioned to democracy beginning in 2006. It rarely comes to mind when one imagines a country that exercises state power by shutting down dissent within its borders. But on several occasions in the past century, ethnic minorities protesting their treatment in Bhutan have faced a dead-end when trying to create internal moments for change.

In this chapter, I cover Bhutan's back story, offering context for the chapters to come. After a brief review of the premodern era and a necessary discussion of the country's demographics, I contextualize the country's lesser-known early incidences of exile politics. With geopolitical changes afoot, I chronicle homeland activism's emergence in the 1950s and the response of Bhutan's powerholders, highlighting the interplay between grievances and state power, and the path that activism took thereafter. The chapter concludes on the precipice of significant changes for the Bhutanese Nepalis.

Early History

Following a prehistoric period "shrouded in a mist of isolation,"[1] sects of Buddhism vied for power in the land we now know as Bhutan. Because the country's religious and political histories were deeply enmeshed,[2] it is not surprising that religious strife bled into sectarian strife, manifested in feuding feudal families.

These clans were loosely united under the rule of Ngawang Namgyal, a monk who fled Tibet in the early 1600s due to internecine conflicts in the Tibetan clergy.[3] There is a certain irony in the way that Bhutan went from being a refugee taker to, centuries later, a refugee maker, but this is hardly a unique phenomenon given the continuous nature of conflict, takeover, and escape that characterizes both traditional and modern polities.[4]

Ngawang Namgyal arrived in what is present-day Bhutan from Tibet, holding fast to the Drukpa Kagyu order of Mahayana Buddhism from which he came. This order was founded in the twelfth century and was so named because of myths that dragons—*druk* in Tibetan—appeared out of the sky when the order was founded. Ngawang Namgyal's effectiveness at consolidating military power and centralizing political administration turned Bhutan into the primary place to practice Drukpa Kagyu, and the country took on the associated enduring name: in the Bhutanese language, Dzongkha, the country is called Druk Yul—the Land of the (Thunder) Dragon—and its inhabitants, Drukpa, connoting the Thunder Dragon sect.[5] The diarchy that Ngawang Namgyal established—with both a spiritual and an administrative head, although deeply tilted in favor of the spiritual ruler—lasted for 250 years, notwithstanding numerous political and civil upheavals, indicated by the rapid succession of administrative leaders that more accurately reflected the power of local chiefs who only nominally paid homage to any centralized authority.[6]

Enter colonial Great Britain. While Bhutan and Nepal were never formally colonized, as India was, the history of the entire region is infused with the presence of colonial officials and local powerholders' relationships with them. Power contestation between Bhutan and British India occurred only twice in the nineteenth century, both times over the lowland Duars region that covers parts of northern India and southeastern Bhutan (see map 1). The second of these clashes, the 1864–65 Duar War, led to the 1865 Treaty of Sinchula, which gave Bhutan autonomy at the same time that it gave Great Britain the power to advise Bhutan on foreign affairs. Later agreements inherited these terms, so that until 2007, Bhutan's foreign affairs were guided first by the British Raj, until 1947, and then by independent India herself.

Domestically, Bhutan was nominally left alone by Great Britain in the nineteenth century. But it has been argued that Great Britain's desire for permanent boundaries and a preference for engaging with a single powerholder led to forces of "semicolonialism," in which "an Asian potentate looking, chiefly, to avert foreign distractions *en route* to settling much more pressing local governance issues" was manipulated by "an Occidental power seeking to set permanent black-line boundaries."[7] That is, the suite of vying powermongers that characterized Bhutan's politics at the time was not appealing to the colonists. The 1910

Treaty of Punakha thus acknowledged Ugyen Wangchuck, leader of Trongsa (a region in present-day central Bhutan), as the country's first hereditary monarch. For the next century, the Wangchuck family followed the tradition of primogeniture: Ugyen Wangchuk is the great grandfather of Jigme Singye Wangchuck, who, in 2006, willingly transitioned the country to democracy and passed the crown on to his son, Jigme Khesar Namgyel Wangchuck.

From the time of Ugyen Wangchuck's accession to the throne, to the transition to democracy, through to today, Bhutan's leaders have had exceptional success in projecting a positive image of Bhutan to the international community, whose view of Bhutan is rose-colored and focused primarily on the positive aspects of the country's road to development. But whether the world has been paying attention or not, the contestation of power has run through Bhutan's history like a live current, manifested in sparks of protest along the way. These were present in tussles between the center and the periphery regarding the position of administrative chiefs from the seventeenth to the nineteenth centuries,[8] and they continued in the twentieth century in a different form, particularly on the southern border, with decidedly ethnic overtones.[9]

Bhutan's expression of power in the twentieth century sets the stage for the rest of the book. Mirroring Esposito's "immunitary dispositif"[10]—a political community viewing a segment of the population as a foreign substance against which the community needs to be immunized—Bhutan viewed early political protesters as "something that threaten[ed] . . . biological, social, and environmental identity."[11] Accordingly, those viewed as threatening were removed or ejected. In this chapter, we see the first signs of protest in the modern era, and the first immunitary reactions by the government. From this, we can identify where and how the first seeds of an ecosystem of exile were planted.

The perspective of power challengers as foreign is made all the more interesting in the case of Bhutan, because, as will become clear, the majority of those who challenged power structures in Bhutan *were* from families that, however many generations prior, had been foreigners. They were also markedly different looking and sounding from the ruling powerholders. To understand this phenomenon, a short detour describing the country's ethnic groups and their historical migration patterns is necessary.

Ethnicity, Population, and Migration

Awadhesh Coomar Sinha (A. C. Sinha) has suggested that present in Bhutan are four different dichotomies: national versus ethnic, king versus parliament, elitism versus populism, and frontier particularism versus universal modernization.[12] Yet it is the ethnic component that seems to eclipse other considerations in human rights reports[13] and in the popular press.[14] In short, and in broad strokes: the ruling class in Bhutan comprises the Drukpa, who are ethnically, linguistically, religiously, and physically different from ethnic Nepalis (hereafter referred to as "Bhutanese Nepalis") in the country's south. The former are Buddhist, speak Dzongkha, and resemble Tibetans, while the latter are primarily Hindu, speak Nepali, and have the darker skin of people from Nepal.

The longer version is that the Drukpa Kagyu order, promulgated by Ngawang Namgyal, created a clear elite population in Bhutan who hail from central Bhutan and of which the Wangchuk family and essentially all of the nobility surrounding the king are a part. They are today called the Ngalong—translated as the "first risen" of the country.[15] A second group is the "people of the east," the Sharchops, who speak Tsangla. Together they make the "Drukpa," grouping together the primarily Buddhist-practicing Ngalongs and Sharchops while excluding other segments of the population, primarily the Bhutanese Nepalis.[16]

The Bhutanese Nepalis—as noted, primarily Hindu-practicing and Nepali-speaking—are the third major population in Bhutan and are broadly referred to as Lhotshampa, or "people of the south." It is difficult to offer an authoritative breakdown of the population by ethnicity for several reasons. The official population of the entire country has been a matter of confusion and contestation. In 1969, the government claimed it had a population of one million, which later seemed to be understood as a notional figure that was considered important for United Nations membership.[17] Thereafter, in a trend that defied normal global population increases, the population estimation was continually adjusted down, until in 1990 the king told a Calcutta magazine that the total population was 600,000.[18] The most recent census, in 2017, counted 735,553.[19]

Contestation surrounding Bhutan's population is also—and more damagingly—about Bhutan's ethnic demographics. The 1988 census, which might have clarified the proportion of ethnic groups in the country, was marred by problems that this book covers in detail. Censuses tie subjects and citizens to official identities, the process of which often causes political conflict.[20] This formalization of knowledge through statistics generates an authoritative representation of the social relations within a state, which is central to the construction of the state itself.[21] In Bhutan, the categorization of a large historical minority as noncitizens corresponds with the nullification of their claims to social and political rights within the state.

The other source of contestation about the population of Bhutanese Nepalis is that more than 80,000 left Bhutan in the early 1990s, and that number certainly changed the demographics of the population who remained.[22] In 1994, after most Bhutanese Nepalis had left Bhutan, Hutt estimated that the ethnic composition in Bhutan was as follows: Ngalongs accounted for 10–28 percent of the population, Sharchops comprised 30–44 percent, and Bhutanese Nepalis were estimated to be between 25 and 53 percent of the population.[23] Hutt repeated these estimates a decade later.[24] The 2017 census did not include data on ethnicity. This is striking considering the extensive and accurate detailing of other demographic characteristics, such as age, sex, and marital status. There is a section of the census that documents the "non-Bhutanese population," which is counted as 53,833, but in this count further identifiers are absent, except the statement that most live in rural areas due to the location of hydroelectric projects, on which they are presumably largely employed.[25] In 2019, the CIA World Factbook stated that Bhutanese Nepalis make up 35 percent of the total population of the country.[26]

Who's Who, and When

This book follows homeland activists who, by and large, wanted to return to Bhutan after they departed. Did they have the right to return? The Bhutanese government asserts that many Bhutanese Nepalis were not citizens and therefore had no right to return because they had come to Bhutan without legitimate documentation that would have allowed them to stay permanently, arriving either as illegal farmers or on short-term contracts to work for the Bhutanese government.[27] This is of course a form of Esposito's immunization, constructing the foreigner in one's midst. Bhutanese Nepalis who left the country—many under severely coercive conditions—insist that they were citizens all along. These debates are spatial and temporal in their character.

In our bordered world, specific dates are reified in order to assess the privileges and rights of migrants and refugees. The 1951 Refugee Convention Relating to the Status of Refugees itself is temporally bound to define as refugees only those who fled persecution before January 1, 1951, although this was modified by the 1967 Protocol Relating to the Status of Refugees.[28] In Bhutan, the year 1958 represents the temporal cutoff. This is when the country passed the Nationality Law, which meant that those who could prove citizenship in 1958 were genuine citizens and those who could not were considered illegal migrants. The debate, then, is not just about *when* Bhutanese Nepalis arrived—few would contest that at least a small number arrived prior to the twentieth century in the ebb and flow of settler migration everywhere—but *how many and at what time*. Proponents of the claims of the Bhutanese government aver that the numbers arriving prior to 1958 were minuscule and that massive illegal migration in the 1980s was at the root of the refugee crisis. Proponents of the refugees' claims maintain that immigration prior to 1958 was substantial and that Bhutanese Nepalis represented a significant portion of the country's population. Because the stakes are so high for the story to go one way or the other, this debate has not receded, but the most authoritative version of events suggests significant immigration prior to 1958.

Information about immigration to Bhutan prior to the twentieth century relies partly on the records of the colonial British Empire, which, because Bhutan was an overlooked outpost, are incomplete relative to British subjects in India, for example. While Bhutanese Nepalis have pointed to the arrival of skilled Newar craftsmen from the Kathmandu Valley in the seventh century to build Bhutan's monasteries as evidence of their long-standing presence in Bhutan,[29] it is widely believed that these artisans, whenever they arrived, likely integrated into the Drukpa population centuries ago.[30] More recent migration of Bhutanese Nepalis (from eastern Nepal and parts of India, such as Sikkim and northern Assam) is surmised to have occurred in notable numbers around the same time as the better-established migration of Nepalis to Sikkim, which occurred from the 1870s onward.[31]

It is impossible to know whether Nepalis actually began arriving around the 1870s or, in fact, arrived earlier but were only recorded around that time, but what is definitive is that colonial records note their presence in Bhutan at the turn of the century. Charles Bell, Britain's settlement officer in Kalimpong (in present-day West Bengal, India; see map 3) from 1890 to 1919, estimated in 1904 that there were 14,000 Bhutanese Nepalis in southwest Bhutan who came "many years past."[32] A "crude estimate" was also offered by Captain C. J. Morris around the same time, who, by visiting markets and estimating households of two southern districts, projected that there were 60,000 Bhutanese Nepalis, not counting the Samtse area in the southwest of Bhutan.[33] This evidence all lends credence to the claims that many Bhutanese Nepalis arrived in Bhutan prior even to the rise of the throne.

Migration continued in Bhutan's southern foothills throughout the first half of the twentieth century with the cultivation of lands that had once been mosquito-infested and ignored by northerners who feared malaria.[34] It is worth noting that, much like population movements facilitated by the colonial British to secure labor for the empire—like Indians to British Burma to cultivate rice, for example, or Nepalis to Darjeeling to work in tea plantations—the Nepalis who moved to Bhutan did not do so covertly; they were not "sneaking in" by any means. As Sinha notes, the Nepali farmers "have actively contributed to the economic development of Bhutan, turning the 'negative' southern area into a vibrant zone of prosperity."[35]

This prosperity benefited not only the Nepalis themselves but also local Drukpa officials, who now had laborers to cultivate the land and more tax revenue from their profits. In particular, the powerful Dorji family encouraged Nepali immigration. Related (if weakly) by blood to the throne, the Dorji family was given a hereditary position by the king in the early twentieth century, as successive members of the family were named as chamberlains and later as the country's trade agents. The responsibilities of the anointed Dorji clan, however, were closer in reality to work ordinarily carried out by heads of state and foreign ministers.[36] The location of the Dorji family homestead in Kalimpong, West Bengal, and not in Bhutan, points to the fact that the Dorjis also played the unofficial but crucial role of ambassadors to India, as their connections with their southern neighbor were significant.[37] The Dorjis married into noble families—both in Bhutan and in the then-independent kingdom of Sikkim—and they were very much part of the aristocratic infrastructure that sought to hold power at the top.

In the early twentieth century, the Dorjis' lucrative duties included administration and tax collection in southern Bhutan, and Nepali immigration was of tremendous benefit. Deo Narayan Sharma Dhakal (D. N. S. Dhakal) and Christopher Strawn note that the Dorjis were "amassing a huge amount of money"[38] from collecting taxes from settlers in the south and further estimated that, had land taxes from Bhutanese Nepalis in the early twentieth century actually made it into the national coffers (which they certainly did not, due to numerous families taking their cut), they would have contributed 20 percent of the country's total treasury income, the rest coming from India's annual stipend.[39]

So, while immigration from Nepal had been long ongoing, and long been of benefit to Bhutan, 1958 represented a watershed year, a line dividing those who could later claim legitimate citizenship and those who could not. While there was significant migration post-1958, those who came as construction workers on large-scale development projects were on strict contracts and were quickly discovered and expelled if they tried to overstay their visas.[40] In fact, these pre-1988 expulsions were actually supported by Bhutanese Nepalis, who considered their citizenship secure. They neither cared very much for the newcomers nor expected that they would one day be pushed out themselves.[41]

There is no one authoritative source that can resolve this citizenship-population dilemma. But Dhakal and Strawn's research suggests that the large majority of Bhutanese Nepalis came before the ever-important 1958 cutoff: taking British estimates of the Bhutanese Nepali population from the early twentieth century and projecting them to the early 1990s, they argue that, "assuming no migration and a reasonably conservative population growth rate . . . the total population of Nepalis in Bhutan would be around 200,000, or one-third of the total population—the exact figure usually given by the government for the [Bhutanese] Nepali population. This substantiates the refugees' assertion that, with few exceptions, the Nepalis were settled in Bhutan by 1958."[42]

If, as is believed today, the population of Bhutan was about 600,000 in 1990, and Dhakal and Strawn are correct that the large majority of them had settled in Bhutan by 1958, then the exodus of 80,000 represents a massive displacement of former citizens—up to one-sixth of the entire population. The immunitary tendencies described by Esposito were carried out on a grand scale. We might call this a mass immunization. What led to it?

The Power's the Thing

Bhutan's combined sheen of great benevolence and good governance do not tell the whole story of its modern trajectory over the past century. First, emerging from a feudal society, the country was, and remains, highly unequal, with access to land, livestock, water, employment, and social services highly variable even while the poorest have responded positively to happiness surveys. This has been called "the enigma of happiness amidst deprivations."[43]

Second, many have noted that there were in the past, and arguably continue to be today, few avenues for challenging political and economic hierarchies in Bhutan due to "theocratic and archaically feudal . . . socio-political conditions."[44] Writing about Bhutan in the first half of the twentieth century, Dhurba Rizal concurred, noting that "administration was feudal, anachronistic, and in a chaotic state. The King appointed, dismissed, and punished civil servants" if they thought too independently.[45] The country's staunchest external supporters have admitted that powerholders were averse to ideas of democratization, let alone acts of it.[46] In the very few instances where people or organizations contested state power, the response was swift and repressive. Therefore, the country may appear to have experienced very few crackdowns against its people, but that is also because the country bred so few challengers.

The most prominent exception to this presumed docility of the people was the relative political awareness of some of the country's Bhutanese Nepalis. Dhakal and Strawn note that this was due to geography (being located near India and accessing external information), education (many Bhutanese Nepalis were educated in India and absorbed messages that challenged imperialistic mores), and ethnicity (the Bhutanese Nepalis were the most recognizably disenfranchised and were most easily able to establish affinities with Nepalis in other countries).[47] Sinha further notes that Darjeeling—a city in the northernmost point of India's West Bengal state, nestled halfway between Nepal and Bhutan—served as a political vector for ethnic Nepalis in the entire region (not just in Bhutan), brewing a heady mix of political contestation, Nepali cultural and literary activity, and labor organizing (see map 3). The ability of Bhutan's population in the south—which is where nearly all Bhutanese Nepalis resided—to reach Darjeeling was of particular importance in countering what was otherwise a "placid political atmosphere."[48] This speaks to the importance of physical location. It is notable that the very few oppositional actors of other ethnicities in Bhutan—primarily Sharchops, whom I cover in later chapters—also regularly crossed the southern border into India.

In this light, the Bhutanese Nepalis look like troublemakers in an otherwise peaceful oasis. But modernizing influences were not far off. Calls to shed the yoke of unrepresentative masters penetrated the entire subcontinent, as Indian subjects demanded independence and ethnic Nepalis promoted autonomy.[49] Vying for recognition in the upcoming shuffle of postcolonial independence, power challengers emerged in India, Sikkim, and Nepal. In Bhutan proper, these groups gained little traction, instead finding expression in nearby states.

The following paragraphs offer a reconstruction of early acts of Bhutanese Nepalis challenging state power, based primarily on the works of Dhakal and Strawn, Sinha, and Hutt,[50] with some additional reflections from activists who lived much later and whom I interviewed myself. But in the absence of triangulated documentation—which Hutt tried, tirelessly, to find—some details in the following paragraphs remain uncertain. Dhakal and Strawn note as much when they aver that "creating an accurate picture is probably impossible."[51] But whether perfectly accurate or not, these stories of protest have value: first, for the way they have been "harnessed to exiles' political cause,"[52] and second, because they reveal more than a kernel of truth about Bhutan's desire to rout out challengers. Importantly, the opposition groups that formed in response to the routing then fulfilled the prophecy of the government: they crossed the border and planted the seeds of an ecosystem of exile politics, which served to further inflame the immunitary response in Bhutan itself. Foreshadowing coming chapters, proximity and precarity were a part of this process.

In 1927, a Bhutanese Nepali village headman (*mandal*), Pashupati Adhikari, protested his high rate of tax in the town of Lamidara (current name Mendrelgang) in Tsirang district. In response, his land was confiscated, and he was beaten up and expelled from Bhutan to India, where his relatives live to this day.[53] Tussling with the same local powerholders (the aforementioned Dorji family), Garjaman Gurung was poisoned.[54] In the early 1950s, Masur Chhetri tried to organize his countrymen to agitate for greater ethnic minority representation in Bhutan, even, according to one source, reaching out to the then prime minister of Nepal, Matrika Prasad Koirala (M. P. Koirala), for support.[55] For this show of disloyalty, he was chased, arrested, and killed by drowning in the Sankosh River in a leather bag (see map 2).[56] While the details of Masur Chhetri's killing vary somewhat depending on the teller of the story, there is always the drowning, always the Sankosh River, and always the leather bag.

A legendary cult status has come to be associated with these three figures. Using Veena Das's term, their expulsion and killings have become "critical events."[57] Such moments in time, Martin Sökefeld has argued, trigger diasporic imaginations, like the way that the Indian army's 1994 storming of the symbolically significant Sikh Golden Temple in Amritsar popularized the movement for an independent Sikh nation-state.[58] Similarly, Pashupati Adhikari, Garjaman Gurung, and Masur Chhetri became cultural touchstones for the exiled community, with stories, songs, and plays enacted in exile to urge remembrance.

The separatist nature of these groups is difficult to assess. One can certainly say that cascading indignant reactions to the deaths of Garjaman Gurung and Masur Chhetri, fueled by the zeitgeist of regional revolutionary movements, ignited opposition to Bhutan's powerholders. But most accounts would suggest that a desire for Bhutanese Nepali representation, and not a separate state, were at the core of two early protest movements: Jai Gorkha and the Bhutan State Congress (BSC).

The Jai Gorkha movement grew out of Garjaman Gurung's early involvement in advancing the cause of a Bhutanese Nepali presence in politics.[59] In about 1947, two village *mandals* in Bhutan sought out material and human support in nearby India to help bring about political change in Bhutan.[60] Bhutanese troops shut down Jai Gorkha almost immediately and tried to arrest all of its leaders. Some escaped and crossed into India.[61] The riveting story told by one of Jai Gorkha's members, Bikh Bahadur Gurung (B. B. Gurung), has been recorded and translated by a later generation of homeland activists. In a 2012 interview for *Bhutan News Service*, B. B. Gurung described his escape from prison, his clandestine journey to India, and his eventual triumphant welcome back to Bhutan as an approved village clerk.[62] Much is left unsaid about B. B. Gurung's time in India, as well as that of his compatriots. While about fifteen BSC activists found immediate safety in their Indian refuge, this was not the kind of protection that would have allowed them to continue to agitate for change in Bhutan.[63]

On the heels of Jai Gorkha, the BSC arose in the early 1950s, with its two most prominent leaders, Dal Bahadur Gurung (D. B. Gurung) and Ganesh Prasad Sharma (G. P. Sharma), emerging from the metaphorical blood of past injustices: D. B. Gurung was a younger relative of Garjaman Gurung and G. P. Sharma was a witness to the events leading up to Masur Chhetri's execution.[64] Spurred by the injustice of these deaths, and riding a wave of Indian independence,[65] the BSC was founded in November 1952 in Patgaon, Assam (see map 3). Over the next several years, the BSC engaged in various activities intended to catalyze change in Bhutan, including speaking with Indian journalists,[66] issuing communiqués to the Bhutanese government,[67] lobbying powerholders from India and Nepal,[68] and organizing demonstrations.[69]

For a group that was seen as a threat to the current architecture of power, its discourse was surprisingly mild. Most of the BSC's communications directed toward home had a conciliatory tone that belied the image of belligerent oppositional leaders. In an appeal to the government regarding representation and taxation, submitted in December 1955, the group called themselves "loyal subjects writ[ing] unitedly with hope and confidence."[70] As Leo Rose noted, this was "scarcely radical" behavior.[71]

The mildness of the language used by the BSC notwithstanding, the reach of the group was further than one might expect. D. B. Gurung and G. P. Sharma traveled to New Delhi to meet with Indian prime minister Jawaharlal Nehru and to Kathmandu to meet with Nepal's prominent dissidents, establishing a lasting relationship with Girija Prasad Koirala, who, after having a hand in overthrowing the Nepal monarchy, would one day become Nepal's prime minister.[72] The BSC also consulted with members of the Nepali Congress and the Indian National Congress to develop its platform and depended on them for "moral, material, and political support."[73] Dhakal and Strawn admit that the Nepali Congress "also sent some arms they had used during the revolution," which led to some "small skirmishes."[74] This example demonstrates how increasingly aggressive expressions of dissatisfaction and increasingly violent immunitary state responses fell into spiraling cycles.

In 1954, BSC leaders turned their sights back to Bhutan, hoping to create the kind of internal energy that could lend power to their movement. They organized a *satyagraha*, a form of nonviolent civil disobedience, to march back into Bhutan and present their complaints to the king, modeled on the Indian National Congress's tactic of filling the jails, or "Jail *Bharo Andolan*." To organize the march, the BSC recruited both Indians and Nepalis. Indeed, the laws of the region "were so flexible across open borders in India, Nepal and Bhutan that Bhutan State Congress collected an assorted crowd of followers from all the three states as its members."[75] Although it took place in Bhutan, this march reflects the ways that an expanding exile politics ecosystem relied on physical proximity to facilitate the passage of activists and activism to nearby places of refuge and influence.

The march to Bhutan, however, where opportunities for protest remained nearly impossible, was ill advised. Imitating the "Jail *Bharo Andolan*" movement of the Indian National Congress proved foolhardy because "Bhutan neither had the police force nor the jails as institutions known elsewhere."[76] Hundreds of people tried to cross the Indian border into Bhutan at the Gelephu gate but were prevented from doing so. The few that did cross had a list of demands to deliver to the king, but as the crowd and onlookers milled, shots were fired, presumably by the police, with subsequent injuries and death. Dhakal and Strawn state that as the protesters tried to escape back over the border, twenty-five were killed and seventeen were wounded.[77] Many were also arrested. In a brilliant piece of political theater that silenced further public opposition, the government paraded the arrestees before a group of Bhutanese Nepali villagers while the king asked them if they were happy with their lives. The silence of the villagers lent little credence to BSC claims of dissatisfaction and made it far easier for the police to justify sending Dalamarden Raye, a member of the BSC's coordinating committee, to prison for life.[78]

Early Political Precarity in India

India did not furnish BSC activists with any kind of permanent official legal status. Instead, activists relied on the informal protection of "blurred membership" that Kamal Sadiq has described so aptly in other parts of South Asia.[79] Further, political precarity—the risks associated with protesting as a foreigner, covered in detail in chapter 5—was prevalent. Public protest for BSC activists was explicitly forbidden. Despite supporting the aims of the movement, Indian prime minister Jawaharlal Nehru wrote a letter to M. P. Koirala, the prime minister of Nepal, about the BSC in March 1954:

> A number of Nepali organisations are organising satyagraha in Bhutan. They have made their base in Indian territory. I have just received news that there was a conflict between them and presumably Bhutan troops. This is exceedingly embarrassing to us as it must be to your Government. Bhutan is your neighbour country and you would no doubt like to have friendly relations with Bhutan. I am aware that there are difficulties in Bhutan for Nepali residents there and that the policy of the Bhutan Government has not been very favourable to the Nepalese. I would welcome progress in Bhutan in various ways. But we cannot encourage Indian territory to be made the base of operations. I am sure that your Government also cannot approve of this method. Governments do not function in this way. I hope, therefore, that you will discourage, in so far as you can, these aggressive activities.[80]

Similarly, some weeks later, the Indian government instructed its local offices in Assam, West Bengal, and Sikkim to prevent collective action of the Bhutanese Nepalis. In a May 1954 letter to Bhutan's king, Jigme Dorji Wangchuck, Nehru wrote: "We told [local officers] that Indian territory should not be allowed to be used for any aggressive movement, even though peaceful, against Bhutan. . . . Your Government must know this fully and in fact we have received letters from officials of your Government thanking the Government of India for the action we took. The agitation subsided then, chiefly, because of the action we had taken."[81]

Tellingly, Nehru differentiated between collective action and individuals. In directing the chief minister of Assam to stop the marches, he explained:

> If organised bands of volunteers endeavour to go from India to Bhutan with the professed object of offering such satyagraha, they will be stopped.
>
> If this has to be done, it should be done quietly and without fuss. There is a difference between organised bands going with this professed object and individuals going through peacefully without declaring their object of satyagraha. Such individuals normally go through and we cannot stop them unless we suspect trouble. Our object should be to prevent this organised movement taking place from India and to make it clear to the Bhutanese Government that we are not encouraging it in any way.[82]

Nehru's advice speaks to the political precarity of BSC members. It also explains why quiet action was possible, even in the context of precarity. That is, public, visible action may have been shut down, but some activities continued. For example, Hutt cites three documents issued by the BSC in 1957–58—a leaflet, a statement, and a letter to Nehru—that indicate that the movement still breathed life, although at a slower and shallower pace.[83] And in 1960, D. B. Gurung was still publishing articles from India that called Bhutan a "despotic regime."[84] Nevertheless, most authors seem to agree that, following 1954, the BSC was a "spent force."[85] Sinha notes that the BSC "tried to organise many misadventures, which all resulted in failure . . . the *Congress* survived more on paper than as an active populist organisation."[86] And Dhakal and Strawn concede that the BSC existed "more on paper than in reality by 1954."[87]

One can surmise that the motivation for BSC members to protest withered because the Bhutanese government granted some concessions to Bhutanese Nepalis, allowing representation in Bhutan's National Assembly and, crucially, offering the possibility of citizenship.[88] The irony of this demand should not be lost on the reader—the BSC, in pushing for greater representation for Bhutanese Nepalis, encouraged the passage of a citizenship law that created distinctions between citizens and noncitizens, and these distinctions, thirty years later, excluded its ethnic members from the rights to national membership. Most of the BSC's leaders were also invited to return to Bhutan. In addition to being officially pardoned, in 1969 three major BSC figures received a rehabilitation package on their return to Bhutan. One BSC leader, G. P. Sharma, "was not qualified for (the King's) clemency" because he had procured Nepali citizenship in the meantime—a rare occurrence, then and now.[89] G. P. Sharma's ineligibility for return foreshadows a paradox of this book, which is that in mitigating precarity through the permanent protection of another country, one forfeits the ability to return home to the country one worked to change.

Dormancy or Death?

Writing about the Zimbabwean political diaspora, Betts and Jones describe the life cycle of diaspora politics, arguing that diasporas may experience a period of death and afterlife when supporters are external to the movement and networks are unstable. "Diaspora death" occurs when funding is withdrawn and meaningful activities cease, and the "afterlife" phase reflects the tragic but ignored efforts of a few remaining stalwart activists looking for a payout.[90]

One way to understand the BSC's acceleration and deceleration is to align it to Betts and Jones's patterns of the diaspora life cycle, with 1954 resembling the death knell for the BSC and the sporadic efforts thereafter as the afterlife phase. But I offer an alternate way of thinking about the movement. The 1970s and 1980s surely represent a low period in the history of Bhutan's homeland activism. But because the problems associated with the original state of repression had not been entirely extinguished—Bhutanese Nepalis were still treated unequally, as the coming chapters will show—homeland activism lay low but did not die completely. Even after the BSC stopped operating some actions continued quietly, subsumed under different names and by individuals no longer using the BSC moniker.

Dhakal and Strawn point out that "a succession of Nepali Bhutanese student movements in Banaras Hindu University [in Varanasi, India] were notable political outlets for Bhutanese frustrations."[91] A student union was formed, for example, and an attempt was made to write, print, and distribute information booklets. Bhutanese Nepalis continued to cross from Bhutan and into India, and they continued to mobilize on behalf of their community at home. Two decades later, when tensions once again mounted regarding the Bhutanese Nepali issue in Bhutan, successor organizations to these original groups were among the first to take a stand. Parashar Parmanand notes the rebirth of the BSC by another name,[92] while Rosalind Evans records that political leaders who had been active in the BSC in the 1950s distributed pamphlets on human rights and democracy some thirty years later in the villages of Bhutan, prior to their flight to Nepal.[93]

Thus, homeland activism neither died nor disappeared nor experienced an afterlife, but instead lay dormant until such time as political opportunities dictated their need. Just as deciduous trees shed their sun-needy foliage in expectation of winter but retain core life systems in their trunks and roots, activism targeted toward Bhutan hunkered down in hibernation.

Britain's political officer (Gangtok), writing in 1932 about power hierarchies in nearby Sikkim, observed that governance was "based on the good old patriarchal monarchy of ancient days of oriental civilization where subjects stand as children of the Ruler; and with the simple hill people unaffected by the virus of democracy and elections, the system works excellently."[94] Bhutan's early decades can be described in much the same way: those in power perceived the system as working smoothly and effectively. The emergence of social and cultural challenges to this status quo was a rude awakening, triggering the government's immunitary response. The subsequent push and pull of claims to power (resistance to it and assertions of it) were not, of course, unique. But given this history, it is interesting how little scrutiny and criticism Bhutan has received. This has been called the "Shangri-la-zation of Bhutan," wherein the captivated international community has for the most part swept aside any discussion of government strong-arming.[95]

This chapter on Bhutan's history attempts to rectify that omission, and it sets the stage for the rest of the book. In demonstrating how expressions of power and protest have always been deeply interlinked, it provides context for the investigations of precarity, proximity, and exile politics that follow. And it has shown the futility of trying to resolve the debate on origin and reaction in the context of Bhutan. Trying to answer the question "Who started this conflict?" brings us no closer to truth; it only tells us something about the bias of the responder.

This examination of midcentury activism in Bhutan has also introduced the ways that protest itself was mobile. In the context of highly porous borders and repression at home, mobilization itself migrated to nearby locations. There, we see the stirrings of how proximity and its less desirable sibling, political precarity, sat uncomfortably side by side as the work of the BSC waxed and waned.

There is no doubt that Sinha's characterization of the BSC as an immature organization is accurate.[96] Its leaders mimicked strategies deployed in other contexts without careful consideration. There was a failure to capture sympathy for the movement from within Bhutan, neglecting the popular opinions of both Drukpas and Nepalis.[97] And the one structural success that the BSC's leaders contributed to—the 1958 Nationality Law of Bhutan—may have ended the possibility of "blurred membership"[98] at the same time that it began to limit other formal citizenship channels, as the coming chapters will show.

Nevertheless, the BSC and preceding protests are worthy of study because they follow spiraling patterns of state power and protest, and moved political mobilization from the inside to the outside. In the face of immunitary action, Bhutanese Nepalis crossed a porous border into India or Nepal on several occasions, resulting in proximate homeland activism. The actions of Bhutanese homeland activists in this bygone era are also valuable to examine because an organization with a title is not the only, or indeed an accurate, measure of the presence of homeland activism. Expressions of dissatisfaction—reflecting real grievances in Bhutan—continued quietly, in limited form, far after the BSC was regarded as dead. Far from representing the end of the movement, these mid-century seeds of activism sprouted anew when grievances grew to a greater pitch. I turn to those events now.

THE PASSAGE OF PROTEST

When I learned of the arrest of my friends who met clandestinely to discuss the political situation, I knew the options for me were limited—either I leave the country or be arrested and possibly be killed in detention. I decided to choose safety and I decided to choose my life. I decided to choose freedom. I left Bhutan on November 6, 1989.

—Ratna Prasad Subba (R. P. Subba)

Yadu (Y. P.) Dhungel, a Bhutanese Nepali, was born in Kikhorthang, Tsirang, a southern district of Bhutan. His father was the Block Headman for Kikhorthang Block and Y. P. Dhungel and his brothers spent their childhood, as many southern Bhutanese did when they were not in school, helping his parents to harvest the fields of cardamom and to work in the orange groves. He attended the prestigious Sherubtse College in eastern Bhutan, studying in both English and Dzongkha, and graduated with a Bachelor of Commerce in 1986. After six months of teaching high school in Sarpang as part of a national work program, he sat the Royal Civil Service Commission exam and, on passing, became a civil servant.

Y. P. Dhungel then began work at the government-run Food Corporation of Bhutan (FCB). Within a few years, he was responsible for the financial management and budget for all of the FCB, which was an enormous responsibility and one that he relished. In 1989, as part of his job, he attended a training program for nine months in Germany to study food policy statistics. When the Berlin Wall fell in November, Y. P. Dhungel knew he was witnessing a momentous occasion. "They were breaking the wall, and they were putting these wall pieces into small glass cases," Y. P. Dhungel recalled. "So I bought it for ten Deutschmarks in a nice glass case, because I wanted to bring that memory of the union, two Germanys uniting. . . . I wanted to preserve that history."[1] When he returned to Bhutan the following month, he brought that piece of the wall with him.

Less than three years later, Y. P. Dhungel was once again caught up in a historic moment. This time it was his own country, Bhutan, and it was a story of division, not unification. The relatively harmonious era between the country's northern ruling class and the Bhutanese Nepalis of the south had come to an end. Y. P. Dhungel fled his native Bhutan with his wife and two children and became a refugee in Nepal. He brought that piece of the Berlin Wall with him, where it remained in his refugee camp hut for seventeen years.

Y. P. Dhungel's story, and others in this chapter, demonstrate that there were varied motivations for Bhutanese Nepalis to leave the country. Some left because they were forced or threatened by the Royal Bhutan Army (RBA), who considered them *ngolops* or "anti-nationals" for taking part in protests against government policies. Others could not reconcile the violence of local militias indiscriminately weeding out these anti-nationals with the king's exhortations for southerners to remain. Others followed relatives or village leaders. There were also people who left due to escalating and increasingly tense situations in the south, feeling "caught in a valley" between government forces and the Bhutanese Nepali political leaders.[2] One refrain was common to nearly all of my interviewees: all mourned some part of the lives they lost in Bhutan, calling to mind their land, their families, and their traditions. To this day, not a single person who left has been permitted to return.

This chapter recounts the events in the decade leading up to the eventual departure and flight of tens of thousands of Bhutanese Nepalis. This is well-worn territory for a number of scholars,[3] human rights advocates,[4] humanitarian aid organizations,[5] and the refugees themselves.[6] I hope, however, to add something new to this discussion by showing how the issue, which I review through primary and secondary sources, quickly crossed borders, in what I refer to as "the passage of protest." In a nod to the dense literature on transnational activism and diaspora politics,[7] I show how the pressures that activists placed on the Bhutanese state shifted to the transnational realm, "over and beyond" the machinations of governments.[8] Here, along with an important contextual discussion of Bhutan's relationship with its neighbors and its policies and practices vis-à-vis the border, we see the origins of Bhutan's most contentious and lengthy wave of contemporary protest, and its transformation into a growing exile politics ecosystem.

Incorporation and Integration

Bhutan's early responses to a growing Bhutanese Nepali population were incorporation and integration. In the 1960s, schools were opened and a road was built linking the north and south. In the 1970s, there was increasing representation of Bhutanese Nepalis in high levels of government.[9] In the first half of the 1980s, a National Council for Social and Cultural Promotion (NCSCP) encouraged north-south integration in the country, with Drukpa and Bhutanese Nepali schoolchildren and college students studying in each other's regions. A cash incentive was even offered for intermarriage between the two groups.

Y. P. Dhungel benefited from these integration policies, when Bhutan willingly and actively worked to incorporate Bhutanese Nepalis into society. He was, in his own words, a "model citizen," devoted to his work, king, and country. But even as some advancements continued, regressive policies were already coming to the fore: increasingly restrictive laws around citizenship, more rigidity in guidelines governing cultural practice, and the 1988 census, all discussed below. By the mid-1980s, the NCSCP was dissolved.[10]

The changing attitudes toward Bhutanese Nepalis—at the individual and government level—are frequently linked to profound regional changes, most notably the 1975 annexation of Sikkim to India. This movement, as well as the rise of the Gorkhaland National Liberation Front (GNLF), highlights one of the most long-standing and entrenched debates about Bhutan's political behavior vis-à-vis Bhutanese Nepalis: the question of "Greater Nepal."

"Greater Nepal"

The Greater Nepal narrative suggested that ethnic Nepali populations—not only in Bhutan, but also in India—were collectively working to create autonomous or independent ethnic enclaves and thus attempting to replace or overthrow incumbent governments. While Hutt suggested in 1994 that the Bhutanese government's fear of a Greater Nepal had largely been "laid to rest,"[11] this discourse remains strongly present in the "Who started it?" blame game regarding the Bhutanese Nepali issue.

The endurance of the Greater Nepal narrative of fear can be explained by viewing the issue through the perspective of the "frayed edges" that characterize Bhutan's southern border.[12] As a state that was largely ignored by colonial Great Britain, Bhutan never suffered the profound "cartographic anxiety" of India.[13] Yet Van Schendel's notion of "apprehensive territoriality"—which he describes as "opacity regarding the territorial dimensions of the state"[14]—is relevant in Bhutan as it is relevant in other countries in the region that David Gellner has termed "Northern South Asia."[15] Van Schendel writes, "Such opacity translates into confusion about the limits of sovereignty as well as about the distinction between what is domestic and what is foreign. Where does 'my' society end and 'yours' begin?"[16] A foray into regional politics further reflects Bhutan's apprehensions, and, indeed, anxieties, about its enormous neighbors.

Bhutan's Relations with China and India

Bhutan sits sandwiched between Asia's two most powerful—and the world's two most populous—states. Since the founding of the modern Indian and Chinese states in the late 1940s, Bhutan has held itself warily in the shadow of both. Eyeing the behemoths strategically, Bhutan saw the Chinese occupation of Tibet in 1950 as a clear and present threat to its own survival as an independent state and, after several Chinese crackdowns on Tibetan uprisings throughout that decade, reinforced the colonial-era India-Bhutan relationship established by the Treaty of Sinchula (see chapter 2) and accepted Indian advances for a closer security relationship.[17] Since then the country has pursued its political, economic, and foreign policy objectives through very close ties with India. Economically, Bhutan and India are extremely closely integrated. The India-Bhutan Agreement on Trade, Commerce and Transit, most recently revised in 2016, establishes a free trade regime between the two countries. India is Bhutan's top trading partner, and its investments in the country comprise 50 percent of Bhutan's total foreign direct investment.[18]

Today, the Bhutanese army is trained in India, and the Indian air force provides military support to Bhutan when required.[19] In June 2017, a Chinese military unit with construction vehicles began extending a road southward into territory that is contested between China and Bhutan. Two days later, in response, about 270 armed Indian troops came to Bhutan's aid to forcefully disrupt the construction. Soon after, India and China announced a joint withdrawal from the confrontation. Tensions ran high over the potential for the conflict to balloon into war, particularly in Bhutan. Locals there, while acknowledging the fear of an annexation similar to what befell Tibet in 1950, also criticized the smothering embrace of India, which they felt was actively sabotaging better relations and stronger economic links between Bhutan and China for its own geopolitical interests.[20]

This trepidation over the tightness of India's embrace was also present in 1975 with the crisis in Sikkim (see map 3). In that year, Sikkim's citizens voted to end the reign of their monarch, Chogyal Palden Thondup Namgyal, resulting in India's annexation of the independent kingdom. At the time, the kingdoms of Bhutan, Nepal, and Sikkim were written about and compared as similar sovereign territories, as the term *Himalasia* suggested.[21] Sikkim's royal lines went back much further than the seventy years of Bhutan's; at the time of annexation, Sikkim's Namgyal family had been ruling Sikkim for 334 years. Thus, Bhutan's leaders took alarmed notice, clearly wanting to avoid the same fate. However mistakenly, they attributed the loss of Sikkim's independence to the significant presence of ethnic Nepalis in the leadership of the two major political parties in

Sikkim, as well as in the voting population at large, who voted to be a part of India.[22] Through the lens of Sikkim, Nepali immigration into Bhutan was a bright red flag. "We live on a day-to-day basis with the fate of Sikkim," asserted one official from the Royal Government of Bhutan in 2005.[23]

But while both Bhutan and Sikkim were kingdoms prior to the latter's annexation, there were significant differences that suggest that Bhutan's fear of a Nepali takeover were wildly overblown. Andrew Duff's *Sikkim: Requiem for a Himalayan Kingdom*, which sympathetically chronicles the collapse of the Namgyal regime and its embattled royalty, notes the many ways that Bhutan was on firmer ground. Sikkim had a significant Indian presence of both military and administrative personnel, where it was minimal in Bhutan.[24] The kings had markedly different personalities. And there were important divergences in the regional geopolitical environment:

> The warm relations between India and Bhutan could not have been more different from the tense relationship between India and Sikkim. Bhutan's leaders had been assiduous in staying close to the Indians and making Delhi feel comfortable with their desire for greater autonomy. Bhutan also had the advantage of a looser relationship with India. The Indo-Bhutanese treaty had been negotiated in 1949, a few months before the first Chinese incursions into Tibet; crucially, Sikkim's had been negotiated more than a year later, when the political environment looked quite different.[25]

Hutt considers, and answers, this question: "Would Sikkim now be one of the world's smallest sovereign states if there had been no Nepali immigration? The most one can say is that this is doubtful."[26] However different Bhutan and Sikkim were, fears of a Greater Nepal were a key part of the Bhutanese government's narrative to justify increasingly restrictive actions in southern Bhutan. Bhutan's apprehensions were also related to the democratic movement of the 1950s (discussed in the previous chapter) and the ascension in the 1980s of the militant GNLF in West Bengal, India, bordering Bhutan. The tactics of the GNLF (violent), as much as their stated aims (the creation of separate Gorkhaland state in West Bengal), were of grave concern to the Bhutanese, as was the anxiety (perceived or real) that some GNLF fighters were hiding from Indian forces among the ethnically similar Nepalis in Bhutan's foothills. Yet Sinha notes that they were "unwelcome guests" in Bhutan.[27] That is, neither northern Drukpa nor southern Bhutanese Nepalis were sympathetic to their aims. What needs to be emphasized is that it hardly matters whether migrants in Sikkim were the reason for its annexation or not, nor did it matter if Bhutanese Nepalis were in cahoots with the GNLF: the narrative of "Greater Nepal" had taken on a life of its own.

Integration to Marginalization

In light of the fears of a Greater Nepal, Bhutan embarked on a national program under the slogan "One Nation, One Policy" that "sought explicitly to compact all ethnic groups into a single cultural strand."[28] This process of Bhutanization aimed to "promote national integration, national consciousness and national identity to profoundly reshape Bhutanese society and national identity with Drukpa values and traditions."[29] In lockstep with this program was the promotion of a centuries-old code of moral and ethical conduct originally suited to the monastic order, called Driglam Namzha. Its application in the 1970s and 1980s, "outside the monastic and ceremonial contexts within which it originally evolved,"[30] led to policies and practices that, many Bhutanese Nepalis charged, abruptly coerced them to change their outer appearance and language. Dress codes were formalized, and Dzongkha was elevated quickly as the Nepali language was eliminated from southern schools and the curriculum.[31]

These changes were not necessarily persecutory in intent. Driglam Namzha's emphasis on inner mindfulness as well as external behaviors suggests the cultivation of practices explicitly unrelated to ethnicity.[32] While the imposition of a dress code was viewed as a form of abuse by some Bhutanese Nepalis, proponents of the government note that public meetings were held around Bhutan, some of which the king himself attended, to discuss what a national dress code might be.

These public meetings did little to assuage Bhutanese Nepali anxieties. Neither the process for determining the dress codes nor the outcome was viewed favorably. The public meetings in the south were less focused on gathering diverse opinions and more about informing southern Bhutanese and thanking them for decisions that were already made.[33] The 1989 edict issued by the king following these meetings seemed a foregone conclusion. It required all people to wear the Drukpa garments of the north at official ceremonies: *gho* for men and *kira* for women. These garments, made of heavy, thick material, were unfamiliar to many Bhutanese Nepalis,[34] and they were uncomfortable for those in warmer climates, as in the south.[35] Outside of official ceremonies, overzealous local implementation led to coercive practices in everyday contexts, with people fined for wearing Nepali dress as their daily attire[36] and Bhutanese Nepali students feeling pressured to cut their hair.[37] The dress code requirement also generated resentment at formal occasions. In one instance documented by a Canadian volunteer, the principal at Sherubtse College demanded that Bhutanese Nepali students put on their *ghos* and *kiras* during an important Hindu religious festival, Durga Puja. It is hardly surprising that the newly *gho-* and *kira*-clad students then celebrated their festival with "an antagonistic undertone."[38]

Language is both a cultural and a practical unifying element for a nation: cultural because it is a repository for the foundational documents of the state as well as its literature; practical so that its laws, rules and regulations—from marriage licenses to street signs—can be universally understood.[39] This is why the demotion of Nepali and the elevation of Dzongkha was viewed by Bhutanese Nepalis as an oppressive act. Hutt argues that the dismissal of well-respected Nepali teachers, whose services were no longer required, and the possible burning of Nepali textbooks were politically and religiously problematic.[40] For some, "the Nepali language represented a citadel from which the malign and corrupting processes of Westernization on the one hand and Drukpaization on the other could be warded off."[41] Practically, too, the emphasis on Dzongkha was difficult. Although the government did introduce classes in Dzongkha, the pressure to learn it was forced and abrupt, especially for those of an advanced age.

Thus, while within the government the process of Bhutanization was viewed as a means to retain Bhutan's unique cultural, religious, and linguistic character and safeguard the country against outside influences,[42] it is not surprising that Bhutanese Nepalis "constructed Driglam Namzha as one of the key instruments of Drukpa oppression."[43] "Then we heard about the fines, if you didn't wear the clothes and speak Dzongkha. We resented this. It might not seem like such a big thing when compared with the torture and like that. It was a very big thing. Like, if suddenly you had to pay money because the government didn't like the way you dressed and the language you talked in. We were like that [i.e., wearing Nepali clothes and speaking Nepali] for our whole lives."[44]

In these same decades, changing laws imposed increasingly stringent requirements for becoming a citizen and disincentivized marrying foreigners.[45] A story of almost mythical status on this issue revolved around Sita Mothe Darjee, a woman who married a Bhutanese citizen and was rendered a noncitizen under the 1980 Marriage Act. When she was told that she had to leave Bhutan without her husband and children, she was so distressed that she committed suicide.[46] This is another of the "critical events" referred to in the previous chapter that stoked the diaspora imagination. Many of my interviewees told the story of Sita Mothe Darjee, recalling her name in a kind of persecution refrain. The new laws governing citizenship and marriage were a "shocking experience to the modernising Lhotshampa elements, who had taken their state-sponsored three decades old linear progress and prosperity for granted."[47]

Clearing the Land: 1988 Census and the Green Belt Proposal

The promulgation of these legislative restrictions and the implementation of Driglam Namzha came to a head in 1988, when Bhutan enacted a census with new strict requirements that no longer relied on village leaders and instead insisted on difficult-to-obtain documentation.[48] Much as with Driglam Namzha and changing citizenship and marriage laws, Bhutanese Nepalis were targeted by policies that, on paper, were meant for all but seemed specifically designed to alienate and push them off their land.

A generous interpretation of the census implementation would suggest that government officials simply wanted to identify illegal migrants among the population, of which, it can be surmised, there were likely some. But this does not explain why the census divided the southern population into seven categories, ranging from genuine Bhutanese citizens to nonnationals.[49] Members of one family were placed into five or six different categories, with the result that even those with genuine citizenship were compelled to leave with the rest of their families.[50] This has been attributed to the stringency of requirements to document citizenship. The only proof that was accepted was a land tax document from the year 1958. Anyone who may have been absent in 1958—a possibility far more likely for Bhutanese Nepalis than for other segments of the population—was denied citizenship. Dhakal and Strawn further note that citizens risked being rendered stateless if they lost documents or had difficulty obtaining such papers from their hometowns.[51] Hutt has documented the stories of numerous individuals with the coveted "genuine citizen" status who had considered their citizenship secure in Bhutan but who were then unable to obtain documentation from truculent local officials, and thus lost their rights of ownership and property during the census.[52] Even Om Pradhan, a pro-government Bhutanese Nepali, admits that expecting families to have preserved these fragile documents, in the humidity of southern Bhutan, was unrealistic.[53]

Another (perceived) means for the government to clear the land of Bhutanese Nepalis came in the form of the promotion of a Green Belt proposal, passed in a resolution of Bhutan's National Assembly on March 19–20, 1990. It was proposed that a one-kilometer forest belt be created on either side of the India-Bhutan border, nominally with the aim of preventing erosion and flooding but which would also serve to "remove the potentials [sic] for criminals and apprehending law enforcers from unknowingly intruding into each other's territory."[54] While in theory this gave people a choice to move or not, in practice the Green Belt buybacks would have forced Bhutanese Nepalis to choose between remaining where they were with no access to schools, health clinics, jobs, or any government services, and leaving their lands, with paltry compensation and limited possibilities to construct new homes in areas where they would be increasingly subject to Bhutanization.[55]

It has been claimed that the Green Belt proposal would have displaced 30 percent of settlers in the south if fully implemented.[56] However, it is difficult to estimate how many people were actually affected by the land buybacks in the end because the scheme never materialized following the Bhutanese Nepali exodus. It may be that, true to the claims of the Bhutanese government, the funding needed to buy back the land was never secured from donors.[57] It may also be that, with so many Bhutanese Nepalis gone, the imperative to clear the land of Bhutanese Nepalis had disappeared. It has been noted that the king did, for some years, desist from redistributing deserted land. But in 2001, Sinha notes that "the resistance to settle the unattended dissidents' land could not continue for long. Of late, the *Tshongdu* [National Assembly] has decided to settle them with shifting cultivators and landless marginal farmers from the interior of Bhutan. It is alleged that influential Drukpas have already taken over certain preferred land in a dubious way."[58]

Another interpretation of the government's land-clearing exercise is that it was a massive resource grab. The lands of the south, formerly malaria-infested and uncultivated, were now literally bearing fruit, and local and central officials saw an opportunity to appropriate these fields.[59] The fast-moving rivers of southern Bhutan provided (and still provide) an ideal place for installing hydropower plants. The first commissioned hydropower plant in Bhutan, Chhukha, gave government officials a taste of how much revenue these lands could bring in. "Chhukha, perhaps, showed the rulers the riches that lay within their grasp but for the Nepali speakers of the south who had the potential of agitating for their share," suggests Kanak Mani Dixit.[60]

Resistance from Inside and Out

The policies and practices of Bhutanization were felt as a slow burn until the 1988 census. But combined with mounting marginalization and a census operation whose methods were opaque and whose outcomes were unjust, resistance emerged, internally at first, and then reignited nearby. The second part of this chapter examines this resistance and its transnational origins in what I call the "the passage of protest." When limited by stringent surveillance in an increasingly difficult atmosphere in Bhutan, activists started crossing the border into India and further into Nepal. The bordering practices described by Ilcan[61]—the surveillance, policing, and increasingly militarized responses to targeted groups—worked to stimulate an exodus of those most active in confronting such forces. As the government increasingly saw all Bhutanese Nepali activity as threatening, it was not only activists who departed Bhutan but huge swaths of the southern population.

The first protest by Bhutanese Nepalis was in the form of an appeal to the government. Tek Nath Rizal, who would become the Bhutanese Nepalis' most famous activist, and Bidyapati Bhandari were the southern representatives of the king's Royal Advisory Council. They had heard about the difficulties that the census had wrought from their constituents and they, along with several other Bhutanese Nepali civil servants living in Thimphu, drafted a petition to bring a complaint about the census process directly to the king. According to Hari Chhetri, a Bhutanese Nepali government official who later left Bhutan, who was present at the meetings where the petition was drafted, this consultation process played out like a Shakespearean drama, with Tek Nath Rizal playing the role of the hot-headed but sincere representative and Om Pradhan—Bhutan's highest-ranking Bhutanese Nepali—playing the role of a deceitful self-serving lackey to the king.[62]

The petition that was submitted—signed only by Tek Nath Rizal and Bidyapati Bhandari—reads as a polite, almost obsequious report of how inaccurate classification methods were affecting the southern population and taking away citizenship from those who should have it. It "humbly beg[s] Your Majesty for protection and relief" and requests amendments to the 1985 Citizenship Act that would restore citizenship to children and spouses and those who arrived in Bhutan before 1985.[63] This kind of language, which continues throughout the document, is benign in nature. Considered on its own, it is a puzzle why Bhutan's National Assembly, meeting in June 1988 after the petition was submitted, charged Tek Nath Rizal with treason. Many speculate it was payback for his role in the Royal Audit Commission, where he aggressively pursued many well-connected senior government officials who had embezzled government funds.[64]

Hari Chhetri sheds additional light on the charge against Tek Nath Rizal. Before submitting the petition, Tek Nath Rizal sought a royal audience with the king. In that meeting, Tek Nath Rizal suggested that many southern Bhutanese officials felt strongly enough about the problems with the census that they were considering conferring with the Indian embassy. Tek Nath Rizal's suggestion that his kin might consort with India, which Hari Chhetri insists was patently false, was viewed as a form of revolt against the government and a threat to Bhutan's sovereignty. Hari Chhetri was furious with Tek Nath Rizal for this thoughtless bravado and brought this up that evening with Tek Nath Rizal and many of the southern Bhutanese leaders:

> Many thought that [Tek Nath Rizal] was perhaps,[sic] trying too hard to impress on His Majesty the King about the "gravity" of the state of

affairs. . . . But . . . the issue by itself was so serious that there was absolutely no need to add grist to it to impress on its seriousness. He had jumped from emotion to speech without reflection at the wrong time, at the wrong place and with the wrong person. So I told them all that I do not know about your "gravity" but if you ask me about our "grave" now, I can tell you one has been dug for us.[65]

Hari Chhetri continues in this vein in his book for several paragraphs, noting how damaging this (at the time, empty) threat of transnational action was. There was not even a whisper of this idea, Hari Chhetri insists. While wanting to neither disparage Tek Nath Rizal nor question his intent, Hari Chhetri nevertheless reemphasizes that "with one insensitive remark [Tek Nath Rizal] had effectively put one very big question mark, perhaps an indelible one on the allegiance and loyalty of all southern Bhutanese to the country and the King."[66]

After the charge of treason, Tek Nath Rizal spent three days in prison. Then, in his own words, he was "coerced" into signing a release form. He then left Bhutan, fearing that he was being watched wherever he went in Bhutan.[67] His passage took him first to India, where he traveled to areas that hugged southern Bhutan in Assam and Sikkim. He met with sympathizers like the chief minister of Sikkim[68] and one remaining BSC stalwart living in Hariduar, India.[69] But he was held at arm's length by potential supporters and his political efforts were viewed darkly by India, who permitted him to stay for only a short time. Tek Nath Rizal then moved to Nepal, remaining (relatively) close but hoping for greater freedom to engage politically. There, he found more sympathetic contacts in Bhadrapur and Birtamod, in eastern Nepal (see map 3), where in July 1989 he established the People's Forum on Human Rights (PFHR).

The PFHR was the Bhutanese Nepalis' first exile organization of the era, and its operation depended on it being located near Bhutan. One activist observed that "people who were involved in some way in giving information to Tek Nath Rizal when he was writing a petition, and when he was still a member of the Assembly, they knew how to find him when he left, and they were in touch with him on a one-on-one basis."[70] Many were students who were among the first to recognize the injustices of their compatriots:

The happenings in southern Bhutan sparked a sharp awareness among the students in all the higher learning centers of Bhutan. Though they were . . . away from the villages where they came from, bad news . . . always found a way into their dormitories and [they] became increasingly alarmed and anxious. They heard that back in the villages, someone had committed suicide because she was asked to leave the country; that wives and children of some village men were deregistered from the census; that others were categorized as nonnationals and their status remained in a limbo.[71]

Subsequent student activism straddled three countries. In Bhutan, at the National Institute of Education (NIE), the Royal Polytechnic Institute (also known as Deothang Polytechnic), and Sherubtse College, students clandestinely distributed pamphlets in both English and Nepali that were printed in India, after conferring with Tek Nath Rizal in Nepal.[72] The Students Union of Bhutan (SUB) at Sherubtse College created a network of concerned students by reaching out about the issues that the Bhutanese Nepalis were facing not only to national student groups in Bhutan but also to students in universities in India, creating a "continuity of activism" that started with the BSC.[73]

The SUB also started to appeal to international groups located in Nepal.[74] Bishwanath Chhetri was the president of the SUB and a founding member of the PFHR. His experiences demonstrate how a sense of marginalization led to dissent, which tied directly into transnational action:

> People were forced to wear *gho*; they were forced to remove their sign of marriage, or all those ornaments. . . . And then people denied their citizenship. All those reports were coming. So, we thought that we should organize ourselves. So just we start[ed] with actually about twenty-five of us. We decided we'll . . . go to the jungle and talk, read some of the literature, and discuss all the news coming from the villages. . . . I was asked to go and find Mr. Rizal in Kakarbhitta, Nepal, and explain him about the situation. . . . We decided to form a human rights group in exile, and then while Mr. Rizal works from exile on human rights issues from outside, we will go inside and expand the network, and start working in a separate way.[75]

The movement was not entirely generated and led by students. First, student activists genuinely saw the genesis of their activities as coming from the thirty-year slumbering BSC. Bishwanath Chhetri reached out to former BSC members who had remained under virtual house arrest since the mid-1950s, and students resuscitated the decades-old pamphlets in their hideouts in the jungle. When I surmised that it might have been difficult to obtain relevant literature within Bhutan, Bishwanath Chhetri specifically referred back to the BSC: "Remember, there was an uprising in 1952 as well; there were some literature from that time."[76] It is not just that the material existed, it is that the activists felt themselves very much tied to those prior events.

Second, university teachers also got involved. Ratan Gazmere, a lecturer at the NIE, published a booklet entitled *Bhutan: We Want Justice*, which encouraged resistance against Bhutanization. A similar Nepali pamphlet translated as "Bhutan: Where Are Our Human Rights?" did much the same. These materials were transnational in character: the data came from inside Bhutan, they were created with support from Tek Nath Rizal and his associates in Nepal, they were printed in India, and they were then distributed back in Bhutan.

Third, some younger Bhutanese Nepali civil servants, mindful that many of the problems in the south might not seem apparent to those in the north, began circulating ideas, letters, and pamphlets to other parts of the country. Bhakti (Prasad) Bhandari, a civil servant at the Bhutan Development Finance Corporation, was considered the Thimphu node of an underground activist network, which distributed the Indian-printed pamphlets and held discussion groups.[77] Bhakti Bhandari, who spent nearly two years in prison for his actions, recalls:

> I was a political animal. You can say it that way. I had studied the systemic violation of human rights and I was telling people about it. . . . I was taking complete care of . . . three different projects for the entire country. I used to be out of Thimphu three months of the year, visiting rural areas and checking on farmers. In Thimphu and in rural areas, I shared the information. Even the Sharchops,[78] I told them that the government was rotten. So that's how I got arrested on a Saturday evening. My own friend arrested me.[79]

These internal activities were part of a transnational current. Members of the network from inside Bhutan frequently crossed porous borders to meet in Siliguri and Kakarbhitta with the dozen or so activists who had already left Bhutan and had taken refuge at the Garganda tea estate in West Bengal, India.[80] In Nepal, Tek Nath Rizal's PFHR was responsible for publishing material that was secretly sent to Bhutanese government officials. This was noted in the 68th Session of the National Assembly of Bhutan: "Though every effort was being made to trace the culprits responsible for such publications, it was not easy to stop these miscreants since the seditious letters and booklets were posted *from outside Bhutan*" (my emphasis).[81]

Although Hutt[82] and Amnesty International[83] note that these informational materials were far from incendiary, they were viewed as such and the government took swift measures to shut them down. A student activist from the NIE, Man Bahadur Chhetri, was killed by the Royal Bhutan Police in November 1989. In the same month, Bhakti Bhandari was arrested in Thimphu. By December 1989, forty-five people had been arrested for their involvement in "anti-national" activities.[84]

Bhutan's eagerness to stop political expression within the country triggered just the reaction that one might expect: activists fled nearby to seek out other means of continuing their work. But the passage of protest was not a panacea.

Ratan Gazmere was arrested on the Indian border. In Nepal, Tek Nath Rizal and two associates, Jogen Gazmere and Sushil Pokhrel, were taken by Nepali police from a residence in Birtamod and transferred to Bhutan's authorities, and from there, sent back to prison in Bhutan.[85] These arrests foreshadow an important tension between proximity and precarity in the chapters to come: while there were benefits to engaging in transnational activism from places physically proximate to Bhutan, this appeal was in direct contradiction to the risks—and the fact—of arrests and deportation.

Violence or Activism? The Construction of the Anti-national

Due to fears of responses from the government, student activists from groups like the SUB were clandestine in their efforts. Many interviewees described to me how, under the cover of dark, they snuck away from campus. In the forest, they discussed recent injustices, read old BSC documents, and shared new material produced by the PFHR. Bishwanath Chhetri reminisced: "We were 155 in the college, from the south. I think what made everyone feel the same way was [that] the oppression was so much. Every family was impact[ed]. It's not just the citizenship. The way it was implemented, it made our job easy. Everybody felt. In some way or other, everybody was involved, everybody contributed, somehow everybody shared the same sentiment of anger."[86]

The clandestine nature of these activities gave fuel to the belief among northerners that students were systematically planning violent tactics. This, of course, heightened the fear of northerners and led to an atmosphere of paranoia and othering, from which it was very difficult to back down. While all of my interviewees vehemently denied their involvement in violent activities, if we are to be fair to the psyche of the northern Bhutanese it is important to note that violence was undertaken by some. The most disturbing example of this was the gruesome beheading, not of Drukpa Bhutanese, but of two Bhutanese Nepalis, Kailash Dahal and Balaram Giri, who had collaborated with the government to help carry out the census. A letter found with the severed heads accused the men of cooperating with the enemy and betraying their own people.[87] The beheadings were never linked to any particular organization, and the activists with whom I spoke insisted it must have been the work of disturbed individuals who had adopted violent techniques from liberation movements elsewhere.

These killings, along with the death by government forces of Man Bahadur Chhetri that preceded them, led to a deeply troubled atmosphere in which even symbolic gestures were sure to be interpreted violently. Thus, Bhutanese Nepalis brandishing traditional Gorkha swords at a Hindu ceremony and, later, during demonstrations was taken as evidence of anti-national behavior.[88] There was little, if any, common ground between Drukpas and Bhutanese Nepalis. "Each half thinks it makes a whole story on its own, and neither side will acknowledge that there is another side," wrote Jamie Zeppa about her efforts as a volunteer teacher to informally mediate her students' opinions of the other side. "I have not heard one person speak of mediation or negotiation or even the listening that is necessary for understanding. There is no recognition of any overlap, any common ground. Already it is a case of two solitudes."[89]

It did not help matters that, at the time, Bhutan had only one newspaper, *Kuensel*, which was a government mouthpiece. Reports about violence were sure to highlight Bhutanese Nepali violence and minimize the abuses of the government. With only word-of-mouth comments and one national source, the "spectral threat" of the anti-national had pervaded work and social settings, and even close friends began not to trust one another.[90] Richard Whitecross powerfully conveys this change when describing how a family who used to consider a Bhutanese Nepali woman as an adopted mother had now, some years later, begun to regard her and all Bhutanese Nepalis with deep suspicion, highlighting "the powerful effect of othering and a fear that intimacy with an anti-national may be dangerous or contaminating."[91]

Inside Out: Demonstrations and the Flight of the People

In September and October of 1990, the anger of southerners and the fear of northerners came to a head when thousands of Bhutanese Nepalis marched against the government in four southern districts: Samtse, Sarpang, Tsirang, and Dagana (see map 2). These marches were organized by the SUB, the PFHR, and the newly established BPP, formed in Garganda by exiled activists. Originally, the BPP tried to organize a demonstration that was to start in India and cross into Bhutan. India prevented this from occurring; it closed the roads and shut down buses that were supposed to take marchers to the protest.[92] Instead, the three organizations together tried to rally people inside Bhutan. The purpose of the demonstrations was to submit a list of thirteen demands at each district headquarters, modeled on mores of human rights and democracy, likely influenced by then-recent similar demands of pro-democracy demonstrators in Eastern Europe and Nepal.[93] But the violence associated with the protests, carried out by both sides, left the most enduring mark.

It is difficult to measure fairly the scale of violence. The government reported that some marchers destroyed property and physically assaulted officers, tearing off their *ghos*. The dissidents allege that some protesters were arrested, beaten, and tortured, and that the police fired on them.[94] The government admitted to one inadvertent death caused by a soldier of the Royal Bhutan Army, while reporting on the brutal death of another soldier at the hands of dissidents. The BPP released a chronology that listed hundreds of gruesome deaths, but the fact that this chronology was later proved to be false damaged the BPP's credibility in the extreme.[95] One activist who attended the demonstration surmised, "There were rumors going on everywhere. We heard about Sita Mothe who suicided and bad news that the government is targeting only the southern Bhutanese. I think the rumors just went out of control. I think [the BPP] heard the rumors and believed them. Many things ended up being true: the census, the suicide. I don't think they fabricated it on purpose. And I don't know if there was really only one death by the government. Maybe they covered it up."[96] It is likely that there is some truth to both sides of this story and that claims of violence have also been used by both sides to justify further action.

The depth of anger against the government among the marchers is also difficult to ascertain. Hutt notes that there were marchers persuaded or coerced into marching, some reluctantly, and others simply confused, not really knowing what it meant to march. Evans, who conducted research among refugee youths in Nepal, noted that "many accounts of the 'peaceful' protests, and indeed the wider political tensions, in southern Bhutan underestimate the level of coercion exercised by members of the BPP over the Lhotshampa population."[97] This included bullying people into attending the marches and demanding membership fees for BPP activities. The head of the BPP, Balaram Poudel, admitted that some BPP members were forceful in informing Bhutanese Nepalis about the coming marches, but he insists that this was the exception rather than the rule. He also argues that violence supposedly carried out by BPP members was not political, but personal, an explanation offered to me by several other political leaders as well.[98]

Om Pradhan, a high-ranking pro-government Bhutanese Nepali government official who never left Bhutan, weighed in on the events of 1990, spreading the blame evenly between BPP members who bullied villagers to attend and zonal administrators who failed to protect those villagers. The common people were not to blame, he insists, but neither was the Royal Bhutan Army; not only did the king give orders that they were not to fire weapons, but directed the chief of the army to withhold giving soldiers any live ammunition, "perhaps the wisest and most far-reaching instruction that his Majesty gave during the demonstrations."[99]

The results of the demonstrations were profound. First, the numbers of protesters—no matter the level of violence—had shocked northerners, who now viewed entire swaths of the population as anti-nationals.[100] Educated Bhutanese Nepalis who avoided the demonstrations entirely were not immune. Despite not attending the demonstrations himself, Y. P. Dhungel began to lose important work opportunities as he devoted more time and resources to prove himself loyal. Another said:

> We were on tour, and we heard what happened in my own district, Chirang [Tsirang], that there was a big demonstration, and security people were going there. What [my boss] told me that day was, "Birendra, we two are very good friends, and I know you have good heart, but I cannot trust you anymore now." . . . I didn't know what to say. We were so good friends. Wow, that is . . . till that time, I always thought I was a real Bhutanese guy. I said, "Something is wrong with us. We are not united. The country is divided. It's not going to work."[101]

Second, dissidents who simply wanted a voice in expressing their dissent were now out of outlets in Bhutan. Bishwanath Chhetri summed this up: "We discussed that we cannot do anything from here. It's too terrifying a situation."[102]

Following the demonstrations, an exodus of Bhutanese Nepalis occurred on a massive scale. The government of Bhutan insists that those who left did so willingly, often selling their land before they left, often before even receiving compensation, and often rejecting the pleadings of the king who, in actual fact, did personally travel to the south on several occasions to ask Bhutanese Nepalis to remain.[103] But departed Bhutanese Nepalis have a very different narrative, saying the king's pleadings could not have been genuine if they occurred in the context of nighttime raids, arrested family members, torture of loved ones, and threats and fines imposed by local officials.[104] Narayan Sharma explained:

> In 1991 when my brother and I came home for winter vacation after tenth grade examination, there was a state of fear in the village. Every male was gone. The army came to the village and demanded our cows. They took my father and beat him in front of the village. They said to me, "Look at your nose, this country doesn't belong to you. You look like Girija.[105] That is the country you belong to." There was a social terror in my town with girls scared of the army. Then officers personally ordered us to leave Bhutan.[106]

These examples are among the many detailed and harrowing accounts I have heard, of hurried and fearful flights from people who considered Bhutan their one and only home, which indicate that voluntary departure was not the norm for this population.

Passage into India and Nepal

The path that most refugees took on leaving Bhutan was through Phuntsholing, on Bhutan's southern border (see map 2). At the start, many tried to remain in India, assuming that they would be returning to Bhutan within days or weeks. "We all felt like that," said one activist who fled immediately after the protests. He never had time to say goodbye to his family, who remain in Bhutan to this day. "I thought I would see them again soon. I stayed in India a little while, but we could not get asylum."[107]

India, in fact, played a decisive role in determining the long-term destination for this significant refugee population. Like Nepal, India is not a signatory to the 1951 Refugee Convention but, unlike Nepal, its ethnic Nepali population is not the majority. India was generally unsympathetic to the Bhutanese Nepali cause and the central Indian government ignored the few local politicians in Assam who sided with the Bhutanese Nepalis. Instead, India practiced what I have called the "shuttle and funnel" approach, rounding up refugees who were trying to remain near the Bhutan border and putting them in vans to be shuttled across the border to arrive in Kakarbhitta, Nepal.[108]

Government sources have also pointed to the flight of several high-level Bhutanese Nepalis, who the government claims absconded with government funds.[109] This is an absurd charge, counter the activists. The resignation letter of one of the highest ranking of these officials, Bhim Subba, is both forceful and pleading in its explanation of why he left: "In view of the current fear psychosis that now pervades among all Southern Bhutanese I have chosen to make my decision known from outside the country. I have always been apolitical, and wish to remain so, but I cannot dare hope that the administrative machinery of the Government would leave me to roam freely within Bhutan. I, therefore, beg Your Majesty's kind understanding and forgiveness in the matter."[110]

Meanwhile, Y. P. Dhungel continued his job at the FCB, well aware of the charges of corruption against others. He felt tremendous pressure to leave Bhutan, but he refused to do so until he had fully balanced the books at the FCB, which he did, daily, for several months, under the harrowing and suspicious watch of a security guard:

> I was scared, but still I didn't leave the office just like that. I then wrote to the Minister saying that we have to do the audit, because I was handling lot of government's money, and if I just leave my office just like that, next day they will probably [be] saying that I fled with so much of government money. Because that was the case with senior friends. . . . They said that they've robbed the bank, and they fled with millions of

government money. So, I thought if I leave just like that, they will put me same sort of thing. . . . Then I did that report. I know what was the position on that day when I left. So that if they come back and they put a charge against me or [say] this was what I did, I can show that at the time, this was the financial position of the corporation.[111]

Even those who considered themselves immune from these pressures because of their loyalty were not. Y. P. Dhungel's father, born in Bhutan, was not present at the demonstrations but he was pressured to leave his village. He initially refused but eventually relented when a friend, *mandal* from a nearby village, was imprisoned, tortured, and killed for refusing to leave: "My father was very, very scared that maybe the same fate will happen to him, and then he went and filled out the forms saying that 'I will leave the country,' and then they give him deadline. 'Okay, twenty-four hours you leave the country.' So, they fled, and then after one month we heard that they were in the camp. Then when I heard that they were there, I felt very, very unsettled, like what to do? Because even in the office, life was totally changed."[112]

That experiences like this were widespread and narrated with relative consistency and affected many socioeconomic segments of the Bhutanese Nepali population suggests, again, that for many, flight was coercive, rather than a willing departure. Y. P. Dhungel, as a model citizen and a loyal employee, never imagined that he would be targeted. And yet, he, too, was gone by June 1992, as he and his wife Ganga Dhungel explained:

> Y. P. Dunghel (YD): So, I was coming out of the office and then there was a police van. . . . The police were waiting in the van and they stop me when they saw me, and then one of the officers, you know, sitting in the front of the car seat, "He's the one we need to target," in Dzongkha.
>
> Susan Banki (SB): But you understood it.
>
> YD: I understood. They thought that I don't understand, but he was commanding his people, "Okay, he's the one we need to arrest." Then I was just falling, you know? Just sickened. I don't know how I came out all the way walking. Then that night I told her [gesturing to his wife]: "Let's pack up everything and move," and around twelve [at] night we just sneak through the border to Jaigaon.
>
> Ganga: What we packed, only two pillows?
>
> YD: Yeah, two pillows.
>
> Ganga: Two pillows. Some documents are there. I put it under the pillows, under the cotton and then I stitched them.
>
> YD: So to save our documents, you know.

Y. P. Dhungel knew the value of documents. He brought with him into exile various kinds of physical proof of his and his family's legitimacy, believing, as tens of thousands of other Bhutanese Nepalis did, that these would later help buttress claims to citizenship. But, unlike the migrants in Sadiq's *Paper Citizens*,[113] who were able to use various forms of documentation to acquire citizenship in India, many Bhutanese Nepalis lost their citizenship despite possessing a variety of documents to prove residence. Neither Y. P. nor his compatriots knew at the time that this would be their last look at Bhutan.

This chapter has set the context for what I have termed the passage of protest. A convergence of geopolitical and individual forces led to a series of actions and reprisals from which the country and its erstwhile residents have never been able to back down. An atmosphere of distrust grew quickly, with actions of good faith and ill intent committed on both sides. There was a king who traveled the countryside to speak directly to his subjects, and there were local officials who sent a different message. There were loyal citizens who communicated earnestly with powerholders and there were agitators who committed violence. There were vulnerable Bhutanese Nepalis who were bullied both by local administrators promoting flight and by radicalized dissidents demanding membership fees. With few outlets available in the country, people who wanted to voice their grievances crossed the border, and their actions took on a transnational hue. Following this passage of protest, the ecosystem of exile politics grew.

Along with two pillowcases and several documents, Y. P. Dhungel brought with him out of Nepal that piece of the Berlin Wall. It was, after all, a reminder of many things that he wanted to carry with him on a painful exit: his impressive educational credentials, an important and useful job, a memorable European trip, and the hope of reunification and return. Y. P. Dhungel was not alone in that hope, and much of the advocacy that followed in the years to come centered on pressuring the government to consider that return. That is the subject of the following chapters.

THE POWER OF PROXIMITY

The advantage of doing advocacy in Nepal was [it was] more fresh, more raw, the stories were right there. . . . British embassy, US embassy, Australian embassy, all the friendly country embassies were involved. I could go to their offices and broach them, and whenever they had visitors . . . they would invite me, also.

—Mangala Sharma

Until his death in June 2022, a small and decorated room in Damak, a small town near the refugee camps, served as the office for Bhampa Rai, a Bhutanese Nepali refugee doctor whose medical services to the refugee community were legendary. Many interviewees told me that they were treated without charge by Bhampa Rai or that he paid for their medicine himself. The desk in his office was piled with medical equipment like stethoscopes and boxes of bandages. There was also a calendar exhorting viewers to eat a fibrous diet for a healthy heart. And right at the center of the desk, elevated on a small stand, was a miniature flag: the yellow and red triangles, adjoined by a dragon, that represent the national flag of Bhutan. "The government of Nepal has been very good to us, but Bhutan is my country," Bhampa Rai told me.[1]

Bhampa Rai indulged me on three separate occasions, during which I peppered him with questions about his personal history, the history of the exiled refugees, and his own role during that time. At one point, after discussing the work that his organization carried out to try to list all the refugees who had owned land back in Bhutan, he sighed and said, "We did all the detail. Useless." I asked him why. He fixed me with a stare and said, "If somebody places a very big plate of food in front of you and you can't eat it . . . we worked so much. It was useless, in the end."

Whether the work of Bhutan's homeland activists was useless is a matter of debate. But more than twenty-five years after the first of Bhutan's refugees departed, Bhampa Rai's organization, the Bhutanese Refugee Representative Repatriation Committee (BRRRC), remains steadfast in its aim, unfulfilled, to get

Bhutan to accept back a portion of its refugee population. While others have moved on to countries of the Global North, members of the BRRRC remain in Nepal, where their gaze is firmly fixed east, back to Bhutan. "If we have any hope of repatriating," Bhampa Rai said to me wistfully, "it has to be launched from here."[2]

This chapter offers an in-depth look at how the efforts of Bhutan's homeland activists were constituted and defined by their proximity. Through behind-the-scenes information gathering and highly visible performances, in locations in both India and Nepal, Bhutan's homeland activists used a range of strategies to try to reform their home country. This examination of proximity rehabilitates the importance of physical space at a theoretical moment when it has been dismissed as essentializing and problematic. While it may be true that the depth of social relations, identity, and lived experiences complexify our understanding of space, the claims of certain theorists that we are witnessing the progressive disappearance of spatial fixedness in favor of interactivity, speed, and intersubjective information go too far.[3] This chapter foregrounds the ultimate importance of physical proximity in the political ecosystem of Bhutanese homeland activists, and in doing so provides a counterexample to the postmodern analysis of Paul Virilio that "everything that has previously been involved in the arrangement of real urban and rural space will tomorrow simply be a matter of organizing the real-time conductivity of images and information."[4] Rather, those spaces proximate to Bhutan constituted the most vibrant arenas of struggle for the Bhutanese Nepali exiles. They are models of the liminal borderlands described by Susan Bibler Coutin as "spaces whose very existence is simultaneously denied and demanded by the socially powerful."[5] These are spaces of exclusion, restriction, and erasure, but also the zones where institutions and norms spring up as both the enforcers and contesters of political power.

Homeland Activism in Nepal and India

A full count of Bhutanese homeland activist groups over time would number more than fifty, but many of these folded into others, went defunct, shifted priorities (or had opposing priorities within the same organization), or fragmented into multiple organizations, often with similar aims and slightly different names. Rather than review the specifics of each, which would resemble a crisscrossed laundry list, I shine a spotlight on the work of all of those that played significant roles in homeland activism. In the pages that follow I organize an exploration of these groups through their three main goals: calls for democracy and representation, the broadcasting of abuses carried out by Bhutan's government and army, and specific calls for Bhutan to accept the return of the Bhutanese Nepalis.

Before turning to these three goals, a discussion of one homeland group is warranted. The Druk National Congress (DNC) merits special attention because of its unique standing as an organization founded and run by Bhutanese who were *not* ethnically Nepali. The DNC's story has been virtually ignored in the scholarly literature and it remains unknown outside of a small circle of local journalists in India and Nepal. Yet its formation and continued existence are very much intertwined with Bhutanese Nepali homeland activist groups. Incorporating the story of the DNC into a narrative about Bhutanese exile politics is long overdue, particularly because the DNC challenges the notion that the Bhutanese government's hold on power was, at the time, exclusively an ethnic issue.

The DNC was founded by Rongthong Kunley Dorji (R. K. Dorji), an ethnic Sharchops businessman from eastern Bhutan, who gained notoriety within Bhutan and popularity within refugee circles for being an outspoken critic of the Bhutanese government on many counts. First, his business dealings gave him a unique view into the ways that a culture of kickbacks and bribery was tolerated in the royal family but not outside of it, and he publicly denounced the simmering, ever-present problem of corruption. Second, he noted the uneven pace of development in eastern Bhutan, where poverty and poor health indicators were well above the national average. Third, he deplored the persecution of his coreligionists in eastern Bhutan, that is, monks who followed the Nyingmapa tradition of Buddhism and who were shunted from their *shedras* (Buddhist learning institutes) in favor of those who practiced the Drukpa Kagyu tradition of the ruling powers. Because he spoke in favor of these monks, they formed the backbone of his support in the DNC.

It was, however, R. K. Dorji's fourth set of critiques against the government of Bhutan that linked the DNC with Bhutanese Nepali exile groups. He marched in the 1990 demonstrations and had an openly critical stance against the treatment of the Bhutanese Nepalis. R. K. Dorji's actions and views landed him in prison in May 1991, where his claims of torture were recorded by Amnesty International.[6] Two months later he was pardoned and released, after which he crossed the porous southern border and, for the next three years, moved between India and Nepal, "painstakingly building up a network of dissidents within Bhutan."[7] He remained close to these networks, collecting stories about corruption and religious persecution. In Kathmandu in June of 1994, with the support of Bhutanese Nepali organizations, R. K. Dorji founded the DNC. Because the DNC demonstrated that the problems of power and representation in Bhutan were not simply the manifestation of troublesome Bhutanese Nepalis, the DNC was outsized in its role in denouncing the government. This is why another DNC leader, Thinley Penjore, said to me in 2007, "We are small, but our grievances are large."[8]

While the DNC differed from the Bhutanese Nepali exiled community in size, it shared with Bhutanese Nepali groups the goals mentioned earlier: democracy in Bhutan, documenting government abuse, and promoting return to Bhutan under safe conditions. I now turn to describing these three goals, noting that they were logically aligned. Bhim Subba of HUROB noted that "as refugees, it would be I think suicidal for us to take a ticket home until and unless there were . . . essential reforms which guaranteed that this thing could not happen again."[9] That is, promoting the goal of return made sense only when paired with the goal of democracy and the protection of human rights.

Democracy and Representation

The early 1990s witnessed democratization campaigns around the world, from Eastern Europe to Africa to South Asia. In Nepal, the Panchayat political system—which since 1962 had rendered Nepal a partyless absolute monarchy—was replaced by the reintroduction of a multiparty democracy in 1990. This ushered in a political leadership substantively and discursively interested in promoting human rights in the form of the Nepali Congress. Reflecting these norms and broader geopolitical ones, many homeland activist groups emphasized the goal of trying to bring democracy to Bhutan. The primary groups using the language of democratization were the BPP, the DNC, and the Bhutan National Democratic Party (BNDP). While Bhutan underwent a democratic transition starting in 2007, much of the work described below preceded the democratic transition. (Nor is this work complete, a topic covered in chapter 6.) These groups projected the image of exiled dissident figures who wanted to be part of a different kind of government.

Nicholas Van Hear, with a nod to Pierre Bourdieu, has pointed out that class and its embedded relationship with social capital is an understudied and critical component in the determination of migration routes and destinations.[10] Even less well studied is the way that refugee activists, differentiated by education and class in their home countries, not only follow different journeys but rely on different aspects of social capital to form exiled organizations. This phenomenon is apparent in the case of Bhutan's exiles. The BNDP, formed by a young guard of college-educated civil servants, attracted a different set of actors than the original BPP, whose senior status and political experience as government officials in Bhutan had early on given them a certain authority in standing up to the government of Bhutan. In exile, however, rifts having to do with formal education and tactical approach grew more pronounced. This is covered in greater detail in the following chapter.

Efforts to promote democracy in Bhutan took a number of forms, and these were most bold when the information about problems in Bhutan was collected and printed in proximate places and then smuggled back into Bhutan. In 1994 the DNC produced a report, "The Silent Suffering in Bhutan," which noted Bhutan's endemic corruption and relayed specific examples of the disproportional and drastic responses by the Bhutanese government, including torture, to peaceful requests for power sharing.[11] In the same year, most of the educated elite of Thimphu received an anonymous pamphlet entitled "Druk [Gi] Selwai Melong" (translated as "The Clear Mirror of Bhutan"), detailing the unchecked power of the monarchy and the deleterious effects on local citizens. The pamphlet also offered specific stories of recent abuse, such as the king's father-in-law, Ugen Dorji, who, willing to "do anything for self-aggrandizement," orchestrated the impoverishment of a sawmill owner so that he could buy out the lucrative factory.[12]

In 1995, the DNC managed to initiate a nationwide poster campaign with the help of local police.[13] The posters were printed in Nepal and one DNC member smuggled five thousand of them back into Bhutan, where they were surreptitiously mounted throughout the country. "Some audacious person pasted a poster up at the top of a cliff, where the road passes through. So everyone could see it. It took some weeks to take down that poster," recalled the poster smuggler with a wry suggestion of a grin.[14]

Homeland activists also released an abundance of documents meant for public consumption outside of Bhutan. Members of the BPP regularly released press statements to local news agencies in India and Nepal, for example, and their ability to get this information printed in local and national newspapers was linked to previously established networks that had developed through the porous borders of the region. Local journalists as well as national media personalities confirmed that their regional knowledge—and prior contact with activists who had crossed the border—helped elevate the Bhutanese issue before other media agents took it up.[15] The publisher of the well-regarded *Himal Southasian*, Kanak Mani Dixit, was able to publish several exposés starting as early as 1992, and to this day they are among the most comprehensive pieces in the popular press about the origins of Bhutan's refugees. Dixit's detailed articles can be attributed to his ability to marshal local anecdotes and information from the leaders of the BPP and the BNDP, as well as politicians in India who were well versed on the topic.[16] At the same time, activist organizations benefited from their access to this credible outlet, demonstrating that networks formed by proximity played an important role in the work of homeland political parties.

Public protests also took aim at Bhutan's lack of democratic principles, and these, too, were furthered by Nepal's spatial role in the South Asian region. As early as 1991, for example, three exiled members of Bhutan's National Assembly held a hunger strike in front of a meeting of the South Asian Association for Regional Cooperation (SAARC) being held in Kathmandu. The trio's hunger fast coincided not only with the SAARC meeting but also the convening of Bhutan's National Assembly in order to highlight the disproportionately low representation of Bhutanese Nepalis in the legislative body.[17] The ability of the activists to elevate their critique of Bhutan to the regional political arena was very much dependent on networks as they capitalized on personal connections for support and even leadership. About the 1991 sit-in, one activist recalled, "It actually [was] helped by the foreign minister of Nepal. . . . He helped to lead these strikes, he went to camp and helped us to form [a] movement."[18]

From then until Bhutan's democratic transition, public protests aimed at highlighting Bhutan's governance problems sprouted periodically in nearby Nepal and India. The most visible and performative of these demonstrations, however, was focused on return to Bhutan, and will be covered below. But one other series of protests in the name of democracy deserves our attention because they occurred back in Bhutan while being closely linked to proximate activists: the exceptionally understudied DNC-organized protests of 1997 that took place in eastern Bhutan.

One has to look very hard to find evidence of the DNC protests, and even the few news articles that exist fail to provide a full account of the timeline, grievances, or responses.[19] From material produced by the DNC, interviews with DNC activists, a paragraph in the proceedings of Bhutan's National Assembly, and one Amnesty International report,[20] a clearer picture emerges. In October 1997, the DNC organized protests in four eastern districts of Bhutan, and an estimated three thousand people participated.[21] While the tone-deaf National Assembly vaguely surmised that the protesters were "motivated by greed and vested interests,"[22] the messages espoused by the organizers reflected legitimate grievances: a demand for democracy and the release of prisoners whose only crime had been to request that Nyingmapa monks be restored to their *shedras*. Pema Tendzin, a DNC leader and one of the protest's organizers, was clear about its goals: "There was the presence of religious persecution by the state. Those who felt persecuted, they said religious freedom will only come if there is a democracy in the country. So . . . they rallied, demanding human rights and democracy."[23]

Pema Tendzin and three other DNC members whom I interviewed all talked to me about the injustice of their peaceful protest being met with disproportionate force. During the crackdown, in which more than one hundred were arrested, one monk, Gomchen Karma, was killed by the dzongdag (the district administrator). There was an eyewitness to lend authority to this extrajudicial killing, so Gomchen Karma's death had the same symbolic resonance for the DNC as the death of Man Bahadur Chhetri had for Bhutanese Nepalis. Even Om Pradhan, the aforementioned pro-government Bhutanese Nepali officer, pointed out that the response to these rallies "went too far in arresting monks and meting out harsher treatment than was called for."[24] In the aftermath of the crackdown, approximately 500 people, mostly ethnic Sharchops, fled the country fearing arrest and torture. Many remain in India today, while several families sought refuge in the refugee camps in Nepal. Thus, Sharchops were never expelled en masse, but some were rendered refugees after their own protests.

While events within Bhutan had laid the groundwork for the 1997 protests, it was events in proximate locations that served as the catalyst for DNC members to take action. For the past six years, up to 100,000 Bhutanese Nepalis had been living proof of a crisis of democracy and human rights within Bhutan, and human rights advocates frequently conducted training programs in the region (eastern Nepal and the area of India adjoining it). One such training program, held in eastern Nepal, brought together Bhutanese Nepalis and members of the DNC. Rinzin Dorji of the DNC recalled: "It was a training on the UDHR [Universal Declaration of Human Rights] and it was for the youth. We had 100 participants, and it was about empowerment and the UDHR and how to advocate. We did the training, and after that, we started the peaceful protests in Bhutan."[25]

Here, the link between public expressions of dissent and proximate places where training took place could not be clearer. It is worth noting that, in the eyes of the Bhutanese government, the training constituted a foreign threat because it took place outside the country. The government newspaper *Kuensel* described how protesters had been paid by those in Nepal.[26] While Rinzin Dorji openly admitted to receiving funds for his involvement in the training, the payment was not to reward with money people who protested, as the government of Bhutan alleged, but for the logistics of moving the participants in and out of Bhutan and providing them with a place to stay during the training.[27] The key factor that permitted Bhutanese to receive training and return quickly to Bhutan to help organize a protest was, of course, proximity.

Raising Awareness: Human Rights Documentation and Publications

The second aim of homeland activism was to highlight the abuses of Bhutan's powerholders: government officials as well as army and police personnel. Raising awareness was also intended to illuminate the effects that the expulsions had on those rendered refugees. The way that trauma became collectivized, because it was so widespread and witnessed so readily, cannot be overstated. "I remember one particular night, because of lack of medical facilities, lack of proper drinking water, forty children died. Among those, my cousin's child also died. We were on the bank of the Maidhar River[28] to prepare bodies for burial. It was a negative impact on my life. I balk at that picture even now."[29]

Even for those with no personal memory of the horror of flight, in the camps it was easy for young refugees to learn what had happened simply by listening to the stories of their parents and grandparents. Several interviewees of the younger generation, whose memories of Bhutan were relatively sparse as they had departed at a young age, explained how the camp's crowded conditions actually fed a sense of collective purpose, because one did not have to go far to glean a sense of shared persecution and the loss of a homeland, even for those who hadn't seen it. "Every day in the camp schools, we would sing the national anthem to Bhutan. We didn't understand a word, but we could pronounce it."[30]

Organized activities to convey the exiles' narrative to the next generation were common. The famed Masur Chhetri—killed by drowning in a leather bag, as described in Chapter 2—arose as a character in camp-based plays:

> For many years, we did a drama in the camp. About Masur Chhetri. A long time ago, he raised the voice to change the country's policy, the democratic policy. Then the Bhutan government attacked him, to make a warning to him, and the government or the Royal Bhutan Army arrested him and put him in the Sankosh River alive. So it is very terrible, this story for us, so we played a drama in that scenario sometimes. . . . I played the most wanted character, I am the Masur Chhetri.[31]

If the camp provided the stage for sharing stories among the refugees, it also provided activists with the material they needed to inform regional and international actors. For example, Bhutanese Refugees Aiding the Victims of Violence (BRAVVE), founded by Mangala Sharma, was an organization supported by local and international NGOs and present in all seven camps. BRAVVE's 2006 "Profile of the Torture Victims in the Prisons of Bhutan" relied on the testimony of former prisoners who had escaped to Nepal to offer detailed and harrowing accounts of their arrest, imprisonment, and torture, including beatings, electric shocks, iron leg shackles, and exposure to cold, insufficient food, and death threats.[32] BRAVVE did not have to go far to collect these stories—they were the disturbing truths of neighbors in the camps. One of BRAVVE's leaders, Birendra Dhakal, recalls that the BRAVVE office "became a very popular place, and whenever UNHCR and the government had some guests, international guests, they started bringing them here."[33] By providing a channel between refugees and humanitarian and human rights actors, BRAVVE capitalized on myriad stories of abuse to criticize Bhutan.

HUROB also collected and published information about Bhutan's persecutory tendencies. Its monthly publication, the *Bhutan Review*, had an alternatingly irreverent and angry tone, and clearly relied on cross-border information for its most detailed reports of goings-on in Bhutan. For example, one article told the story of Shivalal Chapagai, a power meter reader whose job prior to expulsion had permitted him to travel around the south and hear multiple stories of repression. The article included photographs of Shivalal Chapagai's house in Bhutan before he fled and after his exile, attesting not only to the destruction of his property but also to the ability of HUROB to gather photographs from inside Bhutan.[34] Om Dhungel, one of HUROB's founders, confirmed that Nepal's relative proximity to Bhutan permitted the collection of these kinds of stories, as both Bhutanese Nepalis and Drukpas who were privately sympathetic to the refugees clandestinely came to Nepal to share information. The more information HUROB could collect from inside the country, the better. Om Dhungel explained that "we wanted to make sure that we don't write something that we just hear once. That was not something we would ever put it in the paper. We had to double confirm that. Because if you write once, like, if there are two people injured and if I said ten people injured, and if I can't show them, then my credit is gone forever."[35]

Published in Kathmandu and written in English, the *Bhutan Review* targeted both an international and a regional audience, reflecting the diversity of the ecosystem for which it was intended. Each month, after its printing, HUROB members spent a full day walking the streets of Kathmandu distributing it to important international stakeholders, including foreign embassies. But it was also distributed to Nepal government offices, such as the Home and Foreign Ministries.[36] And the publication also made its way back into Bhutan, both into the hands of Thimphu politicians and also into remote villages.[37] Some articles, in fact, addressed the Bhutanese government directly, as in one where Thimphu was assured, tongue in cheek, that an apologist for the government remains a devoted minion.[38]

AHURA also played a key role in documenting the problems that arose as a result of the departure of so many Bhutanese Nepalis. One interesting example was its collaboration with the (since defunct) international NGO, the Centre for Housing Rights and Evictions (COHRE). COHRE wanted to document homes demolished in the aftermath of Bhutanese Nepali flight, and relied on AHURA to collect some of this information, and cited AHURA in its own reports.[39] To substantiate these claims of expulsion as comprehensively as possible, AHURA not only received information from refugees in the camps but returned to Bhutan to gather information from the inside. AHURA's chief coordinator, Ratan Gazmere, explained:

> There was a massive resettlement taking place in southern Bhutan in 2001, 2002, 2003 [i.e., northern Bhutanese resettling to the south to take over the lands of those who departed] . . . and during that time every six months or so I sent people in the Bhutan border, stay there for a few days, talk to their people up there . . . whose houses, whose land has been occupied, those kinds of information. . . . And even sometimes I even got photographs of demolished houses . . . and we used that very strongly for advocacy work.
>
> Some people went inside Bhutan. You know, because they were brazen, brave. Like we took two journalists—two [foreign] activists—into Bhutan. One guy, he was some kind of a madcap, he said, "I will take them to my little village which is just across the border." . . . So there was risk, but a bit of risk taking was in our genes then.[40]

Bhakta Ghimire was one of those "madcaps" who crossed back into Bhutan on several occasions. In one instance, he brought with him a woman I will call "Rikki," who came from an international NGO:

> BHAKTA GHIMIRE (BG): We discussed and we decided to pretend like an Indian farmer. I got a round kind of cap. It is called a Muslim hat . . . I was having a beard and *longyi* [*laughs*].[41] I bought some vegetables like cabbage and something. I just went carrying that bag open like everyone can see. Rikki just followed me. She was having an ordinary woman's dress like long, simple dress. She did not even comb her hair. [*laughs*]
>
> SUSAN BANKI (SB): So, you were trying to just look like peasants?
>
> BG: Yes, yes. So, we went like that and we saw the group in south Bhutan. That was so easy. We didn't face any kind of problem, just going here and there. We went every village. We met with the people. We talked to the Drukpa people too who have resettled when the refugees left.[42]

The collection of information to substantiate problems in Bhutan demonstrates the importance of what might be called tripartite porosity, with the India-Bhutan and India-Nepal borders being open enough to permit the flow of information out of Bhutan and allow pamphlets and newsletters to be circulated inside. Even when activists did not manage to return to Bhutan themselves to collect information, they relied on evidence from others still there, non-activists who nevertheless helped provide information and/or other support to homeland activists, who crossed into India to meet them. Ratan Gazmere explained about some activists: "Often they spent a period of time, not one day or two days, a week or so, in the safety of Indian towns, and people they knew from Bhutan days would come there, during what we call 'Market Days.' . . . People [would] come from inside, and the [activists] . . . would say, 'Okay, next time you come to market, can you bring all these informations?'"[43]

Thus, the region's proximate role proved critical, despite, as we will see later, the precarity that activists experienced there.

(Re)claiming Citizenship and Reversing Exile

A third aim of Bhutan's homeland activists was campaigning for the return of the refugee population to Bhutan. The desire to reclaim citizenship was an omnipresent feature of life for those in exile, and therefore nearly every homeland organization was involved in trying to do so, including those already mentioned (political parties and human rights organizations) and also those explicitly created to promote return, most prominently the BRRRC and the Appeal Movement Coordinating Council (AMCC). These organizations engaged in a wide range of tactics, including protests, lobbying, and documenting citizenship. As elsewhere, proximity played a key role in shaping the timing and tenor of these activities.

Public Protests

Public protests, like rallies and marches, were undertaken by the largest number of homeland organizations and were practiced for the longest duration. Mass rallies and uprisings have a long tradition in South Asian civil resistance movements and many, like the Swadeshi Movement's anti-Bengal partition protests, have their origins in the nexus of power, politics, and geography.[44] The marches and rallies carried out by Bhutanese refugees ranged in participation from a handful of protesters to the thousands. They took place in camps, in Kathmandu, in other places in Nepal, and, quite interestingly from a symbolic point of view, through India. Refugees left the camps together, walked or cycled to the India-Nepal border, crossed into the small wedge of India that separates Nepal and Bhutan, and tried to make it to the India-Bhutan border, a distance of approximately 120 miles that would take several days to walk (see map 3).

In 1996, the AMCC coordinated the most prominent and logistically complex series of these protests, symbolically reclaiming the right to return to Bhutan, as discussed in chapter 1. Over the course of the year, no fewer than seventeen batches of protesters left the refugee camps and tried to march all the way back to Bhutan, where the intention was to make it all the way to the capital, Thimphu, and personally petition the king to accept back the refugees. Ratan Gazmere, one of the AMCC's lead coordinators, stressed the importance of preparing protesters to remain peaceful. "We gave them training in the periphery of the camps, what is nonviolence, how to do it right."[45] The first batch of volunteers, about 150 people, began their march in January of 1996 and were immediately arrested when crossing into India. This continued numerous times, but the AMCC managed to sneak 600 marchers all the way to Jaigaon, India, close to the border with Bhutan (see map 3).

> RATAN GAZMERE (RG): By dawn, we were at Phuntsholing gate.
>
> SB: How did you feel?
>
> RG: I think a feeling of satisfaction that, you know, we adequately demonstrated that we would walk, come home. We took so many risks, we overcame so many political obstacles to come here. India should realize that we want to go home, Bhutan should realize that too, we want to come home. I think that message was loud and clear. Everybody was surprised that we were there, "How did you manage to come here? How did you come from Kakarbhitta to Jaigaon? How did you travel by bus? How did you evade all the police?" You know, because [the route through India] was full of intelligence people, but somehow, we managed to hoodwink them.[46]

Only a few of the marchers ever entered Bhutan, and only for a day before being expelled from the country again. Govinda Rizal, one of the marchers who made it in, writes emotively in his autobiography about this. After coming face to face with police inside Bhutan and trying to explain why they wanted to appeal to the king, he and his fellow protesters were put in vans and tricked into believing they were being taken to Thimphu. Instead, the police drove them into India and physically forced them out of the van. After years of hardship in the camps, arrests in India, and the sickness and death of loved ones, it was this rejection from Bhutan that finally brought Govinda Rizal to tears: "I felt defeated. A pain erupted inside my [cheek] bones, my voice stopped, and tears flowed profusely. I cried. After many years, I cried loud and without feeling ashamed. For the first time, I felt the pain of losing a nation."[47]

I have written elsewhere, with two of the 1996 march coordinators as coauthors, about the impressive logistics of this peace march and how, over the course of a year, the AMCC tried to keep enthusiasm for the march alive and keep the media interested.[48] The AMCC peace march received significant mainstream media coverage from diverse sources, particularly in relation to the mass arrests of marchers in India, and the subsequent strikes undertaken by Indian Ghorka groups demanding their release.[49]

The AMCC protests were the most prominent but by no means the only protests that were undertaken by activists. The BNDP organized a cycle rally around the same time, as well as weekly sit-ins on the Mechi Bridge that stopped traffic for an hour between India and Nepal.[50] In the camps, there were countless public rallies and protests, organized by BRRRC and other groups. Rallies were staged in front of the US embassy in Kathmandu and simultaneously in all seven camps, often on auspicious days such as International Human Rights Day or the National Day of Bhutan.[51] All of these public expressions of dissent had a commonality, which is that proximity played an important role. Ratan Gazmere said: "Now we are 80,000 people in the seven refugee camps, the wound is very fresh and the energy is there, frustration has not crept in and it's not very difficult to do, it's just a matter of mobilizing people."[52]

At the same time, public demonstrations did occur further afield, such as a rally in front of UN headquarters in New York attended by BNDP president and general secretary D. N. S. Dhakal.[53] But no coverage of this event can be found in local or international papers, in contrast to the rallies planned in Nepal and India. This is partly because the glut of protest issues emanating from international organizations diminishes the focus on any one in particular. But it is also because public protests calling attention to particular abuses are far more powerful when the participants are significant in number and protest repression comes from firsthand experience. Y. P. Dhungel participated in some of the public protests that crossed the Mechi Bridge and noted that "many people said how beautiful the marches were. I mean, we were carrying Gandhi's photos and sitting in the bridge, a peaceful march, a *satyagraha*. We were around each other, all of us had the same experience, being expelled. It was totally powerful."[54]

Lobbying Powerholders

A second tactic that focused on return to Bhutan was lobbying powerholders, particularly those in the region. This was important, because as D. N. S. Dhakal told me, "Bhutan presents itself as sort of lost in paradise, but they are shrewd. US diplomats will say that they are the smartest politicians in South Asia."[55] To counter this charm offensive, dissidents relied on their own contacts to share information directly with those in positions of power. In the early 1990s, these contacts were mostly regional and had come from friendships and collegial relationships that preceded the troubles in Bhutan. This is because many of Bhutan's high-level officers—including the king himself—had been educated in India and had established solid friendships with classmates from the region.

This phenomenon—a South Asian version of C. Wright Mills's "power elite"[56]—exposes the ways in which friendships formed at institutions of higher learning provide access to powerholders that far exceed the value of a transcript itself. In South Asia, this has been explored through the examination of the role of tertiary institutions in creating and reproducing elite and highly networked communities by equipping them with the tools to govern, rule, and oppress within the framework of a modern industrial society.[57]

In the context of Bhutan, these proximate connections were not insignificant. For example, prior to fleeing Bhutan, Nar Bahadur Giri (N. B. Giri) held a prominent post in the RBA, for which he had trained at the Indian Military Academy in Dehradun, India. The officer training program prepared him and his classmates for high-ranked duties, and many of N. B. Giri's classmates became well-connected military officers in the Indian army. These military connections gave N. B. Giri access to information about military purchases by the Royal Bhutan Army that he used to critical effect in a book he published about the Bhutanese government's abuses.[58] "These were my classmates, these are my friends," N. B. Giri told me. "One friend is a big commander in the Indian army and he had the Bhutan ambassador to India at his house for dinner. He talked to him, even mentioned my name."[59]

This is only one example; dozens of dissidents described to me how they met with Indian and Nepali politicians on numerous occasions, including (at the time of meetings): Ram Mahat, Nepal's finance minister; Chakra Prasad Bastola, Nepal's foreign minister; Sher Bahadur Deuba, Nepal's prime minister; George Fernandes, the Indian politician who was both in opposition and served as defense minister while meeting dissidents; and various local politicians in both eastern Nepal and northern India. "We took several delegations to India," one activist noted. "We met all the leaders. We met the political functionaries. And then from [the] Communist Party, we met almost everybody, and the journalists, the thinktanks, and then NGOs, the student organizations. We met everybody you could think of."[60]

These lobbying meetings were too frequent to mention comprehensively, but perhaps the most interesting of them were those linked to the ten-year Joint Ministerial Committee (JMC) meetings between Nepal and Bhutan intended to resolve the refugee issue. From 1993 to 2003, Nepal and Bhutan held bilateral meetings that were meant to establish the criteria that would be used to determine Bhutan's "genuine" citizens and the process that would be employed to allow them to return. From the outset, the JMC was plagued with criticism by dissidents, who: complained of Nepal's capitulation to Bhutan regarding the process of negotiations;[61] noted the inappropriate categories that had been established to classify the refugees; critiqued the composition of the Bhutan team (noting the "feebleness of mind" of the Bhutanese Nepali negotiator who had been included);[62] commented on the unjust processes for deciding return;[63] and frequently lamented the constant delays that drew out the talks for years.[64]

Dissidents highlighted these problems and their desire for return to Bhutan through a number of channels. In addition to myriad press releases by various groups and quotes to the local media decrying the JMC meetings,[65] activists organized busloads of refugees to travel to Kathmandu in the hundreds to protest in front of the Sital Niwas (Nepali Foreign Ministry) when the Bhutanese delegation of the JMC was in town.[66] All of these tactics were facilitated by the large number of refugees that could be enlisted to participate, either as "bodies" in a demonstration or to give power to numbers for press releases. But lobbying Nepali politicians provided the activists with their sharpest tools. Those with close ties to high-level powerholders did their best to strengthen the bargaining position of Nepal through frequent meetings with the Nepali members of the JMC. Om Dhungel of HUROB, who had worked closely with many high-level government officials back in Bhutan, had a keen sense of how to plan for negotiation meetings, and prepared those in the Nepali delegation by sharing the backgrounds of the Bhutanese: "We actually built a profile of individual people who would be sitting on the other side of the table."[67]

Documenting Citizenship

A third tactic to promote return was to try to substantiate refugee claims to citizenship. Here, it was necessary to contest well-crafted Bhutanese government narratives. The government claimed that those who left did so voluntarily, pointing to the Voluntary Migration Forms (VMFs) that many refugees had signed before they departed Bhutan. The same organizations that detailed stories of human rights abuses similarly collected stories about the falsity of VMFs. Thus, refugees shared stories that they were either duped or coerced into signing forms that many could not even read, as they were often written in Dzongkha. These stories were easier to collect because those who told them were nearby and very willing to uncover the injustices done to them.

The Bhutanese government also explicitly denied that the refugees were citizens to begin with. To counter this narrative, many of the dissident organizations collected information about the refugee population—where they were born and the circumstances in which they left. Bhampa Rai, for example, explained that "BRRRC started doing documentation. We did all the detail. At that time, we learned how many [had] lands, where they came from, and that information would be signed for the village heads, with a witness, very fine signing. House number, different kind of land, how many number people, when they left Bhutan, what day they entered the camps."[68]

By far the most sophisticated of these efforts was the digital database created by AHURA, which recognized something that theorists have long suggested, that documents and material papers function as markers to assign national identity in place of language and borders enforced by state forces.[69] AHURA's focus on material documents set it apart from other activist groups. In 1999, it commenced building the digital database described in chapter 1: using computers and scanners donated from Nepali friends, teams of AHURA volunteers scanned the documents from Bhutan of willing refugees. These included citizenship identity cards, land tax receipts, and photographs of homes.[70] Hari Khanal, in charge of the collection, was responsible for visiting refugees in their huts, interviewing them, collecting their documents, bringing them to an office in Damak, and returning them to the families thereafter. He explained that "it was not an easy task for me, because I had to be responsible if anything gets missing from there. We had thousands and thousands of documents. At one time I have been carrying documents for maybe forty families, fifty families, and I have to give them back. I am proud that not one document went missing."[71] These scanned documents were then attached to a digital database that included information about each family through their *thram* (land deed number), linking information through block and district levels. The database user, by clicking on one region of Bhutan, for example, could view all families in the region and click further to obtain specific information about each family, including not only scanned documentation but other relevant information such as departure details and village heads.[72]

Ratan Gazmere explained how he came up with the idea:

> I happened to look at this scanner in Kathmandu when I went to meetings [there], scanner/photocopy machines, you know? And, going into the camps, I could see families having their documents. They would say, "this is my evidence, this is my land, ethnicity, this is my citizenship card," and also [there was the] occasional story about people losing them—fire[73]—and I thought this must be preserved somehow and there is technology available . . . and you can put it there. I thought, "Oh, it would be good to have all this data in a CD, putting it in there, go to Geneva, prompt it to open and show: We are Bhutanese. How can you say we are not Bhutanese?" That's how the idea came about.[74]

Ratan Gazmere managed to secure a year of funding from a Norwegian organization to undertake the project. Over the course of the year, AHURA was able to complete documentation from 51 percent of the entire camp population of (at the time) over 96,000, interviewing 4,553 households (49,909 refugees).[75] There are debates about why the remainder of the camp refugees did not have their documents scanned, but many agree that infighting between different advocacy groups was a major factor.[76] "There was also jealousy. Ratan Gazmere worked on the sixth floor [i.e., he had a high-up office] and other groups didn't like that."[77] It can be argued that this was a missed opportunity in the history of dissidence for the Bhutanese Nepalis, because while the depth of documentation allowed Ratan Gazmere to assert on a 2009 BBC program that there was "incontrovertible documentary evidence" to prove residence in Bhutan for 99.8 percent of those interviewed,[78] the database could not demonstrate the breadth of documentation for the 49 percent who were not interviewed. For those who have since lost their documentation in refugee campfires, that documentation is gone for good.

AHURA's digital database nevertheless represents a remarkable instance of homeland activists in a proximate place undertaking significant human rights documentation at a far cheaper cost than would have been possible by other actors. Ratan Gazmere commented that "we did it in a very cheap way. Later on, when I showed it to UNHCR and people in Geneva, they said it was the same work that UNHCR should have done, could have done. But UNHCR, they would have spent millions doing that; I didn't spend that sort of money."[79]

Though produced on the cheap, and even in its incomplete state, the AHURA database was impressive. Years later, even pro-government sources admitted that the proof for citizenship in Bhutan during the census was unreasonable, relying on "tiny pieces of hand-filled paper that had been issued sometimes decades ago . . . papers on which the ink of the handwriting would have deteriorated even if somehow preserved."[80] That more than 50 percent of the refugee population was able to show paperwork at all is an indication of how inaccurate it was to claim that the refugees were not citizens. Ratan Gazmere knew this, and it is why he worked hard to place the database into the hands of important officials. He personally handed a CD-ROM with the database information directly to Mary Robinson, the UN High Commissioner for Human Rights, and showed it to about twenty diplomats in Geneva.[81] Sadako Ogata, the High Commissioner for Refugees, received it as well.[82] One month later, while Ogata was visiting Beldangi refugee camp, she said publicly in front of thousands of refugees, "I pledge that UNHCR will take every effort to return you."[83]

Joint Verification Team

Dissidents hoped that such clear evidence of prior citizenship, combined with Ogata's pledge, would represent a turning point in what by then had been a ten-year problem.[84] But return never materialized. The JMC talks eventually led to the creation in 2001 of a Joint Verification Team (JVT), which was a group of Bhutanese and Nepali government officials who were to work together to interview refugee families for classification of identity to determine those who could return to Bhutan.

In retrospect, the high expectations placed on the JVT process were heartbreakingly hopeful, in light of what occurred: the JVT was painstakingly slow, and after more than two years, had been implemented only in Khundunabari, one of refugee camps with the smallest population. In June 2003, the JVT announced that 2.4 percent of the Khundunabari population was found to be forcibly evicted and, as such, permitted to repatriate.[85] The remainder of the refugees were placed into categories that might have rendered them stateless for years. This was a crushing blow to the refugees who had waited for more than a decade to have their citizenship reinstated and their unfair expulsion vindicated. The myriad problems of the JVT have been described elsewhere, including the exclusion of women from the process, slow processing times, and the intimidating presence of Bhutanese government officials on the JVT.[86] Thus, there was palpable anger at these findings. In December 2003, members of the Bhutanese delegation went to Khundunabari to discuss the results. Some refugee youths threw stones at them and the delegation left quickly, claiming that they had been attacked. One refugee present insisted that the claims of attack were overblown: "When the officers said something very, very rude, some boys threw some stones. Nothing very serious. The JVT team made it very serious. Not serious at all. They wanted some reason to pack up. And they packed up. That's what they wanted to do. It wouldn't have stopped them if they were serious, a few stones."[87] Nevertheless, the JMC/JVT processes were shut down, never to be reinitiated.

When I last interviewed Bhampa Rai in Damak in 2019, he recalled the JVT process with a mix of bitterness and nostalgia. The finality of the departure of the Bhutanese delegation felt like a personal affront to him, and he placed the blame squarely on the delegation that left in a hurry. But he also commented on the energy of the masses at the camp during that time and the shared sense of hope turning into frustration experienced not only by the Khundunabari refugees but by all camp refugees. "At that moment, all had a similar goal: to return to Bhutan."[88]

This collective energy was possible, Bhampa Rai said, because refugees remained nearby. "We were close, we were many, and we were using our connections in Nepal and India."[89] In other words, proximate places provided fertile ground for homeland activism directed at Bhutan. In this chapter, I have shown the many ways that proximity helped activists. Social networks borne of proximate relationships gave activists unusual access. A significant number of people with similar stories substantiated claims of abuse and the revocation of citizenship. And in both India and Nepal, physical closeness permitted symbolic action in the form of rallies and marches that concretized the refugees' claims of abuse and sparked the attention of both local and international media sources.

The spatial emphasis I invoke is reminiscent of the work of Adamson, who has argued that a "dominant spatial imaginary" that elides considerations of physical location can be problematic when it risks misunderstanding the nature of "civil" conflict and consequently ignores broader structural factors feeding that conflict.[90] Similarly, when the center of gravity of a conflict has shifted to a location external to the state, a spatial imaginary that fails to consider the importance of physical proximity in an ecosystem of exile politics neglects to see the ways that all aspects of activism—from tactics to networks to resources—are informed by that proximity. It also fails to recognize another key feature of that location: precarity.

For many refugees I interviewed, the failure of the JVT process represented a moment of profound disappointment. Until then, their stay in Nepal (and to a lesser extent, India) seemed temporary. The precarity that accompanied that stay was tolerable because they believed that they were going back home. Now, more than ten years after leaving Bhutan, many activist refugees felt that the advantages of proximity were finally outweighed by the constant and consistent precarity they experienced. That precarity, which took legal, political, and social forms, is covered in the next chapter.

PRECARITY IN EXILE

They thought we would become beggars in Bombay.

—D. N. S. Dhakal

I met Suk Bahadur Subba (S. B. Subba) in Kakarbhitta, a Nepali town just west of the Indian border and 30 miles east of Damak. It felt like many border towns I have visited: a constant stream of people walking purposefully, in both directions. Pedal-bikes and motorbikes overloaded with plastic bags of any number of food products. Buses crammed with colorful merchandise. Long lines of people holding documents in varied stages of disarray. Just a few minutes from the bus station, where I waited for S. B. Subba to arrive, the Mechi Bridge rose in the distance, a tattered Nepali flag affixed to the bridge's sign. This was the bridge across which thousands of Bhutanese refugees had marched in protest to try to reclaim their rights to citizenship in Bhutan more than a decade before.

S. B. Subba, the former chairman of HUROB, crossed the Mechi Bridge to meet me. I was interested in the way he was able to take advantage of the tripartite porosity (see chapter 4) of the region, as he negotiated the collection and distribution of information across the borders of Bhutan, India, and Nepal. Over cups of tea and the blazing of a small television broadcasting music videos at the small tea shop I had chosen, we discussed how he helps people who are still in Bhutan and who lack citizenship. He described the way they cross into India to meet him, his correspondence with international advocacy groups and Global North diplomats, and his hopes for Bhutan's future. We also addressed, head on, the accusations that he was involved in the disappearance of one refugee and the death of two others. S. B. Subba firmly denied all three, describing in detail his alibis as well as the underhanded motivations of his accusers.

There was possibly another side to the swirling accusations that surrounded him, which was that he was a suspected spy for the government of Bhutan. If so, some activists said, this explained the disappearance and murder of activists by his hand. After all, went this well-trodden narrative, S. B. Subba's wife continued to work for the government in Thimphu. To those unfamiliar with state conflict, this may seem like adequate evidence to pin him as a spy. But family affiliation is a poor marker for determining cohesion during war or conflict; it is not uncommon for siblings, parents, children, and spouses to find themselves pitted against one another in attitudes, ideology, and even in physical conflict.[1] Therefore, S. B. Subba's family relationships with people in government did not convince me of his own affiliations. He said as much, and explained that when he fled, the family made the decision to be physically separated.

After about an hour of our wide-ranging discussion, the volume on the music videos ratcheted to alarming levels and we moved to a small bench outside. I noticed that a woman was leaning quite close on another bench that backed ours. With a start, I wondered if she was a Bhutanese government official. Was I being spied on? I didn't want to give away my alarm, and S. B. Subba seemed happy to continue the conversation in the even, quiet voice with which he had been speaking all along. I tried to concentrate, with only limited success, and steered my questions away from anything controversial. About twenty minutes later, S. B. Subba and I said goodbye and I cast an askance look behind me. The bench-leaner, whose appearance in my peripheral vision gave the effect of a tidy, fair-skinned woman with shiny black hair, was walking away with a gaggle of friends.

Numerous interviews preceded this one and numerous ones followed it; I am no closer to knowing whether S. B. Subba was involved in violence or colluded with the government of Bhutan. I do not know if his nonchalance was feigned, because he was somehow linked to this woman (in cahoots or wary of her), or real, because there was absolutely nothing to worry about on that day. But I share the story because of how this small jolt of fear changed my behavior, even though I was the one who chose the tea shop, and I was the one who suggested we move outside when the music grew too loud. The petite woman behind me was probably just a shopper who chose that bench because there were not many places to sit. On the other hand, it was not impossible that she was a spy for the Bhutanese government. It would have required no 007-modified vehicles for her to come to Kakarbhitta, where she would have easily fit in among the throngs of border shoppers and visitors. And it was certainly not outside of the Bhutanese government's playbook to engage in extraterritorial eavesdropping to stem what it perceived to be anti-national activity.

In an ecosystem of exile politics, proximate spaces offer ample opportunities to collect information and mobilize the masses. But because borderland areas are ripe for the operation of espionage and collusion, they also magnify the experience of precarity. Homeland activists in Nepal and India, who knew very well the story of how their early leaders were abducted and returned to Bhutan (as described in chapter 3), had reason to fear being spied on and turned in because Bhutan was so close, particularly as they lacked legal status where they resided. This also fed the not uncommon sowing of distrust within the ecosystem. Proximity, the very thing that allowed activists to engage in their work, also increased their precarity.

In the previous chapter, we saw how aspects of physical proximity to Bhutan gave homeland activists the networks, institutional access, and symbolic resources they needed to undertake their work. In this chapter, I explore the downside of proximity to Bhutan: three types of precarity that I identify as legal, political, and social. In the coming pages I cover these precarities discretely, but as scholars of precarity have long recognized, the deprivations and threat of exploitation, detention, and deportation common to those experiencing "precarity of place" create overlapping and intersecting categories.[2] The experience of precarity of place is not unique to activists, of course, but relevant for all refugees and migrants subject to these risks.

The three kinds of precarity in this chapter have notable overlap with the tripartite model of precarity identified by Ilcan, Rygiel, and Baban.[3] *Legal precarity* describes a lack of legal documentation and absence of official permission to reside in a place. This aligns clearly with Ilcan, Rygiel, and Baban's precarity of status, "vulnerable and insecure conditions that derive from refugees being assigned a certain socio-legal status by governing authorities such as states."[4]

Political precarity describes the risks associated with challenging power as a foreigner. The nuts and bolts of exile politics require movement, as activists move from physical meetings to lobbying to facilitating the carriage of physical items across borders. Mobility, then, is a key feature of exile politics. This aligns with Ilcan, Rygiel, and Baban's precarity of movement, "controlling the movement of marginal groups, such as refugees, through governing practices and responding to this control through organising or campaigning for the rights of refugees in light of their conditions of precarity."[5]

Social precarity describes the social fragmentation and disunity that come from vulnerability and insecurity. On the surface, this is the most tenuous alignment with Ilcan, Rygiel, and Baban's tripartite model. "Precarity of space" describes "a multi-layered notion that refers to those spaces that are given meaning through the precarious experiences and everyday living of marginal groups."[6] But the meanings that refugee activists ascribe to their work—and the ways that these are dismantled by precarity—demonstrate that social precarity and precarity of space have, at their core, the same instabilities about the source of dignity and comfort.

Legal Precarity

In both India and Nepal, refugees were unable to obtain any form of permanent protection, despite many years of physical residence. In both countries, citizenship and legal protection were elusive and remain so to this day. While the bilateral 1950 India-Nepal Treaty of Peace and Friendship grants equal employment rights and free travel across the borders to citizens of both India and Nepal, two caveats must be noted. First, refugees are of course not citizens, although the southern Terai region of Nepal runs "imperceptibly" into India, and the physical porous border has historically allowed for the free movement of people.[7] Thus, there have been times when Bhutanese Nepalis have been able to cross back and forth with relative ease. But second, over time, and in response to political events such as the Maoist insurgency in Nepal, Naxalite movements in India, and elections in either state, the India-Nepal border is often subject to significant surveillance from both countries. This waxes and wanes over time, but in general, the border has grown increasingly restrictive, with border guards requiring documentation that makes it more difficult for Bhutanese activists, and any refugees, to move back and forth.[8]

India

In India, from the earliest arrival of Bhutanese refugees coming on foot through border crossings (primarily Phuntsholing), it was clear that refugees were not going to be permitted to remain long enough to seek out even temporary forms of residence. As already noted, while local organizations in West Bengal did assist the first waves of refugees, local police engaged in harassment and the destruction of early hastily created camps. It has also been claimed that, on occasion, the Indian police forced some exiles to return to Bhutan.[9] Subsequently, arrivals from Bhutan used India only as a point of passage to Nepal, where both informal and more organized forms of transport took refugees to Maidhar, the earliest of the Nepal camps.[10] "The situation was so bad that time, you know? People were dying of cholera, dysentery, diarrhea, and all that; and I didn't think it was safe for my children to be there. [They were] probably one and a half, two, and four years old."[11]

Given their ethnic Nepali heritage, it may seem logical that Bhutanese refugees ended up in Nepal rather than in India. But most Bhutanese Nepalis, particularly those who lived near the border, had a greater familiarity with India than with Nepal. They had intended in the early days after their flight to remain there temporarily until they returned to Bhutan. "If India would have been willing to give asylum to the people, I am sure that nobody would want to go to Nepal, because India is the next neighbor. We always wanted to go back to our country, because we were born there, we are grown up there, and we love our country."[12] The move from India to Nepal, it must be remembered, was not a foregone conclusion.

An unknown number of Bhutanese Nepalis did avoid being moved on to Nepal in the aftermath of their expulsion, since, as noted, Bhutanese citizens are permitted to travel to and work, study and reside in India. At the time (although increasingly less so today) informality reigned, and while paperwork was technically required to guarantee the security of permitted residence, some number of Bhutanese Nepalis dispersed before being rounded up by Indian authorities and moved on. In 2007, Human Rights Watch reported that Bhutanese refugees in India "live on the margins of society, without citizenship and with no legal status in India."[13] This remains the case today. Several of my interviewees confirmed this, noting that India provided not even temporary protection for refugees, let alone permanent protection.[14]

Nepal

The presence of refugee camps that housed, by 2008, 106,000 refugees from Bhutan indicates that Nepal tolerated Bhutanese refugees as temporary residents. However, the prospects for permanent protection were rare. The anecdotal evidence suggests that very few refugees obtained citizenship in Nepal. The official policy of the government of Nepal was to grant neither permanent asylum nor citizenship to the refugees,[15] even if movement in and out of the camps for undocumented work was permitted.[16] In keeping with what Ellie Vasta has called "irregular formality,"[17] a small number with money were able to purchase land in Nepal and buy a Nepali identity through Sadiq's "networks of complicity,"[18] but this was quite uncommon and clearly not official policy. Even well-established refugees with better resources and connections in government "certainly didn't get passports."[19]

Legal precarity for all refugees is the precursor to subsequent precarities in the political and social realms. The absence of legal status and accompanying lack of legal protection by the state is precisely what makes real the risk of removal. Refugees' lack of citizenship in Nepal and India restricted action and changed political and social behaviors, even with forgiving host state practice.

Political Precarity

Placing political pressure on Bhutan came with its own precarious risks. As hosts, India and Nepal were, at quite different levels, tolerant of some activism, but it must be remembered that any activity that reached into the political realm was accepted solely at the discretion of local and/or national leaders.

India

Activism in India proved precarious in several ways. Public protests by Bhutanese refugees were met with resistance and force, with some devastating consequences. While some forms of lobbying were accepted, there were also instances where meeting with Indian powerholders proved dangerous.

Highlighting their desire to return to Bhutan, homeland activists gained significant media attention and symbolic capital from planning and carrying out myriad demonstrations, protests, and rallies using India as their stage. But these mass public events were not without their risks. Sections 141–49 of the Indian Penal Code limited public assembly in order to prevent public disturbances, and these sections were used to arrest waves of refugee marchers who had crossed into India.[20] This occurred as soon as marchers crossed the Mechi Bridge after passing from Nepal into India, as noted in prior chapters. After being detained and eventually released, marchers kept trying to move toward Bhutan, where they were rearrested in district after district.[21] Eventually, the Calcutta High Court ruled that detaining marchers was illegal, but not before a beating in prison led to the death of one marcher: "One guy, weak and quite old, Mr. Baburam Sengden, was badly hurt during the [beating]. He was taken to the hospital inside the jail and after three or four days he died. . . . I want to remember his name with honor in this relation," one refugee said to me.[22]

A later march in India also proved fatal. In 2007, during another set of marches, one marcher drowned as he tried to cross a river without being seen.[23] Another was killed by police. "A young guy lost his life because we were organizing and he was participating. He was shot dead by the Indian police. Then it was tough time, like how we had to deal with the family there, because he was from [my camp] and I was representing that camp, so I had a lot of problem managing that, and of course somebody is losing life because of us. It was very hard for us to remember. He was committed to march and they kill[ed] him, started shooting."[24]

India also reined in the activities of Bhutanese Nepali students who were studying temporarily in India. Most of these students had come from Bhutan originally, spent time in the refugee camps, and had raised sufficient funds to pay for lodging and tuition in Indian universities. While they may have wanted to be involved in homeland politics, they were wary of Indian police and kept their political activities to a minimum. Said one refugee of his time as a student at Banaras Hindu University, "We were living in the hostel [dormitory] and there was a scary environment. Some of the Indian police, if they came and they know that this is the Bhutanese student and they are involving in the demonstration or something, they would catch us and they would put [us] in jail."[25] Another made the point that even moving from place to place was difficult. "Transportation was relatively cheap and easy though not safe sometimes. Surveillance by Bhutanese security forces traveling in plain clothes in India was not uncommon during those days. We had to be careful and take the cover of local population."[26]

Given the many important Indian figures that activists met with in India, mentioned in chapter 4, one might think that lobbying was less precarious than other activities, but even the most prominent Bhutanese political activists were not immune from precarity in India. At both local and national levels, activists found themselves in precarious positions. One senior politician in Delhi, Lal Krishna Advani, told a group of activists that while he was personally sympathetic to them, they had no business in Delhi. "He suggested we do our work in Thimphu! We shouldn't feel comfortable doing it here!" noted Govinda Rizal with a mix of frustration and bemusement.[27] In north India, where local officials were often said to be sympathetic to activists' claims, meeting directly with leaders was also risky. One activist surmised that, while there was much sympathy for the activist movement at both national and local levels, Indian police officers could be, and were, bribed to target the Bhutanese: "It was not safe in the border areas. There were instances where Indian police picked up the people and handed [them] over to Bhutan. [Delhi was] a little more safe. I would say that it is more hassle to go through the extradition process, and hand them over than just grab a person. I think it's just a headache. It was in the border areas where it was more scary."[28]

Whether in border areas or capital cities, India's proximity to Bhutan proved politically precarious. The most pointed example of the dangers of engaging in political activism in India is illustrated by the case of the DNC leader R. K. Dorji, who was arrested and nearly extradited to Bhutan, effectively silencing this important political figure. In 1996, waves of Bhutanese demonstrators were crossing into India to highlight their desire to return to Bhutan, hope was turning to frustration, and leaders from many of the organizations that were coordinating the demonstrations were bickering, anxious after months of leading marches and failed attempts to make change in Bhutan.[29] The main exiled human rights groups and political parties agreed to work together under the aegis of a unified organization, which they called the United Front for Democracy (UFD).

R. K. Dorji was elected as chair of the UFD, and its members immediately began to plan for high-level lobbying action in India to supplement and complement a year of demonstrations. In April 1997, the UFD's leaders traveled to New Delhi on a lobbying mission to meet with Indian national political parties and foreign embassies. But on April 18, one day after the UFD met with members of the Dutch, German, and Austrian embassies, Indian authorities arrested R. K. Dorji for failure to produce travel documents in India. This was a disingenuous excuse given the aforementioned 1950 India-Nepal Treaty of Peace and Friendship, but the action by India reveals the tenuous nature of political action. In the following days, India nearly extradited R. K. Dorji to Bhutan, pointing to a new well-timed extradition agreement between the two countries that placed virtually no limits on those who could be extradited.[30]

It was only with yet more risky refugee activism that R. K. Dorji's extradition was stopped. Narad Adhikari from the BNDP visited various political leaders in India and even went to the house of the Nepali ambassador to India late at night to ask for help.[31] Om Dhungel of HUROB met with the former Nepalese prime minister in Kathmandu, whose contacts with India's leftist government were helpful in accessing other important stakeholders in India. Thanks to these efforts, a stay order was issued from the Delhi High Court, and as a result R. K. Dorji could not be extradited immediately.[32] Further advocacy efforts after this initial phase stopped him from being extradited altogether, including public protests outside the jail and appeals to then opposition leader George Fernandes, who showed up at a protest in solidarity.[33] R. K. Dorji was released on bail in June 1998, under the stipulation that he stop political activities and report to the Delhi police periodically. When his case finally came to a close in 2009, all charges were dismissed, though he had to remain very cautious about engaging in any political activity. He died of natural causes in Assam, India, in 2011, sending shock waves through the activist community.[34]

It is worth quoting at length from Karma Dupthob, who was R. K. Dorji's assistant before his death, on how precarity and proximity were interwoven in the aftermath of Dorji's arrest, and how that very precarity gave the situation greater attention:

> Mr. Dorji's struggle for human rights came into limelight, so the UFD and his case became widely known throughout the world. . . . The Red Cross became interested, and several European countries [were] interested in him. They wanted him to be [given a] one-way pass, one-way ticket to their country, because if he return[ed] to Bhutan . . . [he] would be given capital punishment. So that was Western countries showing interest to him to resettle in their country, but he refused. He stayed,

because he thought there was issue, political issues, there; so, if he go[es] [to Western countries], the political issue dies. . . . This issue was pressing behind his mind. . . . Everything happened in Bhutan assisted by India, so if you want the democratic process in Bhutan, India needs to be involved. So, there's a case against you in India, if you just run away, then . . . the cause of democracy is over. So, this is the reason he stayed behind.[35]

The tension Karma Dupthob describes above—the desire to remain nearby and the difficulty of doing so under circumstances that permit action—is at the core of political precarity. Significantly, the restrictions on political activity in India have been explained by commentators through analyses of India's *physical* position in the region, explanations that are related to proximity. India's desire to ensure a compliant buffer with China[36] required the proximate in-between country of Bhutan to serve as just that buffer. Similarly, Indian fears of a pan-Nepali insurgency[37] were related to the physical adjacency of that jigsaw region located at the intersection of eastern Nepal, southwest Bhutan, and northeast India (see map 3). India also wanted to keep Bhutan in its good graces to help with expelling India's Bodo insurgents from Bhutan's east,[38] exposing how the very proximity that activists and rebels liked to take advantage of was the reason that the countries in that proximate region were inclined to stem those homeland actions. This proximity-precarity nexus is encapsulated in the words of Hari Kishore Singh, India's minister of state for foreign affairs during the 1990 demonstrations, who was quoted in the *Hindustan Times* as explaining that those who had crossed the border "have no political right to agitate against a friendly neighbor."[39]

Nepal

The volume of Bhutanese refugees in Nepal's refugee camps and its environs created a very different drive for political action in Nepal than in India, and the previous chapter details the many ways that refugees did engage in activism in Nepal, both prior to the collapse of the Panchayat ruling system (described in chapter 4) in 1990 and thereafter. While there were far more precarious consequences for activism during Panchayat, political precarity remained throughout, as detailed below.

The most pointed example of Nepal's political precarity prior to 1990 was the arrest and extradition to Bhutan in November 1989 of Tek Nath Rizal, the activist community's best-known and longest-imprisoned individual. Let us not forget that Tek Nath Rizal came to Nepal after his initial arrest and release from prison, first crossing the border to India and then, when authorities there found his agitations inconvenient, moving to Nepal. But as already detailed, Tek Nath Rizal was taken by Nepali police and handed over to Bhutanese authorities, sending the strongest possible message that activism was dangerous.

Even post-Panchayat, Bhutan's homeland activists experienced political precarity. Nepal did not have the same explicit laws forbidding demonstrations as India and, in practice, Nepal was more inclined to look the other way when refugees took up the mantle of activism. But one can locate a pattern of discretionary permission that can act as a kind of early warning system and social pressure-release valve, which scholars have described as preempting and preventing the sort of overwhelming mass protest that can drive institutional and political change.[40]

Refugee camps operate with a unique logic of governance, generally with local enforcement from the host country both physically and metaphorically at the periphery of the community.[41] Nepal's camps were no exception: each had a guard house and wooden boom gate (generally in the open position) near the entrance to the camp, but few other signs of an assertion of power by Nepali officials. Indeed, daily activities in the camps, whether political in nature or not, were not overly constrained. In the early morning of a work day, so many refugees were leaving on bicycles that the main road out of camp resembled what one might imagine a bike race would look like if the racers replaced their Lycra with faded cotton and the bikes all had to be at least fifteen years old and in some state of disrepair. Many of the activists who moved through the camps to document Bhutan's abuses confirmed that they were left relatively alone by Nepali authorities. Thus, they traveled easily both within and between camps to garner the stories about ill treatment, flight, and expulsion that formed the basis of activists' claims of systematic abuse.

Nevertheless, refugees who engaged in these activities were careful to play down the political nature of their organizations. For example, the Bhutanese Women and Youth Empowerment Program (BWYEP) emphasized capacity building and self-sufficiency in their mission statement, despite the fact that they brought forward the stories of those who had fled Bhutan.[42] Likewise, Mangala Sharma's organization BRAVVE promoted itself even in its name as a humanitarian organization devoted to service, even though a key aspect of its work was documentation, as well as advocacy both within Nepal and overseas.

Refugee organizations with a political bent had to be careful. Those groups involved in collecting stories about abuse at the hands of the Bhutanese government were eager to have formal training in documentation and reporting but were worried about the risk of the organizations being considered too political. Consequently, they "named the training programs as 'Creative Writing workshops.' It was really reporting and journalism. That's how it started in the camps," Indra

Prasad Adhikari (I. P. Adhikari), an editor for several news and commentary publications, pointed out.[43] Newsletters within the camp were a common way of reproducing rhetorical pieces about injustice in Bhutan, as well as communicating future protest events, but these newsletters were targeted for closure on several occasions. I. P. Adhikari recalled being harassed for his newsletter by district officials, and he frequently used a pseudonym to protect his identity.[44] Another remembered how he was treated when he was called in for interrogations:

> They are saying to us, you are staying in the refugee camp and you are not allowed publicity, newspaper, you cannot challenge the other country. . . . We tried to tell them that we have the rights and we're not going to stop the newspaper. They want us to stop publishing the newspaper, right? We say, we don't want to stop, we will continue publishing the newspaper. We don't want to be hit by an ax in our own knees. This is our rights, refugees have the right to information. They were sending us to each and every division. They tried to convince us and make us, okay, we will not publish the newspaper. . . . I took a kind of risk, because there were people who wanted to participate, and there were people who did not like us doing that one.[45]

Outside the camps, political activities occurred with frequency, but generally without permission. For example, activist leaders regularly made efforts to motivate the masses by inviting lecturers from Nepali universities to speak in Damak, near the camps. But notifying people of an event like this could be done only by word of mouth and on the sly. "Nepal authorities don't allow this to carry on. . . . We would sneak a little bit. They don't allow legally, but illegally we can do."[46]

One formalization of political activism was the organizing of the mass demonstrations noted earlier, where organizers obtained permits to engage in the marches that moved into India but began in Nepal. These were not only legally permitted but were often sent off with an address by a local politician or religious leader.[47] Yet with both the demonstrations and with Damak-based activities, like the visits of university lecturers, the activities could be, and were, stopped when local or national authorities deemed it prudent, either because of security issues or because of fears that the refugees would disrupt local businesses.[48] Curfews were imposed periodically and, in these instances, no outside movement was permitted. Those found out of camp had their ration cards taken away.[49]

For activists based in Kathmandu, such curfews were not a problem. But even there, permissions changed with shifting political environments. This was because, in line with Betts and Jones's emphasis on the importance of institutional strength,[50] dissident organizations required specific permissions from the government in order to operate. One activist explained:

One organization I wanted to establish, and work through that, the government of Nepal didn't allow me. . . . We had made a constitution of the organization, a proper Board, members, but we cannot register. But this organization can be registered by Nepal citizens. So, I put [citizens] in the Board, president, all these things, all Nepalese citizens should receive everything, photocopy, everything. The proper system was to adopt it to register the organization. It goes through the CDO [Chief District Officer]. First the CDO, then it goes to Home Ministry, and Home Ministry finds out, checks out all the constitution, and if it's ok, then after they can allow, then you can work. But then you have to do what the Nepal Board is telling us to do.[51]

For dissident diaspora organizations in Nepal, ceding control of the organization to citizens was not as onerous a challenge as the difficult conditions that other precarious activists faced in other countries, but it did mean that when disagreements arose between Nepalis and Bhutanese Nepalis, as occurred most commonly over discussions of resettlement, the latter risked losing their funding and recognition. Like other kinds of precarity, this precarity of organizational operation—what I have previously identified as institutional precarity—did not necessarily mean that exploitation or arrest was always imminent, but it did mean that the possibility was ever-present, and as a result, organizations could be shut down.[52]

Governments are not monoliths, and there are frequently tensions between different government departments. The priority to shut down activism was often more of a focus for those who worked directly with refugees rather than those who were involved with matters of state. This was why Hari Khanal, one of the chief coordinators of AHURA's digital database, was exceedingly careful not to antagonize the National Refugee Coordination Unit (NUCRA), the government body that coordinated refugee affairs in the camps, notwithstanding the fact that the foreign minister of Nepal himself was interested in the completion of the database. Hari Khanal explained: "The foreign minister, he told, can you complete [the database] 100 percent, which was not possible, because . . . we need support from everywhere, and we need nobody to stop us from doing it. It was a very useful work that we have done. But even the foreign minister could not say to NUCRA [that they should] leave us alone. Because, really, we were not supposed to do these political things."[53]

I have already described how Ratan Gazmere was successful in passing on the contents of the AHURA database to powerholders in Geneva during an international meeting. But this points to another important discretionary barrier for Bhutanese activists: the ability to travel internationally. Telescoping the work of proximate activists at international conferences is an example of the way that proximate activism interacts with a multispatial human rights community, providing a good illustration of the complexity of the ecosystem of exile politics. But this political path from proximate to international and back again could be severed and was on numerous occasions. R. K. Dorji of the DNC and Balaram Poudel of the BPP both had their travel documents refused, essentially preventing them from traveling to anywhere other than between Nepal and northern India.[54] Ratan Gazmere himself was detained in Nepal when he tried to return to the country after being resettled to Australia.[55] Thus, the ability to build a transnational bridge between local and international activism was in the inconsistent hands of Nepal's visa regime.

Finally, Tek Nath Rizal himself was subject to discretionary treatment. After his release from prison in 1999, his actions were permitted on some occasions and constrained on others. The government tolerated him very well, he said in an interview to me, but given that generosity, he is careful about what he says and does. And like the other activist leaders mentioned above, he has been prohibited from traveling internationally.[56]

These many examples point to the political precarity experienced by Bhutanese activists in Nepal, despite the fact that many in the Nepali government were supportive of the cause. And this precarity, similar to that in India, was related to Nepal's physical proximity to Bhutan. Ram Sharan Mahat, Nepal's former finance minister, was explicit about this relationship. While his book explains the ways that he tried to personally advance the cause of Bhutanese activists,[57] the government preferred silence and invisibility from the refugees for reasons related to physical proximity. In an interview with me, Ram Sharan Mahat noted that "we were not supporting political activists. Bhutan is our neighbor." When pushed further, he explained that, for diplomatic purposes, it made no sense to antagonize a neighbor by actively facilitating the work of people that Bhutan viewed as anti-nationals. "We supported their calls on a humanitarian ground, not political. . . . They were the victims of ethnic cleansing [and] we didn't encourage them to be activists at all."[58]

The UNHCR also discouraged activism, although the organization was not in a position to legislate policy in Nepal. But explanations for this stance, communicated to me in interviews, were similarly related to physical geography.[59] First, UNHCR staff noted the potential for the radicalization of refugees in the context of Maoist rebellions in Nepal between 1996 and 2005. It was the refugees' physical proximity to Nepal's Maoists, whose strength emanated from rural areas including those near the camps, that raised this concern.[60] Political activity of any type was not looked on kindly during this explosive era, when officials in charge of the camps could not necessarily differentiate between those engaging in violence and those who were involved in peaceful actions. Often, in fact, these different events involved the same actors.[61]

Second, UNHCR pointed to the much older population of refugees from Tibet, who had the potential to cause major geopolitical problems with China if they were to be vocally critical of their home country.[62] In outward-facing policy, Nepal was consistent in prohibiting all political activism from refugees. This is why a high-level official in the Home Ministry in Nepal told me that refugees "from anywhere in the region" are not supposed to be political at all, referring to both Tibetans and Bhutanese.[63] Encapsulating the mindset of many refugee activists, the deputy secretary of one camp said that "we know that we are not supposed to do political [actions], but we find a way."[64]

Social Precarity: Trust Destroyed

Refugees—and particularly activists—experienced a form of underexplored social precarity: distrust and disunity borne of proximity. I admitted at the start of the chapter to changing my behavior when I was worried that a woman sitting nearby might have been a Bhutanese government official sent across the border to listen to my conversations. For Bhutanese activists in Nepal, their fear of being spied upon was far worse. This spawned an atmosphere of distrust and disunity among activist groups, much to the detriment of the movement.

I note here that intragroup rivalry is certainly not unique to Bhutanese activists, and a firm body of knowledge has detailed the ways that even those with the same goals can be torn apart by disagreements of strategy and ideology.[65] Similarly, they can be riven by fights over resources, identity, social hierarchy, or even just personality differences.[66] Certainly, fragmentation among politically aligned groups in South Asia is not uncommon. For example, caste, economic and social class, and regional identity all contributed to factionalism and schisms within the Tamil resistance movement in Sri Lanka, which often spilled into open conflict and blood in the streets.[67] Infighting among the northeast Indian ethnic independence movements (particularly the Naga and Bodo) has been endemic for decades.[68] Internecine conflict also frequently emerges in anticipation of a coming accommodation with the national government and a drive to become the main bargaining partner in any future agreement.[69] Given its commonality, it is important to emphasize that the infighting behavior detailed below is neither meant to paint activists as petty, nor to exceptionalize fragmenting behavior. Instead, infighting and fragmentation ought to be read as a rational response to precarity and its challenges.

As early as 1992, the editor of *Himal* noted the fractious nature among the two main groups in the then-developing movement. "The politico-bureaucrats (of the

BNDP) . . . criticise BPP leaders of harbouring idealistic visions of a 'free Bhutan' without searching for realistic ways to push forward the agenda of return. . . . The BPP stalwarts regard the BNDP as a party of well-to-do interlopers out to wrest away a movement that they have nurtured from the start," wrote Kanak Mani Dixit.[70] Indeed, differences in ideology and tactics lay at the heart of the infighting, with the BPP preferring to spur a mass movement and the BNDP wanting instead to work to negotiate with elite political leaders in the region. One astute refugee, not formally associated with either party, described the difference as follows:

> The BNDP group happened to be more educated ones, and the BPP happened to be the ones that moved first—they were the first people to form a party and not many of them were college educated. They were seniors, they knew more about politics, and they didn't want to listen to [the BNDP, who were] these young bureaucrat type of people, who wanted to do more in the proper way. BPP sometimes liked to give press releases with criticism—you know, their sense of public relation was little bit being direct, whereas the BNDP people wanted to please India, please this one and that one. They were very cautious about what to say and what not to say.[71]

In an interview with me, Kanak Mani Dixit elaborated on these divisions, and highlighted the way that spatial divisions exacerbated ideological strategic ones. He pointed out that the BNDP was oriented toward India—which he indicated with his right hand—and that the BPP, represented with his left hand, made better use of connections in Nepal. Clapping his hands together and then separating them, he observed, "Each side wants to stick with the places they know best." He made a motion indicating they wanted to dig in their heels—a physical as well as ideological position.[72]

Suspicions among and between activists were bred as well by accusations and counteraccusations of threats and violence. I have already noted that a few violent events were carried out by Bhutanese Nepalis protesting Bhutan's treatment of its southern population. The government of Bhutan highlighted these incidents to its diplomatic advantage, painting the entire movement as violent. But many exiled activists whom I interviewed strenuously objected to this narrative. They insisted that the few situations of extreme violence were related to personal feuds onto which others had projected the story of political rebellion. These may have been personal vendettas against those who had cheated them in the past or rivalries about the use of land. But the proximity of activists made it easy for the Bhutanese government to attribute this violence to the broader exile movement and to magnify it. Hutt notes: "Clearly, the Bhutanese government wishes the world to believe that it has a terrorism problem on its hands, but . . . many of these incidents appear to be criminal acts of assault and theft, not politically motivated murder or sabotage."[73] Disagreements and accusations were thus heightened among and between groups with differing strategies, as the optics of violence complicated the goals of activists. A regular refrain among my interviewees was the frustrated regret of those who found it difficult to know whom to trust and, literally, *where* to find reliable messengers and conveyers of material back inside the country.

Related, proximity eased the possibility for the government to send spies across the border. Refugee camp residents received visits from family members and friends from Bhutan, who came to the camps secretly under the guise of visiting markets or holy temples. But were visits from those who remained in Bhutan simply family members wishing to reunite or did they represent a sinister attempt of pro-government sources to infiltrate the camps? It is much more likely that it was the former, but the very stealth that visitors practiced (necessary if they were to return home to Bhutan and not be harassed) encouraged whispers about how far "loyal Lhotshampas" might go to secure their own protection in Bhutan.[74] To be clear, I heard virtually no stories where this fear of collusion actually proved to be accurate. One unsubstantiated suggestion emerged from the circumstances surrounding the arrest and imprisonment of Nandalal Katwal, a refugee who tried to raise the Gorkha flag on a march back to Bhutan. For this act he spent fourteen years in prison in Bhutan. But one activist suggested that this was because he was unjustly framed for his role in physically violent activities by "someone, even one of our own."[75] Even family visits took on a hue of secrecy. I heard many people admit that their relatives or friends had visited them in Nepal, often secretly, but when they learned that another person's relatives had visited, they grew suspicious. Thus, the intragroup rivalry that can occur in any situation was heightened by a distrust borne of proximity.

The potential for abduction by the Bhutanese government, carried out in Nepal and attempted in India, was never far from the minds of many activists. I have described a powerful moment of unity that emerged with the rise of the UFD, led by R. K. Dorji. But his arrest and attempted extradition, which initially saw several groups working together to secure his release, eventually shattered that unity. The specter of the proximate arms of the Bhutanese state aggrieved many. To some groups, it was never clear who was working for whom. Some high-level leaders refused to return to India after R. K. Dorji's arrest, worried that they, too, could be targets for abduction or extradition. "So they never set foot in India again," said one activist about several exiled leaders.[76] More detrimentally, the breakdown of the UFD represented what many leaders, on reflection, perceived to have been the very last chance for a unified movement that might have placed sufficient pressure on the Bhutanese government to produce permitted returns under safe conditions.[77] When the UFD lost its staying power, a significant hope for unified activism died.

I am not suggesting here that proximity directly caused the disunity that prevented activism from being successful. But it is clear that heightened distrust associated with being nearby made more difficult the job of placing consistent pressure on relevant actors, something that would have been vital to upending status quo power structures. Intergenerational fragmentation, common in all refugee situations, took on extreme forms in Nepal's refugee camps, as some youths turned to violence borne of distrust and frustration, and directed not only at the Bhutanese government. In 2001, the president of the BPP, R. K. Budathoki, was attacked by several youths with a traditional Nepali sword during a strategy meeting being held in Damak. He died several hours later. Interviewees were divided about who was to blame—some told me it was members of a group called the Bhutan Revolutionary Free Students' Force. Others said that the secretary general of the PFHR, S. K. Pradhan, was behind the attack. And others who defended S. K. Pradhan argued that jealousy lay behind the accusations. "S. K. flew to Geneva, South Africa. That was enough to make others jealous. Enough to mess [up] the movement."[78]

Indeed, activists fought over access to resources. This is hardly unusual, and an abundant literature acknowledges the ways that resources matter to activists, and the ways that groups compete for these resources.[79] In the case of Bhutanese activists, disagreements about resources were exacerbated by other forms of precarity that limited the ability of activists to access funds and other opportunities necessary to further their work. Refugees were unable to obtain jobs through legal means, an aspect of financial precarity that I do not cover here but that is amply treated in the literature about migrants and refugees who work without documentation.[80] While activists were creative in raising funds for activism—requesting donations of rice from refugees,[81] or renting out their personal cars to locals, as HUROB leaders did[82]—it is clear that competition and jealousy frequently characterized these interpersonal and political relationships, often to the detriment of the movement. I have already referred to the possibility that infighting prevented AHURA's database from reaching the maximum number of refugees, and therefore from reaching its most useful potential. Bhampa Rai told me ruefully, "The database project failed because the people failed. The people failed because the trust failed."[83]

Rivalry over resources also took the form of fighting over who were the legitimate spokespeople to broadcast the exiled Bhutanese cause, expressed through disagreements about the ownership of names and symbols. The leader of one branch of a homeland activist group, for example, accused another group of misusing his party's name and flag.[84] And two different groups claimed the name Druk National Congress, with one eventually differentiating itself by calling itself the Druk National Congress-Democratic (DNC-D). These two groups, the heirs of the work of the powerful R. K. Dorji, hardly communicate with one another today, preferring to pretend the other does not exist. I have had conversations with the leaders of both groups. Their differing narratives—about the rise of the DNC and the necessary tactics to ensure its continuation—demonstrate a sublimated struggle for legitimacy into which precarity and proximity are interwoven.

Examples of this proximity-precarity nexus abound. The human rights training in which some DNC leaders participated in eastern Nepal (described in the previous chapter) was risky in the way it exposed its participants to potential capture by Bhutanese forces, and both DNC groups took ownership of the unique costs this imposed on them and their families. The continued lack of documentation for DNC members who remained in India and Nepal was a product of remaining nearby, which both groups wanted to do. In another instance, Bhutanese Nepali groups potentially damaged their chance to have an international platform because of infighting. N. B. Giri explained to me in detail what happened when he decided to get involved in the dissident movement, and managed to gain the attention of Socialist International (SI), an organization with significant global resources to broadcast the exiled cause:

> We formed a socialist organization and we wanted to explain, first tell the world what problems we are having, what we want to do, and what support we need against the government of Bhutan. Not against the people. Not against the country. But against the government. In a very frank statement that we wanted to give to the world. And then I requested Socialist International to give me a platform. And maybe they understood [because] they were really, really interested to know, since we are talking truth, in rough language maybe. I was given a platform to come to New York, with Luis Ayala, the secretary general of SI.[85]

N. B. Giri described how he received funding from the Nepali Congress to attend SI's national convention and was told that, with the letter of invitation from SI, he would be granted a visa. Making efforts to be inclusive, he contacted all the other exile groups so they could work together to prepare a strong speech.

> I was very, very happy. I'd never . . . done this type of work. So how to do it? How to prepare it? It is a big, big thing. So, I called people. Very frank. . . . I need all cooperation and support. . . . I tell them to help. But instead of helping, I don't know, they started requesting, writing

something somewhere. . . . A month before, just 15–20 days before convention came a letter from SI, from Luis Anaya. Our team was cancelled. And what he has written? I was told that since there are many political parties claiming to be final organizer of the movement, nobody will go. What I know is that some other groups [had written] to SI, they said, "Why you want to invite Giri's group and Giri's socialist party? We are already here, started a movement in Bhutan, and we should be invited first for such an important meeting to present the issue." . . . So everything was cancelled [for us] by SI. And since then, no exiled political party has been seen by SI. That is a sad thing. . . . [*Pause, deep breath in*] And I just kept quiet. And I dropped all those things.[86]

The stakes here were high. The chance to be recognized by a global solidarity organization whose membership included governing parties across Europe, Africa, and Latin America represented a huge opportunity for the Bhutanese Nepalis. It was a period of relative strength for SI at the time. The Indian National Congress had recently been admitted to the organization in 1993, and support from SI had been instrumental in rallying international awareness and solidarity around the struggle of political movements advocating human rights, democracy, and counterhegemony in Central America in the 1980s and 1990s. But the stakes were also personal, like the chance to be funded to travel to New York. Squabbles over legitimacy, visas, and what might seem like insignificant funds for travel thus stymied a much larger project.

Throughout my field research, I heard stories from all sorts of activists who had personal connections with famous Indian and Nepali politicians. They called each other by diminutives. They smoked cigarettes with each other. They had late-night meetings in their personal residences. One activist borrowed clothes from a well-known politician. Their access to powerholders was surprisingly good and, where they could, activists capitalized on that to garner support for their cause.

But even refugees with direct connections to those in the highest levels of office still experienced legal, political, and social precarity. Their protection was neither guaranteed nor permanent and their activism was curtailed. Many experienced a breakdown of social cohesion as distrust and jealousy emerged. In this chapter, I have shown how these precarities were related to the very thing that kept a focus on the homeland at the forefront of their attention: physical proximity. In other words, proximity was a boon and a bane at the same time.

The discussion in this chapter has mostly focused on the ways that Bhutan's proximate refugees were limited or influenced in their activism directed to Bhutan by their precarity, which came in legal, political, and social forms. But, like refugees everywhere, they also suffered a more direct form of personal precarity, with profound and devastating effects on the lives of their families and their community. In the early days of their exile from Bhutan, before camps were officially set up, hundreds died of malnutrition, lack of sanitation, and disease. I heard heartbreaking stories about the deaths of children on the banks of the river, just days after they and their parents arrived in Nepal. In later years, refugees suffered deprivations of livelihood and dignity.[87] While many arrived better educated than their Indian and Nepali counterparts, they could not obtain secure work, nor could they guarantee education for their children. Tens of thousands arrived with no resources and no education, and their vulnerability as noncitizens was magnified, making them susceptible to harassment, exploitation, and trafficking.[88]

These personal precarities, overlaid with the others I have described in this chapter, meant that, over time, refugees' orientation changed. While all were firmly focused on returning home in the immediacy of the expulsion, the years in the camps "languishing"—a word I heard from nearly every refugee I encountered, no matter how poor their English—shifted the focus of many refugees away from Bhutan and toward the possibility of resettling in countries of the Global North. That opportunity arose in the mid-2000s and changed the ecosystem of exile for Bhutan's homeland activists. That process, and the resulting ecosystem, is the subject of the next chapter.

EXPANSION OF THE ECOSYSTEM

I feel that whatever we are trying to forget, that is the biggest asset that we're losing.

—Vidhyapati Mishra

From my field journal on December 5, 2007:

> The word is "languishing." Every refugee knows it, no matter how little English. That's how they describe their lives, "languishing" for years and years. Some leaders deploy [the word] daily, hourly, their sights trained on resettlement. Others harken back to the cardamom fields and the orange groves, encouraging people to hold out and fight the good fight. But is it a good fight? Those fields are long gone or owned by someone else. What would [mass] resettlement mean after years of trying to get the government to allow refugees to return? I see it both ways.

From chapters 2 to 5, this book has examined an ecosystem of exile politics that remained relatively stable. While the ecosystem underwent incremental shifts through increased activity in the distant diaspora, the pace and volume of this expansion were limited. Furthermore, the aims of homeland activists remained the same, as their efforts were focused on the tripartite goals of promoting democracy in Bhutan, highlighting human rights violations, and, above all, advocating and agitating for return to Bhutan. But the mid-2000s brought two events that led to significant changes. First was a massive and rapid expansion of the ecosystem through the process of resettlement, highlighted in my field journal entry above. Second, there was political change in Bhutan.

This penultimate chapter examines the ecosystem of Bhutan's exile politics from the mid-2000s onward. It begins by exploring the processes that led to resettlement, laying out the ways that precarity eventually triumphed over proximity. It discusses the complicated narratives that surround the origins and endpoints of Bhutan's democracy trajectory. Along the way, the chapter exposes several paradoxes that activism, resettlement, and new democracy have wrought.

The Triumph of Precarity

The previous chapters have shown how proximity and precarity existed in an uncomfortable but necessary tension, wherein homeland activists in India and Nepal experienced both the advantages and the risks of remaining near Bhutan. Over time, the frustrations of impermanent life in countries that denied citizenship not just to activists but to all refugees grew in tandem with increasingly limited opportunities for the expression of political opposition. Work opportunities on the sly—both those associated with homeland activism and other livelihood pursuits—began to dry up, particularly in light of Maoist desires to rid the country of foreign workers.[1] There were increasing restrictions and clampdowns in Nepal's seven refugee camps. The advantages of proximity began to pale in comparison to the problems of precarity. "All these things were happening in the camps, pathetic stories, in every family, and I asked, how long can we wait to repatriate? It's two decades now."[2]

At the same time, conversations began in humanitarian circles to offer Bhutanese refugees the possibility to resettle en masse to countries of the Global North. Refugee resettlement describes a specific process offered by a small number of wealthy countries to accept refugees permanently from their countries of refuge. This process is facilitated by UNHCR and is a coveted goal for refugees living in protracted precarity, that is, those living for years in countries where they cannot secure citizenship. Each year, countries of resettlement accept only a very small number of refugees. In 2008, when resettlement became a real possibility for Bhutanese Nepali refugees in Nepal, only 65,862 refugees worldwide departed for resettlement, representing 0.43 percent of refugees globally.[3] The prospect of mass resettlement—when countries agree to offer the possibility of resettlement to an entire refugee population (barring security and health risks)—is even more rare. But mass resettlement indeed emerged as a possibility for the Bhutanese refugee population in Nepal, which by 2008 had reached more than 100,000.[4] Those in India, who had never registered with UNHCR and were therefore not part of a process of international refugee protection, were not eligible for resettlement. By 2020, the resettlement program of Bhutanese refugees had closed (i.e., any remaining refugees in Nepal could seek to move to countries of the Global North only through family reunification). All told, 111,697 refugees were resettled to eight different countries, including 94,663 to the United States and 6,825 to Australia (see map 5).[5]

I have argued elsewhere that a discourse espoused by UNHCR that focused on durable solutions opened the resettlement door when other possibilities for citizenship (returning home or permanently integrating in Nepal) seemed closed.[6] It has also been suggested that large-scale resettlement occurred because the international community was ready to wash its hands of this long-standing problem.[7] However, I offer a supplemental perspective here, mostly ignored until now, that reveals several paradoxes.

A close examination reveals that resettlement occurred partially because of the efforts of Bhutan's homeland activists who, in casting a light on the Bhutanese refugee issue, spurred the international community to action. Interviews with members of both the US and Australian governments confirm that it was not just the presence of refugees in the camps that created the impetus to find a solution for refugees, but the specific details about the injustice of their expulsion that advocates had brought to their attention.[8] One US State Department official said, "No one else was interested in Bhutan until now. We heard the stories and saw the evidence."[9] Ratan Gazmere, the creator of the ingenious database discussed in previous chapters, points out that as much as he developed the database to promote return, "That CD really changed the whole game actually. Then the international community began to believe they are Bhutanese, you know, what Bhutan is saying is not right, and if we cannot push Bhutan to take them back then we better do something for them, they can't be living in the refugee camps forever and ever."[10]

Homeland activists—those promoting democracy, human rights, and reclaiming of citizenship—all had return as their main goal at the outset. But in collecting, analyzing, and distributing the information that was supposed to secure their return home, they helped facilitate a resettlement process that would distance them—metaphorically and physically—from their goal of return. This is the first paradox.

From an outsider's perspective, resettlement may seem to be a wonderful solution to the problem of protecting refugees. But mass resettlement can have problematic consequences, particularly for those who remain in refugee camps after others have left—either because they have not yet resettled or because they will not resettle at all. Resettlement has been found to deplete refugee camps of leadership, skilled workers, and morale.[11] Even more relevant here, resettlement represents a double-edged sword for refugees who have been focused on improving the homeland, potentially depriving homeland political movements of their fuel.[12] One commentator, writing during the early days of the Bhutanese resettlement process, argued that resettlement would be problematic if it negatively impacted "the future of the refugees' movement to claim their right to return to their homeland," and, more broadly, the "possible imitation/replication of the brutality against . . . minorities in other countries in the name of ethnic nationalism."[13]

This second paradox speaks to the fact that resettlement, in efforts to protect refugees, has the potential to encourage the kinds of behavior that lead to refugee flows in the first place. For nearly twenty years nearly all Bhutanese refugees, both activist leaders and the refugee population at large, had lived and breathed a narrative of return. This explains why, despite refugees' ongoing precarity and the rarity and general desirability of refugee resettlement globally, the offer of resettlement was initially met with skepticism by many. Resettlement let Bhutan off the hook by relieving the pressure on return. For activists whose entire political careers were built on pushing for repatriation, this felt like a profound loss: "If the refugees go, their constituency is gone," noted one political commentator.[14]

The resettlement offer divided an already fragmented population. Pro- and anti-resettlement groups argued openly and sabotaged each other surreptitiously. Refugee leaders who had spent years pushing for return were sidelined and surprised, and as they came to understand the consequences of resettlement, they were also divided on the best way forward.[15] UNHCR made efforts to communicate clearly the resettlement offer, but this was a challenging endeavor. Lack of information and misinformation were rife, and rumors abounded.[16] Refugee youths strongly opposed to resettlement engaged in threats and acts of physical violence to dissuade others from resettling, including burning effigies and brandishing weapons.[17] Far from discouraging resettlement, however, this violence increased refugee precarity, as curfews in the camps grew simultaneously with sporadic attacks. Refugees on the fence now felt more precarious, and more likely to opt for resettlement.

Complicating matters, some used the specter of violence to try to improve their chances for early resettlement. That is, some refugees who were unsure of the resettlement process and wanted to guarantee themselves a resettlement spot by highlighting their vulnerability created the semblance of an attack. "They will pay a radical boy 12 thousand rupees [nearly US$200 at the time of the interview] to dismantle their hut, just so that the victim will be resettled first," noted one refugee leader.[18] This is the third paradox of the chapter: Some of those who felt most strongly about insisting on a right for Bhutanese refugees to return home catalyzed a more precarious environment in Nepal, eventually pushing more people in the direction of resettlement.

I spoke to many homeland activists who echoed concerns about the ways that resettlement would weaken Bhutanese refugees' claims to return. But there was a counterargument as well: Resettlement had the potential to strengthen the distant diaspora, giving resettled refugees access to resources, international attention, and multiplied networks so that they could continue to highlight Bhutan's abuses and push for safe return from a physical distance. One of the earliest activists to move to the United States, Mangala Sharma, noted that "the advantage of doing it [in the United States] was I was doing it with politicians, with the governments, with the State Department, so the impact was more."[19] Another published his decision to resettle in the *Bhutan Reporter*. After submitting his resettlement application, Hasta Bhattarai was "shattered by the sense of dislocation and loss of identity and unity." But he chose to resettle anyway and, on the verge of leaving Nepal, hoped that

> our scattered resettlement in various parts of the foreign land may give us easy access to raise our pathetic voice to the world communities inspiring them for their immediate helping hands towards the solution. . . . Going abroad may breed better minds. This may be of great help for the country and our suppressed, subdued and discarded brothers and sisters residing in southern Bhutan expecting great help from us. Our mission should not be other than emancipating our siblings from prolonged slavery, exploitation and discrimination.[20]

Scholars have debated the idea of "long-distance nationalism" both theoretically and empirically, through the lenses of transnationalism, diaspora, identity, and migration. On the one hand, theories of assimilation and incorporation suggest that over time, when refugees and migrants move far away and obtain citizenship elsewhere, orientation toward the homeland will lessen and interest in political activity toward the homeland will dissipate.[21] On the other hand, those who study nationalism,[22] political conflict,[23] and deterritorialization[24] have demonstrated that distant diasporas can hold dearly to narratives and images about the homeland that catalyze political (and military) action, expanding the spatial dimensions of war, conflict, and political struggle. The factors that temper or further activism from distant locations have also been studied. Resources from a wealthy resettlement country may increase political mobilization.[25] Education, gender, elite status, and contexts of exit and reception also play a role.[26] It has been found that homeland political action in the Nepali diaspora in particular also relies on a multicultural discourse in the host country.[27] While this last finding points to Nepalis focused on Nepal, rather than Bhutanese Nepalis focused on Bhutan, the importance of host-country conditions—in this case, the relative precarity or lack of precarity in Nepal and resettlement countries, respectively—is relevant to both.

In the context of mass resettlement of Bhutanese refugees, homeland activism could have decreased, as feared by those opposed to resettlement, or increased, intensified, or otherwise expanded, as suggested by those in the pro-resettlement camp. Which occurred? Before we answer that question, it is necessary to introduce the second significant change that impacted Bhutan's homeland activists. In 2008, in the same year that the resettlement program of Bhutanese refugees began to gain momentum, Bhutan held its first democratic elections. The origin of Bhutan's democracy, the reasons for it, and the direction in which the country has moved since these elections, are up for debate. I discuss these issues in the next section.

Democracy in Bhutan

At the same time that the resettlement discussion was gaining ground in 2006, the revered fourth king of Bhutan, Jigme Singye Wangchuck, willingly abdicated his absolute power to his son, with the promise of constitutional democracy to follow. Two years later, around the same time that the first Bhutanese refugees were resettled, Bhutan adopted a constitution and held its first set of elections. While the two parties that ran against each other were virtually indistinguishable in policy and philosophy, the general consensus among the international set was that Bhutan had managed the transition to democracy gently and gracefully. Most scholars of democratization were impressed by the absence of conventional factors in Bhutan that ordinarily lead to political transition and democratization. Mark Turner, Sonam Chuki, and Jit Tshering observed that "there were no elite pacts, no traces of regime disunity, no economic crisis, no international pressure and no popular mobilization for democratic rights."[28]

It will perhaps come as no surprise that the feel-good story about a king willingly permitting democracy to enter the country in gradual forms to reach a pinnacle of complete democracy is contested by exiled activists, as well as by some scholars. One can point to three competing narratives about Bhutan's democratization, both its origins and its endpoint. These are summarized below.

The first narrative is best encapsulated in a 2020 book by Sonam Kinga, who traces the efforts of the third and fourth kings in decentralizing and modernizing the country from the 1950s onward.[29] He points to the establishment of the National Assembly in 1953, nodding to five decades of parliamentary elections. He notes the devolution of power to the village level as early as 1976 and suggests that the handover of the king's executive power to a cabinet in 1998 introduced the idea of the state and the government as separate entities. He describes the king's development of a constitution starting in 2001. With the impressive detail that comes from being a member of the inner circle of Bhutan—Kinga served on the National Council and as its chair and is now a teacher at Bhutan's Royal Institute for Governance and Strategic Studies—the book highlights the "innovative leadership"[30] that the royal family, and especially the fourth king, exhibited, which allowed the country to flourish in the context of a vernacularized democracy.

A second narrative emerges from Dhurba Rizal, whose stance is fairly clear from the title of his book: *The Royal Semi-Authoritarian Democracy of Bhutan.* Unlike the beneficence attributed to the royal family that Kinga espouses, Dhurba Rizal—a Bhutanese Nepali refugee scholar—argues that the sheen of democracy was initiated in order to protect the king from a true devolution of power. He points to three elements—the surfeit of political conspiracies and regional pressures that surrounded the royal family to which the throne wanted to respond, the hypocrisy of the king "gifting" a constitution to its people, and the timing of the king's willing abdication of his throne—that all demonstrate that the reforms were a means for the royal family to consolidate power.

> Considering all these perilous situations, King Jigme decided unfalteringly that it would be for the greater good of his dynasty to leave the throne to his son, so that the transition would take place very smoothly. Thus, it was not a virtuous gesticulation and benign move that the GNH King Jigme exhibited by abdicating the throne as highlighted by frenzied national, regional, and Western media, hitchhiker tourists, academics, and scholars; rather, he left it reluctantly, and he wished to be king for many more years to extend his grip in the country.[31]

These two competing narratives are not easily resolved. Dhurba Rizal claims that there was no consultation on the constitution, for example.[32] Kinga claims that every household received a copy of the draft constitution.[33] Not surprisingly, they disagree on the origins of the refugee situation. But even Kinga agrees that the move to democracy had the effect of strengthening the monarchy, not weakening it. In comparing today's royal family to a legendary Buddhist king who gave up his kingdom and family, Kinga writes that "the notion of the King sacrificing his power to empower the people imbued Bhutan's democratic transition with a strong moral dimension. By giving away the King's right to rule, the monarchy's 'moral right to reign' has been reinforced."[34] Kinga himself identifies the fourth paradox of the chapter: by gifting the people with democracy, the royal family reinforced its image as the source of justice and welfare. "The strengthening of monarchy by introducing democracy creates an interesting paradox."[35]

A third narrative suggests that changes came because of the pressure imposed by exile activists, reforms from which those exiled have of course never been able to benefit. Unlike accounts (by Kinga and others) that democracy emerged in the absence of mobilization or external pressure, several scholars have foregrounded the important role played by ethnic minorities.[36] This pressure has a long history. Homeland activists point out that the creation of the National Assembly in 1953 followed the early requests for representation that emerged from the BSC in 1952.[37] Against the assertion that the king's beneficence was the catalyst for change, they point to the 1990 demonstrations as a popular movement. And while Kinga claims that there was no external democracy assistance to trigger the king,[38] we know that democracy training did, in fact, take place across the border, as noted in chapter 4. On the role of exiled activists, one of them, R. P. Subba, wrote to me:

> It was projected that constitutional democracy that ushered in Bhutan in 2008 was a gift from the palace. They said that the Bhutanese people were not ready for democracy. The refugees believe otherwise—that the democracy that came in Bhutan is the result of the work they have done. They formed political parties, they raised voices for human rights and democracy and campaigned internationally, enough to raise questions and international concern against the autocratic, absolute regime that governed Bhutan. It was hard to insulate Bhutan from globalization and the spread of ideas of human rights and democracy. The king yielded to this unseen force and agreed to introduce democracy.[39]

The trajectory of this narrative, in its purest form, argues that Bhutan has not achieved full democracy today. R. P. Subba continued: "The drama of abdicating the throne in favor of democracy is but a display for credit taking and of appearing benevolent in the eyes of the public. . . . What we hear of as 'change' inside Bhutan especially after 2008 is still largely a display made for international consumption."[40]

The extent to which changes in Bhutan are cosmetic is difficult to resolve. An assessment of the progress of democratization carried out in 2014, six years after its initiation, offered an analysis of mixed results.[41] Civil society organizations, though relatively small in number, had grown in the years since democratization. The regularity, openness, and acceptability of elections were deemed to be positive. The weakness of political parties and the capacity of alternate parties to influence the system were regarded as clear negatives. The rule of law had become more robust and judicial independence had been demonstrated on several notable occasions.

Later research has confirmed some ambivalence concerning Bhutan's democratization. Traditional dispute resolution mechanisms, for better or worse, have nearly disappeared, in favor of modern resolution techniques carried out by local officials.[42] The language of human rights is still viewed with suspicion, particularly because its role as a means to make claims on the state sits in deep tension with a traditional view of the individual-state relationship, in which the individual should show "unwavering humility and respect" to the government.[43] In 2017, the Economist Intelligence Unit ranked Bhutanese democracy as a "hybrid regime," scoring it ninety-eighth out of 167 countries assessed, highlighting low political participation rates as a main factor for this score.[44]

Cultural reasons have been cited to explain low participation. Freedom of expression, while guaranteed in the constitution, was less practiced not because citizens did not want to be represented but because they were unaccustomed to challenging authority.[45] An anecdote from Lisa Napoli's autobiographical account of volunteering at a youth radio station in Bhutan during this time is telling. She noted that while people traveled from far distances in the rain to witness the signing of the new constitution, some did it not because of the historic significance of the constitution but to be in the presence of the king and accumulate merit by being in proximity to a *thongdrel*, a centuries-old religious scroll, that was being exhibited at the same time as the new constitution.[46]

These behaviors explain why S. D. Muni describes Bhutan as a "deferential democracy."[47] Among his critiques, he points out that the political parties still take their cues from the monarchy, and that "parliamentary seats may only be held by people with college degrees—a highly restrictive condition in a country with a literacy rate of no more than 60 percent and a narrow educational base."[48] Despite a tendency toward reverence of authority, overall Muni believes that Bhutanese democracy has a high chance of long-term success.[49]

Thierry Mathou, writing in 2018 in *Asian Survey*, notes the culture of consensus, but argues that signs are emerging of more robust political debate, driven by democratization and increasing rates of social media uptake, and notes that Bhutan has jumped ten places, to eighty-fourth out of 180 countries, in the World Press Freedom index since 2015.[50] Joseph Mathew, from the University of Jammu in India, makes a tougher assessment, pointing to the fact that only two parties were allowed to contest the first election in 2008. Reflecting on their campaigns, he says that "both parties ended up vying to show loyalty to the king and the ruling establishment."[51] Mathew then circles back to the issue of the Bhutanese Nepalis: "Even the draft constitution is meant to deflect international attention from the Bhutanese of Nepali origin who have been forcibly expelled and are living as refugees in eastern Nepal."[52]

Line Kikkenborg Christensen's report describing seven months of field work living with university students in Sherubtse College between 2013 and 2015 is telling. She notes an undercurrent of fear when it came to speaking about the refugee issue—including and particularly among Bhutanese Nepalis.[53] She observes a religious culture of uniformity that elides discussion or understanding of ethnicity.[54] And she finds a "cancellation of memory" when it comes to discussions about the Bhutanese Nepali issue; silence and omission, rather than hostility, created "closed versions" of the past.[55]

The issues associated with the refugee population are the ones that, at the writing of this book, remain unresolved.[56] First, an estimated three dozen political prisoners remain behind bars for promoting democracy.[57] Some have been released since 2010, and the government asserts that those who remain imprisoned are those who engaged in violence.[58] But a 2023 report by Human Rights Watch argues that the "vague and overbroad provisions" of the National Security Act and a lack of due process that these prisoners experienced in a predemocracy era mean that there are significant lingering governance concerns about political prisoners.[59] Second, Bhutanese Nepalis who remained in Bhutan who never received citizenship after the 1988 census—either because their paperwork was not found to be legitimate or because they had relatives involved in the demonstrations—remain in an untenable situation. They have been unable to access a range of opportunities, including government employment, education, and overseas travel. Freedom House's 2019 report on Bhutan notes that "citizenship rules are strict, and many Nepali-speaking people have not attained citizenship, effectively disenfranchising them. International election monitors have noted that Nepali speakers have been turned away from voting."[60] I have not been able to obtain an exact figure for those who remain without citizenship in Bhutan because accurate figures are not made readily available. In 2005, Bhutan's National Assembly stated that there were 81,986 "non-nationals" in Bhutan.[61] From 2006 to 2019, *Kuensel* stated that 10,220 were granted citizenship.[62] From this, we can infer that more than 70,000 remain in the country without citizenship. These noncitizens

> cannot openly criticize the policy. They cannot say. They feel the pain. Their relatives are here in exile. They want to see, they want to come freely, talk about the injustice freely. That cannot be done. You can be ostracized, even by your own friends, right away, if you talk about supporting the people who left the country. Right away. All those laws, and policies, and ordinances, and decrees are still there. They have not been annulled; they are there. People are still categorized. Many of them have lost their citizenship; they have never got it back. So, it's a long way to go. It's a long way. Unless people inside Bhutan can stand up and say what they want to say without fear of prosecution, it's very difficult to say that there is democracy in Bhutan.[63]

Finally, as flagged numerous times, for refugees who remain in Nepal waiting to return to Bhutan, not one has been permitted to do so. About 2,750 people expressed their eagerness to return to Bhutan in mid-2019 after UNHCR sent out a questionnaire seeking the interests of remaining camp residents.[64] This group includes about 100 non-Bhutanese Nepali refugees who are associated with the DNC or DNC-D, whose citizenship was never in question but who are still waiting to know if they can return safely without being arrested. Karma Dupthob of the DNC insists that "repatriation means everybody has to be repatriated, including us. But we will go only under certain conditions." He lists these as safety on return, religious freedom to practice the Nyingmapa tradition of Buddhism, and the registration of the DNC as a legitimate political party.[65]

Homeland Activism Post-2008: Sunset or Sea-Change

Researching homeland activism in the postresettlement era presented new challenges for me as a researcher. Prior to this time, collecting information on activism was relatively straightforward because the center of gravity rested in the region, where I shuttled between Kathmandu, the environs of the refugee camps, and the India-Nepal border to observe advocacy events, meet with stakeholders invested in the Bhutanese refugee issue, collect and analyze advocacy materials produced and distributed in the region, and interview homeland activists. The story was localized, and I knew where to look for evidence of it.

Following resettlement, that changed drastically. As will be clear from the discussion below, the sites of activism are now disparate and diffuse. My methods changed to reflect this: I expanded my interview coverage to include refugees who had resettled. I sought out advocacy materials from a greater range of sources, including coverage of the issue in local newspapers in resettlement countries. And I conducted a thorough media analysis of one of the primary online websites for Bhutanese refugees, *Bhutan News Service*, analyzing and coding the entirety of its 2,575 articles written between 2008 through 2020, noting trends on the coverage of certain topics and paying special attention to all 182 articles that referred to activities conducted by homeland activists.[66]

This research neither fully supports nor fully dismisses the prediction that resettlement would lead to a decline in movement activity. There is no denying that human rights documentation, lobbying, and public protests decreased considerably, over time, after 2008. In 2019, the Beldangi camp secretary said such activity was "like a sunset."[67] But this does not mean that all efforts have diminished. Instead, homeland activism adapted to a new political and physical environment.

A Gradual Erosion of Old Activism

In proximate countries, appeals to political stakeholders, public protests, and information collection have gradually eroded, although they have not ceased entirely. In 2013 in Nepal, I met several times with Harka Jung Subba, a leader who represents elderly refugees who do not want to resettle, of whom Harka Jung Subba is one himself. He detailed for me the petitions and lobbying efforts that he has conducted. As part of the Senior Citizens' Group, he has collected thousands of signatures of elderly refugees who want to return to Bhutan. Several years running, he has organized a "Black Day" annually on December 17, Bhutan's national day. He and his group have sent letters to foreign embassies. "The embassy of Sri Lanka, India, Norway, Denmark. They write back to me." These letters, like ones written in past years, have not yielded change. "They do nothing. It is like the elephant who has two tusks, to show and to chew."[68] That is, while foreign governments may tell activists that their complaints are reasonable, they do nothing to address the problems. While Harka Jung Subba continues to promote the issue occasionally, speaking to the press or meeting with stakeholders, these incidences have declined.

The leaders of other groups, like the BRRRC, DNC, and BPP, have also continued activities in altered and smaller forms. On important occasions they meet for public events, but they are small affairs.[69] Periodically, they meet with important Nepali government officials or the heads of humanitarian organizations to continue to push for return.[70] Several refugees told me that they continue to hear about problems in Bhutan through proximate sources—by those who cross physical borders (under the guise of shopping or visiting holy sites) to share information in person, because phones and computers are not considered secure.[71] This is important because proximity still matters, even today. In 2019, I met a Bhutanese Nepali in Beldangi camp who had just traveled clandestinely from Bhutan to attend his cousin's wedding. He had never left Bhutan before, and he has spent his entire life without citizenship and without the opportunity to obtain an education or meaningful work. "Only manual labor," said a relative sitting nearby.[72] In sharing his difficulty as a noncitizen with camp leaders, this Bhutanese Nepali was adding to the years of documentation that activists undertook.

Most individuals who remain in Bhutan under difficult circumstances, however, do not want to have their individual problems broadcast. Instead, the infrequent but nevertheless continuing publication of reports critical of Bhutan by refugees touch on systemic changes. In February 2019, a newly formed group called Bhutan Watch—comprising an amalgam of leaders from both nearby and the distant diaspora—produced a forty-eight-page document called *Rights under Shadow*.[73] The publication, funded by a German NGO, draws on already public information to cover the situation of political, economic, and social freedoms in Bhutan today. Reports like this indicate that some forms of homeland activism remain salient, even if their intensity and frequency have eroded. The marches that assembled thousands together are a thing of the past. One resettled refugee observed that "that kind of activism, I don't think it will be on foot. Most of the people . . . the number is simply not there."[74]

Same Aims, New Sites, Diverse Forms: Resettlement Country Activity

One of the central hopes of resettlement for homeland activists was that resettled refugees would have the capabilities and access to new powerholders so that they could continue to place pressure on Bhutan. This activity has taken diverse forms, both old and new.

As noted in chapter 4, refugees published a wide range of materials in Nepal and India to underscore their experiences at the hands of the government of Bhutan. In the distant diaspora, refugees have continued to tell their stories to new audiences. Sometimes the details of Bhutan's abuses are central to the story, such as when Dhruva Mishra spoke to the University of Richmond chapter of Amnesty International about the political and ethnic discrimination against the Bhutanese Nepalis.[75] Sometimes, the focus of the story is life in the resettlement country, with fewer mentions of Bhutan's role in the exile of the population, such as a TedX talk delivered by Bikash Regmi.[76] Local media have also written about refugees in ways that, to a greater or lesser extent, tell a story that implicates Bhutan. There are numerous feel-good stories about refugee success—helping the community, gaining citizenship, graduating with honors—while stories about the difficulties that refugees endured in Bhutan serve as a backdrop. Two examples are Sushil Niroula sharing his story with ABC Adelaide just before taking his citizenship oath[77] and two brothers going to college just four years after arriving in Atlanta.[78]

Chapter 4 pointed to the lobbying undertaken by refugees in India and Nepal. In resettlement countries, there have been pockets of lobbying, such as European-based diaspora organizations that have sent delegations to the European Commission, the UN Human Rights Council, and the Global Forum on Refugees to highlight the continued need for pressure on Bhutan.[79] Coming from the United Kingdom, Germany, Denmark, and the Netherlands, these resettled refugees have taken advantage of their European location to travel easily to Geneva, The Hague, and Berlin, where these meetings have been held.

Ram Karki was the first refugee from Bhutan to receive asylum in the Netherlands.[80] Since then he has lobbied both European bodies and those in his adopted country. "After I came to Holland my main mission was to bring awareness. I was in eastern Bhutan in high school. I [was] used to a lot of foreign people, lots coming from Netherlands, to work in hospitals, to build projects, animal husbandry. Many government projects were run by Dutch institutions. I also learned that the Dutch government gave lots of money for development purposes. But lots of money was used to suppress us."[81] Ram Karki started by testifying in the Dutch Lower House of Parliament, aided in networking by a human rights organization based in The Hague that focuses on human rights in South Asia. Since then, he has been meeting with Dutch parliamentarians periodically. But when he shares information with them about events in Bhutan, he continues to rely on those who live nearby, in Nepal, to learn salient facts. This is a key point, because it suggests that even with the Internet, proximity to Bhutan still matters. Ram Karki does use the Internet—both to communicate with those in Nepal and to communicate with former classmates in Bhutan—but not all will share political or human rights information with him online for fear of being found out in Bhutan.[82] Thus proximity to new centers of power has supplemented, not replaced, proximity to the site of abuse.

Prisoners and Disappearances: A Truly Transnational Ecosystem

Some of the examples thus far have described activities that can be carried out in relative isolation. One does not need to be deeply embedded in a broader ecosystem to write a letter to a local newspaper, for example. But advocating for the better treatment and release of political prisoners and the search for disappeared activists illustrates a truly transnational ecosystem focused on Bhutan. Political prisoners and disappearances have received, and continue to receive, attention by activists all over the globe. Often someone who lives locally in Nepal or India is the first person to let those further afield know about a person who has disappeared or the treatment of a prisoner. This information may come from family members who have visited the prisoner or from former prisoners who have been released, as I detail below. The DNC, for example, managed to obtain some information about a prisoner whose treatment they had been tracking because the prisoner's guard was friendly enough to permit a photograph to be taken, which was then passed on to the DNC. For his kindness, Karma Dupthob of the DNC told me, the guard himself was put in prison for nine years.[83]

Information is then shared more widely. Shantiram Acharya was a refugee journalist who was arrested and imprisoned in 2006 after he crossed into Bhutan and took photographs of an army post. The letters he wrote to his family, passed on by the International Committee of the Red Cross, were published by *Bhutan News Service*. Advocacy carried out by other exile journalists, in conjunction with international organizations like the International Federation of Journalists, helped secure his release in 2014.[84] Information about Shantiram Acharya came from sources in Nepal as well as from family who eventually resettled in the United States.

Another example is the disappearance of Lok Nath Acharya, who was last seen in October of 2014. Lok Nath Acharya went missing after he told family and friends that he intended to attend a human rights meeting in Siliguri, India. Sites of activism around the globe were activated in the efforts to locate him: in Beldangi refugee camp, his sister and other family members shared information with the International Committee of the Red Cross.[85] Govinda Rizal in Kathmandu tried to use contacts within Bhutan to obtain information about his presence in prisons within Bhutan.[86] Family members in the United States reached out to contacts in India to determine when he was last seen.[87] Resettled refugees in Australia who were attending meetings in Geneva prepared documents to present to the Human Rights Council.[88] These documents turned into source material for the Council's Working Group on Arbitrary Detention.[89] As of this writing, Lok Nath Acharya has not been found, but the widespread efforts to locate him speak to a functioning ecosystem of exile activism.

Starting in late 2019, another transnational effort was undertaken. The Global Campaign for the Release of Political Prisoners in Bhutan (GCRPPB) was founded by activists in nodes all around the globe, including its founder, Ram Karki, in Holland, I. P. Adhikari in Australia, and Govinda Rizal in Nepal. The organization has engaged in many efforts to call for the amnesty of Bhutan's remaining political prisoners under the Royal Prerogatives provision of Bhutan's constitution. In 2019 the group created a common petition to be sent to host government representatives in Australia, the United States, United Kingdom, Holland, Canada, and Denmark, as well as to human rights bodies such as the Human Rights Council.[90] They also created an online petition to be sent to the king of Bhutan. In part, the petition reads: "The elderly parents of those political prisoners are . . . dying without see[ing] the face of their beloved sons. . . . Children of those prisoners who were just born have . . . great wishes to see their fathers." By June 2023, it had been signed by 534 people in thirteen countries including those in resettlement countries, as well as in Nepal, India, and Bhutan itself.[91]

The GCRPPB has also lobbied at international levels. In June 2020, Ram Karki raised the issue of Bhutan's political prisoners with the United Nations High Commissioner for Human Rights, Michelle Bachelet, during her presentation of the 2019 UN Human Rights Report. In the online meeting, Ram Karki highlighted the suffering of these long-standing political prisoners, asserting that "we see no reason for them to suffer in prison when the very reason for their arrest was the demand for human rights and democracy which has already been introduced in the country." He further noted the previous year's visit of the UN Working Group on Arbitrary Detention to Bhutan's prisons, pointing out that the visits to prisoners were monitored by Bhutanese government officials and therefore not independent.[92]

Meetings such as these are posted on the GCRPPB Facebook webpage, along with information about public protests—like one in December 2022 in the Pennsylvania capital, Harrisburg, where approximately forty activists stood outside the Capitol building with photographs of relatives still in prison and signs urging their release. A letter-writing campaign to the king was also advertised on the webpage, encouraging Bhutanese Nepalis all over the globe to write to the king and take a picture of the letter to post on social media. The campaign has also produced numerous appeal videos released on social media linked to auspicious occasions, such as the annual National Day of Bhutan, Human Rights Day, and the birthday of the king, in which Bhutanese Nepalis from all over the world ask for the release of family members.

Detailed information concerning the health of prisoners has buttressed GCRPPB's claims, and these data have been supported by information collected in Nepal, even during and after the COVID-19 pandemic. A research project carried out by Human Rights Watch and supported by GCRPPB members resulted in the March 2023 release of the first in-depth report to cover the issue of Bhutan's political prisoners.[93] By the completion of writing this chapter, the king had yet to respond directly.

Activism Adapts: New Aims, Shifting Focuses

Resettlement has brought significant changes not only to the demographics of the Bhutanese refugee population but, as foreshadowed, to its primary areas of concern. These issues can be divided into two categories: integration and memorialization.

INTEGRATION

The first category of activism described here steps away from the homeland target. There is now, decades on from the original source of refugee flight, an increasing desire to turn away from Bhutan and focus on improving lives where refugees live. For those in resettlement countries, this kind of advocacy comes in the form of improving the communities of resettled refugees. Many of the resettlement country organizations now engage in work of this nature, such as hosting cultural and community events that elevate the achievements of Bhutanese refugees and lobbying politicians, to improve lives not for those in Bhutan, but for those in resettlement countries. For example, in 2018 in Massachusetts, refugees submitted a memorandum to the Massachusetts governor Charles Baker that requested improved worship facilities, better access to English as a Second Language (ESL) classes, and a greater attention to the physical and mental health needs of Bhutanese refugees.[94] Another example occurred in 2015 in New Hampshire, where three resettled refugees testified at a New Hampshire Senate Committee meeting to support a resolution that focused on integration *and* on homeland activism.[95] The resolution began by recognizing the contribution of Bhutanese refugees in New Hampshire. Then it requested "that the United States government work diligently with the governments of Bhutan, Nepal, India, and other interested parties, to resolve the refugee crisis, reach an agreement to allow the option of repatriation, and promote human rights and democracy in Bhutan."[96] When the resolution passed, one of the refugees who initiated the lobbying suggested that similar strategies could be replicated in other US states.[97]

In Nepal, advocacy toward integration has also increased over time. When refugee leaders meet with Nepali politicians, they request improved conditions in Nepal at the same time that they request continued pressure for Bhutan to permit return. Meetings with UNHCR and advocacy organizations are similarly double-pronged.[98] There has also been, since resettlement, an increased focus on the fate of unregistered refugees, of whom there are an uncounted number in Nepal and India.[99] The issue has been highlighted by refugees in Nepal who, for example, in 2011, organized a "fast unto death" to fight for refugee status.[100] Refugee leaders who remain in the camps meet with local officials from NUCRA who then make the case to central authorities.[101]

Given the lack of other options post-resettlement, the increased focus of activism targeting the host country is logical. It mirrors patterns identified in the Syrian conflict, where external factors (security imperatives and a behemoth international aid machine) channeled Syrian refugees away from grassroots mobilization focused on change in Syria and toward an aid-based model in which activists focused their energies on improving lives in Jordan.[102] It also conforms to what I have previously identified as the "logic of the activist," in which individual choices about pursuing meaningful activities in the here and now may trump a broader "logic of activism," which in turn might suggest a collective action wholly focused on the future.[103]

It is also important to recognize that resettlement has brought a new understanding of "homeland." While those aged forty years or older would have memories of Bhutan, the younger members of the refugee population knew only Nepal as their home prior to moving to new countries. For this generation, homeland activism then shifts focus away from Bhutan and toward Nepal. Many resettled refugees who engage in lobbying or writing articles include recommendations for what Nepal could do to improve the situation of Bhutanese Nepalis in Nepal. This is hardly surprising when the prospects of return are absent; refugee compatriots simply want to find some avenue for helping their brethren who remain in Nepal, by lobbying and, of course, by sending money back to friends and relatives. There is a substantial literature covered elsewhere on remittances; in short, resettlement has brought, at the very least, a significant influx of cash to at least some of the remaining camp refugees.[104] But resettled refugees also engage in fundraising for causes in Nepal more generally. Many of the activists most attuned to current policies in Bhutan, such as Ram Karki, regularly raise money to send to Nepal.[105] Several drives were organized in the aftermath of Nepal's terrible earthquake in 2015.[106] While it was not their first priority, this shift indicates that many leaders eventually adopted flexible goals that reflected the stalemate regarding the issue of return.

MEMORIALIZATION

When memories of persecution are assembled collectively, some narratives eclipse others, which implicitly or explicitly assign sources of blame. Thus "memory entrepreneurs" who craft and present such memories play a deeply political role.[107] For Bhutanese homeland activists, the processes of memorialization began with the publishing of the first recollections of expulsion in the early 1990s, as described in chapter 3. But new forms of memorialization have emerged. I describe two forms here.

First, online outputs produced by Bhutanese Nepalis have worked to capture the histories of the refugees. I. P. Adhikari started *Radio Pahichan*, a Nepali-speaking show broadcast out of Adelaide, Australia, as a way to retain the stories of Bhutanese who have now resettled. *Pahichan* means "identity" and by focusing on the bygone stories of the elder generation, I. P. Adhkari and his colleagues are intentionally seeking to preserve collective memories of and retain a unique identity for the Bhutanese Nepali community. This form of "defending memory"[108] does not simply relay the traditional stories of farming the cardamom fields. Instead, it includes self-told mnemonic narratives that reveal rich personalities and include much "emplaced knowledge" about Bhutan, information that legitimizes identities that are still linked to Bhutan, years after displacement.[109] Another example is *Bhutan News Service*, which published many articles that captured the never-before told narratives of Bhutanese refugees. Some of these are harrowing, difficult accounts, made no easier by the passage of time. But these articles—many as part of a series called "Untold Story"—are unique as pieces of memorialization because of the way they produce reverence for the people, places, and objects that are the history of the movement. One autobiographical account tells the story of the escape from prison of B. B. Gurung, who was active during the late 1940s Jai Gorkha movement and imprisoned as a result.[110] Two other articles recount the life, both in Bhutan and in Nepal, of the son of the famed Masur Chhetri, the iconic figure who was drowned in a leather bag for challenging authority.[111]

Masur's son, Ranjit, eventually resettled in 2012. *Bhutan News Service* portrays his departure from the refugee camp with stirring words:

> "I am never happy to move to a completely strange place. My dream to die in Bhutan, where my father ended his life for the common cause, is going to shatter," Ranjit lamented, a few minutes before he stepped into the IOM [International Organization for Migration] bus. Tears trickled down his cheeks as he waved hands to bid farewell to his relatives and neighbors among those spectators. The bus moved away quickly, leaving a cloud of dust behind, aboard the living luminary, Ranjit and the family.[112]

After operating for more than fifteen years, *Bhutan News Service* closed in January 2020.[113] Its last editorial, unmistakably lugubrious, observed that a cadre of volunteers could no longer continue to do the work effectively "with the passage of time, changes in physical situations and dislocation of communities into different countries."[114] This is of course a clear reference to the way resettlement had weakened a prominent exile publication. Another opinion piece mourning its closing pointed out that "the maintenance of BNS in Nepal, where nothing was affordable and its discontinuance now from the US, where everything seems doable, offers a sharp contradiction and a stranger paradox."[115] Here is yet another paradox, the chapter's fifth: *Bhutan News Service* was starved of its lifeblood only after most of its writers and readers had moved to rich resettlement countries. It is worth noting that another online diaspora publication, *Bhutan News Network*, continues to operate and covers issues relevant for those in Bhutan, Nepal, and in resettlement countries.

A second form of memorialization is firmly located in Nepal, near the refugee camps, and was still in development at the completion of this book: a museum dedicated to memorializing Bhutan's refugees, called the Bhutanese Refugee Cultural Complex. A bright blue two-story building tucked behind a golden Brahmin Temple in the small town of Charali near the India-Nepal border, the museum rests within a compound with high walls topped with barbed wire fencing. The entire compound also serves as the personal residence and office for its founder, D. N. S. Dhakal, who was also the founder and president of the BNDP. The idea of a museum came to him when he traveled to Armenia some years ago and visited a museum there to commemorate the Armenian genocide. "Until this day, there are countries that have not recognized the genocide of the Armenians, which happened more than 100 years ago. I don't want to wait that long for people to know what happened to our people."[116]

The bells and chanting from the adjacent temple, known locally as the Bhutanese temple, wafted over continually when I visited in March 2019. Large black granite blocks affixed with plaques greeted me in the entrance to the compound. One reads, "We Salute the Martyrs of Human Rights and Democracy in Bhutan. May Their Soul Rest in Peace." A long set of panels, running along the border of the compound wall, stands next to this plaque, listing the names of said martyrs. The list, with sixty-four names in total, is divided by dzongkhag—the district from which the victim originated—highlighting the connection to a physical homeplace. Next to each name, one word describes their death. Most say "shot" or "tortured." The very first name, however, is unique: the word next to it is "drowned." This first name is, of course, Masur Chhetri who died by forced drowning in the early 1950s, more than sixty-five years before the creation of the museum.

The compound also includes an orange building that appears to hold supplies, and on the outside wall hang reminders of the refugee camps that once housed more than 100,000 residents. There are signs of some of the organizations that operated in the camps, onto which are painted the camp names and the logos of donors. Juxtaposed against the list of martyrs, these signs project a curious nostalgia, as if to say: Remember when we were young and hung out at the camp Vocational Training Centre?

On the walls of the airy second- and third-floor balconies are dozens of framed photographs and press clippings. The press clippings are a collage of hope and despair: one headline reads, "Bhutan agrees to take back all willing refugees," while the next one reads, "Bhutan-Nepal talks break down." Photographs of meetings between the Nepalese and Bhutanese ministers are interspersed with pictures of Bhutan's kings, from the first to the fourth. This is a curiosity, perhaps. In what other museum dedicated to commemoration of an oppressed people are the photographs of the royal oppressors framed with reverence? (Then again, I asked myself, what other homeland movements send annual birthday wishes to the king of the country that oppressed them?) This reveals an ambivalence about the role of royalty in the treatment of those who were imprisoned or departed, about which there are very divided opinions: some say the king actively conspired to disempower Bhutanese Nepalis, others say he did all he could to temper the xenophobic streak in the National Assembly. There are also many photographs of activist leaders themselves, where the viewer sees just how close to the corridors of Indian and Nepali power the exiled leaders were.

The photographs are not labeled, and while I could identify about three-quarters of the individuals from my research, I believe this is unusual: activists and older refugees would be able to identify all of them, while anyone not affiliated with the Bhutanese refugee movement would recognize only a few. Whom is the museum targeting? On the one hand, there are no exhibit labels that introduce the full story of the Bhutanese refugees to an uninitiated visitor, suggesting that the museum is holding a rather exclusive conversation with Bhutanese refugees.

On the other hand, most of the articles framed are in English, suggesting a desire to attract outsiders.[117]

Perhaps the best interpretation is simply that this has not yet been decided, because the museum is not yet complete. One room on the third floor is filled with boxes and files still to be sorted, including the records, publications, and press clippings from some of the most important movement actors. While visitors are certainly welcome to the museum, D. N. S. Dhakal has not advertised its existence widely and does not plan to hold an official opening ceremony until "the leaders of Bhutan and Nepal are shaking hands at its entrance."[118] Neither wishing to antagonize his hosts in Nepal nor put Bhutan on the defensive, the museum, like the refugees who remain in Nepal, awaits a hopeful sign from governments consumed with other matters.

The period since 2008 represents a new era for the Bhutanese Nepalis, when Bhutan entered an era of democratic transition and the center of gravity of the refugee population physically shifted. Along with hopes for more secure work, freedom of movement, and better education for their children, many refugees expected that the Global North would give them better opportunities to place pressure on the Bhutanese government to improve the situation for those who were not the immediate beneficiaries of the fledgling democracy. The sprouting of Bhutanese Nepali communities all over the globe certainly represents an expansion of the ecosystem, as activists and their constituencies are now dispersed far and wide. But the nature of that ecosystem—where its hub is located and whether its homeland orientation remains the same—is less certain.

This chapter has reviewed the activism of Bhutanese Nepalis in the era since 2008, both those who remained near Bhutan and those who moved further afield. It found declines in some areas of activism, most notably in public protests. And we cannot point to nearly as many newsletters in the camps or meetings with Indian and Nepali politicians. But the letters written, petitions initiated, and political bodies lobbied in the post-2008 phase are not completely isolated incidences. Given the small number of refugees who remain in Nepal, in fact, it may be argued that the intensity of homeland activism has not changed significantly, proportional to the claims of abuse and numbers of those who desire reform.

But the chapter has also identified new kinds of activism, representing adaptive modes of mobilization. Refugees target powerholders proximate to their new vicinities. Political action has become more transnational, as nearly all actors still rely to some extent on information collected near Nepal and India, highlighting the continued importance of proximity for those focused on Bhutan. Most difficult for those who remain committed to change in Bhutan, the "homeland" has come to mean something new, with many young people thinking of Nepal as the homeland that they want to improve. There is also a new kind of activism, which is not focused on the homeland at all, but which seeks to improve life in the here and now. In this way, resettlement has produced activities that run counter to the original aims of exile politics: the unmitigated celebration of life in one's new country with no reference to return or to the problems that remain. This does not signify the collapse of the ecosystem, but it does indicate a shifting view of the location of home.

Given that no refugees have been permitted to return to Bhutan, some may be tempted to call the entire homeland activist project a failure. And certainly, the return issue remains a painful sticking point for many who always dreamed of their cardamom fields and orange groves. But another way to think about Bhutan's exile politics is to consider the changes it arguably facilitated in a slow-moving kingdom. The country has embraced at least some democratic elements, it has released a few of its political prisoners, and certainly some Bhutanese Nepalis who remained in Bhutan for the past two decades are slowly being incorporated into the polity.

A wholesale condemnation of exile politics is therefore unfair. This is important to note, particularly in light of the fact that, from the distance of resettlement, many activists have been excoriated by those in the diaspora for their ineffectiveness. The following comment posted on an article in *Bhutan News Service* is characteristic of a small vocal segment of the diaspora: "The so called leaders were beating around the bush for last two decades. I feel quite ashamed when people call them leaders."[119] This book demonstrates, however, that, far from "beating around the bush," despite factionalism and flaws in strategy, the exile politics in which activists were engaged had a significant impact, though potentially not the impact the exiles expected. Refugees advocated for democracy in order to return safely to Bhutan; instead, there has been democratization without return. While critiques of ineffectiveness partially ring true, advocacy *did* result in resettlement, of which a very large portion of the population is the beneficiary.

Following resettlement, the ecosystem that activists helped to build, and which expanded thanks to their efforts, dispersed so quickly that the central hub near Bhutan lost its centrality. Distant sites have been nourished by renewed attention. Sites proximate to Bhutan have struggled to retain their importance. The original aims of the ecosystem have not disappeared, but they sit alongside new, adaptive forms of activism.

The ecosystem—expanded, dispersed, changed—nevertheless remains.

CONCLUSION

I think in the long run, we have to build bridges. The time will come.
—Birendra Dhakal

Bhutan is known for stunning mountain temples, a benevolent king, and a creative approach to measuring the country's progress through the creation of the Gross National Happiness index. Few people know its fraught history with its ethnic Nepali population. Up to one-sixth of the country's entire population departed Bhutan in the early 1990s and became refugees in Nepal and India. Not one has been permitted to return.

Whether this massive outflow represented a willing departure for those who left, as the government of Bhutan claims, or an expulsion, as the refugees claim, is a matter of contestation. This book tells that contested story. It also tells the story of the refugees who *told* the story: it examines, in fine detail, the work of Bhutan's homeland activists, who, on leaving the country, sought to place pressure on their homeland. These homeland activists documented human rights abuses, collected information to prove legitimate Bhutanese citizenship, wrote petitions to the king, and protested publicly to gain media attention. From sites both near Bhutan and further away, they used multiple strategies to challenge the narrative tropes deployed by the government of Bhutan.

These physical sites of exile politics—in India, Nepal, and, over time, in resettlement countries of the Global North—offered specific place-based opportunities. The sheer volume of refugees in the camps in Nepal made it easy for activists to go from hut to hut to ask for material proof of abuse and the stripping of citizenship, as when activists collected and scanned old identity documents from Bhutan. Prior relationships with high-profile politicians in India and Nepal facilitated lobbying, as when a late-night meeting between activists and

Nepal's ambassador to India helped stop the extradition of Bhutan's most seasoned dissident at the time. Membership in new polities emboldened public requests, as when forty refugees stood in front of the Pennsylvania Capitol building to call for the release of Bhutanese political prisoners.

These different physical sites were also defined by their precarity, or its absence. In India and Nepal, refugees experienced legal, political, and social forms of it. In India, Bhutanese refugees lived with no formal protection or documentation, while in Nepal, those registered with UNHCR received identity cards that offered protection solely contingent on their stay in the refugee camps. In both countries, there were risks involved in planning marches, printing pamphlets, and meeting sympathetic powerholders. These risks heightened distrust and aggravated tussles over resources, leading to social fragmentation among homeland activists. Despite legal, political, and social precarities, the potential for mobilization was ripe. In resettlement countries, physical distance and permanent protection significantly diminished the risks of activism at the same time that they turned down the volume on refugee pressure to return to Bhutan. Nevertheless, in resettlement countries, adaptive forms of homeland activism continue to survive, even dispersed across the globe. Whether physically proximate or further afield, whether few or many, sites of exile play different roles in homeland mobilization.

An Ecosystem of Political Exile

Through a detailed examination of Bhutanese homeland activists, this book shows that exile politics function very much like a physical ecosystem, with hubs in different physical locations interacting in visible and underground ways. These sites, which may thrive or weaken, remain connected to one another through at least a partial common purpose. While transnational social movements are already understood to be interconnected, the relationships of Bhutanese homeland activists go far beyond the links between, say, different hubs of a network.

Organisms within a physical ecosystem rely on one another for survival, but they also compete with one another, particularly when resources are scarce. The same is true of mobilizers, whether as part of an exiled community or not.[1] In a physical ecosystem, the availability of nutrients improves organisms' chances of surviving, as does protection from predators. In an ecosystem of exile politics, sites of activism are similarly concerned with nutrients (resources) and protection (being safe in the host country). For homeland activists, physical proximity provides certain resources (chiefly a mass of potential agitators and access to information) that help to facilitate their work at the same time that their protection is limited by legal, political, and social precarity. In that situation, key hubs of a homeland movement may shift from sites near the homeland to more dispersed communities in resettlement countries, just as base plants release seeds that travel to distant locations. It is no coincidence that the word "diaspora" comes from the Greek word for "scatter" or "disperse."

Thinking about homeland activism as functioning within a transnational ecosystem is a useful way to understand how migrants and refugees located in differentiated sites of activism attempt to make claims against more powerful actors, working from the outside in. The circulation of power—from states' immunitary expressions of it to homeland activists' resistance to that power—operates across all sites of an exile politics ecosystem. The relationships among these sites are dynamic temporally and contingent on physical space. The importance of these locations—as physically proximate or distant from the homeland—challenges those who trumpet the rise of the Internet as signaling a decline of the physical world. While our virtual world has grown in importance, we still need physical channels and corridors to move objects and people from place to place. The full range of activities that constitute mobilization cannot occur without it.

Further, the seasonal and cyclical nature of ecosystems usefully draws us away from static thinking about the permanence or prominence of political diasporas. In line with Betts and Jones, I see diaspora mobilization as moving through temporal stages.[2] But rather than the diaspora death and afterlife that they have proposed, conceptualizing such dynamics as an ecosystem reflects the reality that homeland mobilization waxes and wanes over time and space, but rarely dies outright. These rising and falling arcs of activism may be short or long, and they may change in tenor and tone. Sites of activism may recede in importance. Homeland activists may produce shifting sets of priorities, and they may become more or less strident in their demands, but even when individual activists slow or stop their work, a focus on the homeland passes from one site of exile to another.

The Matter of Physical Space

While viewing exile politics as an ecosystem certainly acknowledges its transnational nature, the centrality of physical location in that ecosystem also complicates what we understand "transnational" to be. It is not simply "beyond borders" in some ethereal, evanescent way. The nonstate actors who challenge their home countries do not operate in a diaphanous realm where the physical world is relegated to the background. To the contrary, transnational politics, like the homeland activists that carry it out, must touch down somewhere.[3] Ecosystems of exile politics are very firmly grounded in physical space, and directly impact both the way mobilizations are carried out and the precarities that those mobilizers face.

First, physical space matters because homeland activism is oriented toward a home country, and relationships with home are rooted in the physical. The connections that diaspora populations have created about their home country are deeply material.[4] Diaspora literature is replete with symbolism that elevates physical space and ties it to nostalgia. Rituals are tied to memory of land and places.[5] Immigrants call to mind the trees and the fruits of the motherland.[6] Refugees describe the buildings that weigh on their memories.[7] This is important for exile politics because it not only illuminates the motivations that drive homeland activism (even in situations of great precarity) but it also cues us to better understand why conceptualizations of home change over time and across generations. For homeland activists who remember the cardamom fields and orange groves, home is Bhutan, and many remain fixated on a desire to improve the country and return to it, even temporarily. For younger activists who spent nearly their entire lives in Nepal, ideas about home are more complicated. Their homeland orientations have shifted to include Nepal and the people and physical spaces where their memories were formed, including refugee camps and their environs.

Second, physical space matters for the repertoires that activists undertake, for the resources available to them, and for the networks on which they most rely. Just as physical space structures geographies of power—a point made repeatedly in the literature on spatial politics[8]—it also determines what happens at sites of *resistance* to traditional forms of power. Put another way, just as violations are multispatial in nature, so are responses to them.[9] This is partially an issue of scale, as activists try to create levers for change through local, regional, and international institutions, but it is also about physical proximity to the home country, where one is more likely to find large numbers of those who have fled, and whose stories provide the fuel for continued activism. Proximity is a specific aspect of physical space that, until now, has been largely overlooked.

Third, physical space matters for experiences of precarity. Physical locations and spaces shape the risks of living, working, socializing, and mobilizing. The host country is a key part of this, but localities matter also. This is, once again, a nod to scalar differentiation. Border towns have a different risk profile than capital cities. Small towns render undocumented populations more visible, while cities, because of their hunger for labor, subject migrants to exploitation and "permanent temporariness."[10]

Proximity and Precarity

Even where physical space has been conceptualized in its relationship to mobilization, physical proximity, as an aspect of physical space, has been largely overlooked. But proximity deserves our attention as a factor of homeland activism. As a concept, it is necessarily messy: it does not have the binary quality of either being *within* a country or *outside* of it. Quite deliberately, I have not defined proximity to mean contiguous to another country or to be located within an exact distance of it. This is because the power of proximity comes from multiple sources. It is not a force field that works only within a certain range. Instead, it emerges both from geography and from a complex set of political, social, and economic relationships, often historical in nature, that drive how neighboring entities—states, municipalities, individuals—treat one another. For example, activists sneaking back into Bhutan to see for themselves what had happened to their families' land holdings found power in proximity not just because of the porous borders between Bhutan and India, but also because of the personal relationships in border towns that facilitated their passage. Power also stemmed from regional proximity, as activists capitalized on historical and kinship-related ties to access well-known journalists and politicians in the region, as well as institutions like SAARC.

One of this book's most salient contributions is its exploration of the relationship between proximity to the homeland and the precarity that this engenders. The advantages of proximity for homeland activists, described in tension with the precarities of these physical locations, illuminates not only the work of exile politics but also reveals the understudied geospatial configurations of migrant and refugee protection. To be very clear, precarity is an experience currently woven into the lives of the displaced who lack the resources to travel to physically distant locations. It is a question for further research whether the link between long distance and permanent protection is an intentional design of our current refugee and migrant regimes or only one of happenstance.[11] Either way, the tension between proximity and precarity leads to a set of difficult paradoxes for homeland activists: proximate exile represents both the best and most difficult opportunities for reversing exile and/or reforming one's home country. Resettlement, with its (rare) promise of permanent protection in distant lands, permits political action at the same time that it reduces the urgency and centrality of the homeland struggle.

Resettlement's production of a distant diaspora prompts us to return to the ecosystem. What can we say about elements of an ecosystem that are physically cut off from their roots? In the physical world, ecosystems can be massive, but they require some channel, some material way, to move nutrients from place to place. Exile politics are no different. People crossing borders and, more recently, sharing information on the Internet provide the channels for maintaining a homeland orientation, even if home is very far away. The ocean, as the planet's largest ecosystem, moves food and oxygen throughout the ecosystem. Transborder activity is like its riptides and currents. Resettlement demonstrates that while physical proximity matters, an ecosystem of exile politics can be quite expansive in the physical sense. Physical distance from home does not end activism but merely reshapes it, as the diaspora itself is reshaped over space and time.[12]

Despotic Power and External Pressure

Thinking about how homeland activists contest state power is not merely a theoretical exercise. Those who agitate from outside the state often represent the "canary"—the initial alert to the international community that something is amiss in the home country. The voices of homeland activists can expose state actions in a way that may not be possible within the country. This is true not only of highly authoritarian states, which practice outright repression and flagrant human rights violations, but also of those where practices of "lesser" crimes like corruption and unrepresentative holds on power can silence or discourage internal dissent, particularly as modern technologies have sharply refined the surveillance, policing, and targeting of critics.

Countries practicing these "lesser" crimes are distant neither temporally nor geographically. Despotic regimes, John Keane argues, use the trappings of democracy to "conceal . . . their larcenous features through crafty statecraft."[13] Elections and abundant information flows lull citizens into complacency, yet genuine power-sharing is absent. Keane stirringly warns that these "new despotisms," linked across borders through multinational corporations and entangled economics and politics, are contagious. Smug watchers of autocratic regimes may fail to notice that countries traditionally considered safe from authoritarianism have been shaped by—and may be moving in the direction of—despotic forms of power. In short, "there is plenty of despotism inside states that consider themselves democracies."[14]

It is not necessary to read academic literature to recognize that "democratic" countries are embracing a range of authoritarian practices.[15] In these contexts, a fear of speaking out may not be the fear of death or torture, but may include state practices of livelihood stripping, political ostracism, and trumped-up trials. It is therefore easy to understand why people who have left their country can play a role that may be difficult for those who remain inside. This may be increasingly true of countries that we have heretofore considered democratic. If this is the case, exile politics—and a nourishing ecosystem to support it—may take on a new urgency as it responds to new despotisms.

Deeply ingrained ideas about the sanctity of citizenship may provide (potentially false) reassurance to those in all but the most authoritarian countries.

Would-be dissenters may ask: Why leave my country for the wilds of noncitizen precarity? Indeed, they may not, particularly if the places most easily accessible (often proximate) offer significant risks for dissenters.

But another force is at play here, which is that even those with citizenship are at risk of losing it. Because the hurdles to obtain citizenship are often so great, there is a view that once it is gained it cannot be revoked, as if by reaching the peak of a difficult mountain, there is no chance of falling off. Historians and scholars of statelessness know this not to be the case. Most famously, Hannah Arendt and Giorgio Agamben relied on the empirics of stripped citizenship to theorize the impact of statelessness.[16] And the revocation of citizenship has staged a comeback. The example of expelled Bhutanese provided in this book is not an isolated occurrence.

It is hard to imagine in the modern era that a citizen could have her or his passport taken away and then be pushed across the border, but that is what the United States has undertaken against Americans of Mexican heritage.[17] Australia permits the stripping of citizenship based on the criteria of conduct and conviction.[18] The United Kingdom, the Dominican Republic, and Yemen all have policies and practices that have the potential to deprive citizens of their nationality.[19] India has amended its Citizenship Act to target Indian-born Muslims and has built a network of detention centers in which to house them following the (now-stalled) implementation of a national census.[20] These examples point to a worrying trend that, combined with the rise of despotic practices, suggests that the need for protection for homeland activists has never been higher.

Protecting the Canary

Making explicit the relationship and inherent tension between proximity and precarity serves an important practical purpose in thinking about how to protect that border-crossing canary. A first-take examination of the ways that precarious homeland activists function may falsely suggest that the power of precarity fuels their transnational actions, including their transborder exchanges of information, lobbying, and demonstrations. In fact, I had this unnuanced view several years ago when I suggested that precarity possessed a "paradoxical power."[21] There is some logic to this, as those without protection have less to lose and may have more motivation to change the country from which they have come.

However, in light of the research undertaken to complete this book, I have come to see that the power of homeland mobilizers comes not from their *precarity*, but from their *proximity*. And while our migration and refugee regimes are currently structured such that proximate populations are nearly always precarious, that need not be the case. Must proximity and precarity always live in tension? Is there a way to separate them? What if there were a way to shift the balance such that homeland activists near their homelands were more secure, rather than less?

I do not mean to suggest that this is an easy thing to accomplish. Host states have decades-long precedents that prevent nearby populations from becoming permanent residents immediately,[22] while the international community has no jurisdiction in sovereign host states to demand something as precious as permanent protection. And neither state nor international actors have been sympathetic to precarious homeland activists. However, prior to a contemporary bias against proximity, history suggests that dissenters seeking refuge from persecution who fled to nearby places were protected.[23] There is no linear path to describe a protection trajectory, and just because nearby activists are at risk today does not mean that they must be.

One reasonable response to the suggestion that proximate host states improve protection for proximate activists is that these states already shoulder a disproportionate burden in hosting refugee populations across the world. But efforts to mitigate precarity for mobilizers need not always ask a great deal of host state actors. One response to activists critical of home is the effort to protect them as human rights defenders. This recognition is an important step, but much more could be done to advance the work of human rights defenders who remain near home countries. It is understandable that, for their protection, some have to be flown far away, but this presents a similar proximity-precarity problem identified earlier in this book. In an ideal world, homeland activists could receive protection and be able to remain nearby. The specific mechanisms that might ensure this protection are outside the scope of this book, but they might include the provision of documents that permit mobilizing actions (similar to the Nansen passport and its successors, which permit refugees to travel); the development of specific guidelines that allow homeland activists to develop homeland-oriented political communication; and access to virtual regional and international conferences that allow refugees to participate more fully in discussions about resolving crisis situations.[24]

Individual Reconciliation, Collective Forgiveness: Some Speculations

In chapter 3, I told the story of Y. P. Dhungel's escape from Bhutan, and the small piece of the Berlin Wall that he had obtained in Germany in 1989, brought back with him to Bhutan, and hurriedly packed with limited belongings when he escaped a few years later. That piece of the dismantled Berlin Wall stayed with Y. P. Dhungel in a refugee camp hut in Nepal for seventeen years, where it remained a symbol of his hopes for reconciliation with and return to Bhutan. When he departed Nepal to resettle to Australia, however, he left that piece of the Berlin Wall behind, concerned about Australia's strict quarantine laws.

Y. P. Dhungel's Berlin Wall memento represents homeland activists' desires to effect change in Bhutan: ever-present in nearby India and Nepal but peripheral, considered with some nostalgia, from the physical distance of a resettlement country. Indeed, interviews with many resettled activists indicated the mellowing imprint of physical distance. Several told me that they are now in touch with former Drukpa colleagues and, on both sides, palpable anger and fear have been replaced by a desire for closure and a curiosity about forked paths taken thirty years ago. Families divided by contested histories are beginning long-silenced conversations in the distant diaspora. Both Drukpa and ethnic Nepalis who still reside in Bhutan are now meeting up with resettled refugees in places as far away from Bhutan as one can be: Sydney, Atlanta, London.

Even refugees who remain closer to Bhutan are moving toward reconciliation, indicating that it is not just physical distance that has tempered old tempers, but temporal distance. Crossing the India-Bhutan border, a handful have unofficially visited their hometowns for short visits, with all-seeing district administrators looking the other way. There is no doubt that social media, notably Facebook, have played a critical role in these personal rapprochements, allowing old friends to find one another after many years. Yet it is important to note that difficult political conversations are not happening online. Even when the homeland project shifts to reconciliation, rather than challenging power, physical proximity remains central.

Personal conversations in proximate locations are a far cry from national reconciliation and resolution. Bhutanese refugees in Nepal and India still see no hope of safe and permanent return to Bhutan. Efforts by homeland activists to create official means of visiting Bhutan through a "nonresident Bhutanese" platform have thus far been unsuccessful. Political prisoners remain in Bhutanese prisons. And while democracy has indeed progressed in Bhutan, the granting of citizenship to tens of thousands of ethnic Nepalis has moved at a snail's pace.

However, the opening up of individual conversations, abetted by physical distance, might signal a ray of hope. Bhutan is a small country and it is possible that private reconciliations could take on more public hues. If personal dialogue moves up the chain of power, it could lead to more promising results, influencing mainstream media and National Assembly members. There is room for collective forgiveness and listening. The conditions for a gentle form of collective action focused on reconciliation are better now than they have been in thirty years and might overcome the silence surrounding the issue within Bhutan.[25] This is potentially the best gift that resettlement could offer to the expanded eco-system it helped create.

Homeland activists mobilizing around a platform of reconciliation would expand the ecosystem again, this time to include sites not only near and further away from Bhutan but *within* it. This would also indicate the continuing potential for adaptive forms of activism focused on Bhutan. In this hopeful but not impossible scenario, the weight of old narratives might lift, and the links between those nearby and further away would work to create new conversations with powerholders inside Bhutan. For a generation of refugees whom I interviewed in this book—among them the bookended activists Y. P. Dhungel, Ratan Gazmere, Bhakta Ghimire, and Mangala Sharma—who remember much of Bhutan with great fondness, this reconciliation would signal a new beginning.

Notes

1. INTRODUCTION

Epigraph: Michael Hutt and Gregory Sharkey, "'Nepalese in Origin but Bhutanese First': A Conversation with Bhim Subba and Om Dhungel (Human Rights Organization of Bhutan)," European Bulletin of Himalayan Research *9, no. 4 (1995): 38.*

1. Interview with Bhakta Ghimire, January 2019, online interview.

2. Interview with Mangala Sharma, January 2019, online interview.

3. Dhurba Rizal, *The Royal Semi-Authoritarian Democracy of Bhutan* (Lanham, MD: Lexington, 2015), 72.

4. Nicole Curato and Diego Fossati, "Authoritarian Innovations: Crafting Support for a Less Democratic Southeast Asia," *Democratization* 27, no. 6 (2020): 1006–20.

5. Steven Levitsky and Lucan A. Way, *Competitive Authoritarianism: Hybrid Regimes after the Cold War* (Cambridge: Cambridge University Press, 2010); John Keane, *The New Despotism* (Cambridge, MA: Harvard University Press, 2020).

6. See, for example: Barbara Harrell-Bond, *Imposing Aid: Emergency Assistance to Refugees* (Oxford: Oxford University Press, 1986); Gaim Kibreab, "Myth of Dependency among Camp Refugees in Somalia, 1979–1989," *Journal of Refugee Studies* 6, no. 4 (1993): 321–49; Jennifer Hyndman, *Managing Displacement: Refugees and the Politics of Humanitarianism* (Minneapolis: University of Minnesota Press, 2000); Clara Lecadet, "Refugee Politics: Self-Organized 'Government' and Protests in the Agamé Refugee Camp (2005–13)," *Journal of Refugee Studies* 29, no. 2 (2016): 187–207.

7. Clifford Bob, *The Marketing of Rebellion: Insurgents, Media and International Activism* (Cambridge: Cambridge University Press, 2005), 7.

8. Emphasizing its crossborder aspects, Luis Guarnizo, Alejandro Portes and their colleagues have conducted numerous studies about "transnational political activism" or "transnational political engagement," examining contextual factors and highlighting its importance relative to its infrequency among migrants. See Luis Eduardo Guarnizo, Alejandro Portes, and William Haller, "Assimilation and Transnationalism: Determinants of Transnational Political Action among Contemporary Migrants," *American Journal of Sociology* 108, no. 6 (2003): 1211–48; Alejandro Portes, Eduardo Guarnizo, and Patricia Landolt, "Commentary on the Study of Transnationalism: Pitfalls and Promise of an Emergent Research Field," *Ethnic and Racial Studies* 40, no. 9 (2017): 1486–91; Luis Eduardo Guarnizo, Ali Chaudhary, and Ninna Nyberg Sørensen, "Migrants' Transnational Political Engagement in Spain and Italy," *Migration Studies* (2017): 281–322. "Transnational political action" is a term used by Ali Chaudhary and Dana Moss to highlight sources of constraint, that is, when mobilization is expected but does not occur. See Ali R. Chaudhary and Dana M. Moss, "Suppressing Transnationalism: Bringing Constraints into the Study of Transnational Political Action," *Comparative Migration Studies* 7, no. 1 (2019): 1–9. The term "diaspora politics" is common, usefully deployed by Fiona Adamson in describing how diasporas can be both the victims and the perpetrators of the other side of transnational activism: transnational oppression. See Fiona B. Adamson, "Non-State Authoritarianism and Diaspora Politics," *Global Networks* 20, no. 1 (2020): 150–69. The term has also been used by Alexander Betts and Will Jones, who describe the life cycle of diaspora politics and point to the

institutional factors that drive diaspora mobilization. (See Alexander Betts and Will Jones, *Mobilising the Diaspora: How Refugees Challenge Authoritarianism* (Cambridge: Cambridge University Press, 2016).) Sharon Quinsaat variously employs "diaspora activism," "transnational contention," and "homeland politics" to offer many rich examinations of the Philippine diaspora, drawing on political process theory to explain its emergence and relying on theories of assimilation to uncover shifting identities and actions in receiving states. See Sharon Madriaga Quinsaat, "Diaspora Activism in a Non-Traditional Country of Destination: The Case of Filipinos in the Netherlands," *Ethnic and Racial Studies* 39, no. 6 (2016): 1014–33; "Migrant Mobilization for Homeland Politics: A Social Movement Approach," *Sociology Compass* 7, no. 11 (2013): 952–64; "Transnational Contention, Domestic Integration: Assimilating into the Hostland Polity through Homeland Activism," *Journal of Ethnic and Migration Studies* 45, no. 3 (2019): 419–36.

9. Anne McNevin, *Contesting Citizenship: Irregular Migrants and New Frontiers of the Political* (New York: Columbia University Press, 2011); Noelle Kateri Brigden, *The Migrant Passage: Clandestine Journeys from Central America* (Ithaca, NY: Cornell University Press, 2018). It is also possible to refer to all of these individuals as migrants, in recognition of the fact that determining the extent of coercion in departure is difficult. David Scott FitzGerald has done just this: David Scott FitzGerald, *Refuge beyond Reach: How Rich Democracies Repel Asylum Seekers* (Oxford: Oxford University Press, 2019).

10. Henri Lefebvre, *The Production of Space*, trans. Donald Nicholson-Smith (Oxford: Blackwell, 1991); Doreen Massey, *Space, Place and Gender* (Minneapolis: University of Minnesota Press, 1994); Edward Soja, *Seeking Spatial Justice* (Minneapolis: University of Minnesota Press, 2010).

11. Nigel Thrift, "Space: The Fundamental Stuff of Geography," in *Key Concepts in Geography*, ed. Sarah L. Holloway, Stephen P. Rice, and Gill Valentine (London: Sage, 2003), 95–107.

12. Fiona B. Adamson, "Spaces of Global Security: Beyond Methodological Nationalism," *Journal of Global Security Studies* 1, no. 1 (2016): 28.

13. Terrence Lyons and Peter G. Mandaville, eds., *Politics from Afar: Transnational Diasporas and Networks* (London: Hurst, 2012).

14. Betts and Jones, *Mobilising the Diaspora*.

15. Maria Koinova, "Beyond Statist Paradigms: Sociospatial Positionality and Diaspora Mobilization in International Relations," *International Studies Review* 19, no. 4 (2017): 597–621; "Can Conflict-Generated Diasporas Be Moderate Actors during Episodes of Contested Sovereignty? Lebanese and Albanian Diasporas Compared," *Review of International Studies* 37, no. 1 (2011): 437–62; "Diasporas and Secessionist Conflicts: The Mobilization of the Armenian, Albanian and Chechen Diasporas," *Ethnic and Racial Studies* 34, no. 2 (2011): 333–56; "Sending States and Diaspora Positionality in International Relations," *International Political Sociology* 12, no. 2 (2018): 190–210.

16. Koinova, "Beyond Statist Paradigms"; "Sending States and Diaspora Positionality."

17. Maria Koinova, *Diaspora Entrepreneurs and Contested States* (Oxford: Oxford University Press, 2021).

18. Koinova, *Diaspora Entrepreneurs and Contested States*, 3.

19. Roberto Esposito, "Immunization and Violence," in *Terms of the Political: Community, Immunity, Biopolitics*, ed. Rhiannon Noel Welch and Timothy Campbell (New York: Commonalities, 2013), 59.

20. Roberto Esposito, *Communitas: The Origin and Destiny of Community Cultural Memory in the Present* (Stanford, CA: Stanford University Press, 2010), 25.

21. Osten Wahlbeck, "The Concept of Diaspora as an Analytical Tool in the Study of Refugee Communities," *Journal of Ethnic and Migration Studies* 28, no. 2 (2002): 223.

22. Margaret Keck and Kathryn Sikkink, *Activists beyond Borders: Advocacy Networks in International Politics* (Ithaca, NY: Cornell University Press, 1998); Idean Salehyan, *Rebels without Borders: Transnational Insurgencies in World Politics* (Ithaca, NY: Cornell University Press, 2009); Heather Johnson, "Moments of Solidarity, Migrant Activism and (Non) Citizens at Global Borders," in *Citizenship, Migrant Activism and the Politics of Movement*, ed. Peter Nyers and Kim Rygiel (New York: Routledge, 2012), 109–28; Jeffrey Davis, *Justice across Borders: The Struggle for Human Rights in US Courts* (Cambridge: Cambridge University Press, 2008).

23. David N. Gellner, *Borderland Lives in Northern South Asia* (Durham, NC: Duke University Press, 2013).

24. Brigden, *Migrant Passage*, 14.

25. Suzan Ilcan, "Fleeing Syria: Border-Crossing and Struggles for Migrant Justice," in *Mobilities, Mobility Justice, and Social Justice*, ed. Nancy Cook and David Butz (London: Routledge, 2018), 54–66.

26. Willem Van Schendel, "Making the Most of 'Sensitive' Borders," in *Borderland Lives in Northern South Asia*, ed. David N. Gellner (Durham, NC: Duke University Press, 2013), 266–71.

27. Guy Standing, *The Precariat: The New Dangerous Class* (London: Bloomsbury Academic, 2011).

28. Luin Goldring and Patricia Landolt, "Caught in the Work-Citizenship Matrix: The Lasting Effects of Precarious Legal Status on Work for Toronto Immigrants," *Globalizations* 8, no. 3 (2011): 325–41; Luin Goldring, Carolina Berinstein, and Judith K. Bernhard, "Institutionalizing Precarious Migratory Status in Canada," *Citizenship Studies* 13, no. 3 (2009): 239–65; Meghan L. Eberle and Ian Holliday, "Precarity and Political Immobilisation: Migrants from Burma in Chiang Mai, Thailand," *Journal of Contemporary Asia* 41, no. 3 (2011): 371–92.

29. Hannah Lewis et al., *Precarious Lives: Forced Labour, Exploitation and Asylum* (Bristol: Policy Press, 2015).

30. Suzan Ilcan, Kim Rygiel, and Feyzi Baban, "The Ambiguous Architecture of Precarity: Temporary Protection, Everyday Living, and Migrant Journeys of Syrian Refugees," *International Journal of Migration and Borders* 4, no. 1/2 (2018): 51–70.

31. Ilcan, Rygiel, and Baban, "The Ambiguous Architecture of Precarity."

32. Susan Banki, "Precarity of Place: A Complement to the Growing Precariat Literature," *Global Discourse* 3, no. 3–4 (2013): 450–63.

33. Louise Waite, "A Place and Space for a Critical Geography of Precarity?," *Geography Compass* 3, no. 1 (2009): 412–33.

34. Waite, "Place and Space for a Critical Geography of Precarity?," 424.

35. Personal communication with Michael Hutt, March 2019.

36. Sonam Kinga, *Democratic Transition in Bhutan: Political Contests as Moral Battles* (London: Routledge, 2020); Parashar Parmanand, *The Politics of Bhutan: Retrospect and Prospect* (New Delhi: Pragati, 1998).

37. Nicole Bergen, "Narrative Depictions of Working with Language Interpreters in Cross-Language Qualitative Research," *International Journal of Qualitative Methods* 17, no. 1 (2018): 1–11.

38. Interview with Parsuram Ghimire, June 2018, Harrisburg, Pennsylvania.

39. Graeme Rodgers, "'Hanging out' with Forced Migrants: Methodological and Ethical Challenges," *Forced Migration Review* 21 (2004), https://www.fmreview.org/return-reintegration/rodgers.

40. Elena Fiddian-Qasmiyeh, "*Representations* of Displacement from the Middle East and North Africa," *Public Culture* 28, no. 3 (2016): 457–73.

41. Charmian Brinson, *The Strange Case of Dora Fabian and Mathilde Wurm: A Study of German Political Exiles in London during the 1930's* (Berne: Peter Lang, 1996).

42. Martin Jones, "Protecting Human Rights Defenders at Risk: Asylum and Temporary International Relocation," *International Journal of Human Rights* 19, no. 7 (2015): 935–60.

43. Brigden, *Migrant Passage*, 138.

44. Thomas Faist, "Toward a Transnational Methodology: Methods to Address Methodological Nationalism, Essentialism, and Positionality," *Revue Européenne des Migrations Internationales* 28, no. 1 (2012): 51–70.

45. Abimbola Odugbesan and Helge Schwiertz, ""We Are Here to Stay": Refugee Struggles in Germany between Unity and Division," in *Protest Movements in Asylum and Deportation*, ed. Sieglinde Rosenberger, Verena Stern, and Nina Merhaut (Cham: Springer, 2018), 185–203; Carmen Delgado Luchner and Leïla Kherbiche, "Without Fear or Favour?: The Positionality of ICRC and UNHCR Interpreters in the Humanitarian Field," *Target: International Journal of Translation Studies* 30, no. 3 (2018): 408–29; Giorgia Donà, Cigdem Esin, and Aura Lounasmaa, "Qualitative Research in Refugee Studies," in *SAGE Research Methods Foundations*, ed. Paul Atkinson et al. (London: Sage, 2022), https://doi.org/10.4135/9781526421036849022.

46. Van Schendel, "Making the Most of 'Sensitive' Borders."

2. THE BHUTAN BACK STORY

Epigraph: *Thinley Penjore,* The Quest for Democracy: Against All Odds *(Bhutan: A. K. Books and Educational Enterprises, 2010), 67.*

1. Bikrama Jit Hasrat, *History of Bhutan: Land of the Peaceful Dragon* (Bhutan: Education Department, 1980), 22.

2. Leo E. Rose, *The Politics of Bhutan* (Ithaca, NY: Cornell University Press, 1977), 24.

3. Michael Hutt, *Unbecoming Citizens: Culture, Nationhood, and the Flight of Refugees from Bhutan* (Oxford: Oxford University Press, 2003), 18–19.

4. Many countries in the modern era serve as both refugee makers and refugee takers, even simultaneously. Pakistan, the Democratic Republic of the Congo, and Malaysia, for example, all have produced refugee populations at the same time as they have accepted other refugees within their borders. Guglielmo Verdirame and Barbara E. Harrell-Bond, *Rights in Exile: Janus-Faced Humanitarianism* (New York: Berghahn, 2005).

5. For an explanation of the origins of this name, see Rizal, *Royal Semi-Authoritarian Democracy of Bhutan*, 74n10.

6. David Field Rennie, *Bhotan and the Story of the Doar War* (New Delhi: Manjusri, 1970); Hutt, *Unbecoming Citizens*, 19–20.

7. Michael Peil, "Semi-Colonialism and International Legal History: The View from Bhutan," *Völkerrechtsblog* 28 (2019), https://voelkerrechtsblog.org/de/semi-colonialism-and-international-legal-history-the-view-from-bhutan/.

8. Rennie, *Bhotan and the Story of the Doar War.*

9. Challenges to power are, of course, in no way unique to this region or period. Specific to Bhutan, there are myriad stories about families or tribes who vied for control (of land, resources, laborers) by revolting against the local hegemon. See Michael Aris, *Bhutan: the Early History of a Himalayan Kingdom*, Aris and Phillips Central Asian Studies. (Warminster: Aris & Phillips, 1979). I begin my examination in the twentieth century, with the creation of the modern Bhutan state in 1907, where one can more comfortably view dissension as a sociopolitical force rather than a military one.

10. Esposito, "Immunization and Violence," 58.

11. Esposito, "Immunization and Violence," 59.

12. Awadhesh Coomar Sinha, *Bhutan: Ethnic Identity and National Dilemma* (New Delhi: Reliance, 1991).

13. Human Rights Watch (HRW), "'We Don't Want to Be Refugees Again': A Human Rights Watch Briefing Paper for the Fourteenth Ministerial Joint Committee of Bhutan and Nepal," Human Rights Watch, New York, March 13, 2003, https://www.hrw.org/sites/default/files/media_2021/08/202108asia_bhutan_refugees.pdf; Amnesty International, "Bhutan: Human Rights Violations against the Nepali-Speaking Population in the South," Amnesty International, December 1, 1992, ASA 14/004/1992, https://www.amnesty.org/en/documents/asa14/004/1992/en/.

14. Thomas Laird, "Going Nowhere," *Asia Week*, November 30, 2000.

15. Hutt, *Unbecoming Citizens*, 4.

16. See D. N. S. Dhakal and Christopher Strawn, *Bhutan: A Movement in Exile* (Jaipur: Nirala, 1994), 47. There are smaller populations of ethnic communities in Bhutan who speak a range of dialects, but these will not be treated here. For more information, see Rizal, *Royal Semi-Authoritarian Democracy of Bhutan*, 5.

17. Hutt, *Unbecoming Citizens*, 6.

18. Michael Hutt, "Introduction," in *Bhutan: Perspectives on Conflict and Dissent*, ed. Michael Hutt (Gartmore: Kiscadale, 1994), 7.

19. National Statistics Bureau of Bhutan, "2017 Population and Housing Census of Bhutan," ed. Kuenga Wangmo, Thimphu: National Statistics Bureau, Royal Government of Bhutan, 2018.

20. Bruce Curtis, *The Politics of Population: State Formation, Statistics, and the Census of Canada, 1840–1875* (Toronto: University of Toronto Press, 2001).

21. Curtis, *Politics of Population*.

22. Eighty thousand is a conservative estimate. In January 1993, there were 76,774 refugees in the camps in Nepal; see HUROB, "Media Scan," *Bhutan Review* 1, no. 1 (1993), 3. But this does not take into account an unknown number of Bhutanese Nepalis who left Bhutan but never registered with authorities and remained outside the camps, living in Nepal or India. In 2007, the unregistered population of Bhutanese Nepalis in India and Nepal was estimated at between 15,000 and 30,000. See HRW, "Nepal: Bhutanese Refugee Tensions Erupt into Violence," Human Rights Watch, New York, May 31, 2007, https://www.hrw.org/news/2007/05/31/nepal-bhutanese-refugee-tensions-erupt-violence. Fifteen years prior, in 1993, I estimate that there would have been at least 5,000 unregistered. The Bhutanese government claimed for a time that some in the camps were in fact not from Bhutan at all but were Nepalis who had entered to enjoy the services of the UNHCR. I address this claim, and how Bhutanese Nepali homeland activists countered it, in later chapters.

23. Hutt, "Introduction," 7.

24. Hutt, *Unbecoming Citizens*, 7.

25. "Demographic Characteristics," in National Statistics Bureau of Bhutan, "2017 Population and Housing Census of Bhutan," 3–9.

26. Central Intelligence Agency, "Bhutan," https://www.cia.gov/the-world-factbook/countries/bhutan/.

27. Kinley Dorji, "Bhutan's Current Crisis: A View from Thimphu," in *Bhutan: Perspectives on Conflict and Dissent*, ed. Michael Hutt (Gartmore: Kiscadale, 1994), 77–96.

28. The Convention in its original form was also geographically limited to the borders of Europe. The 1967 Protocol Relating to the Status of Refugees removed those restrictions, but temporal considerations are still very much at play when it comes to the identification and treatment of refugees. Time continues to function as a border, "privileg[ing] some at the expense of others." Shanthi Robertson, "The Temporalities of International Migration: Implications for Ethnographic Research," in *Social Transformation and*

Migration: National and Local Experiences in South Korea, Turkey, Mexico and Australia, ed. Stephen Castles, Derya Ozkul, and Magdalena Arias Cubas (Basingstoke: Palgrave Macmillan, 2015), 52.

29. Bhutan National Democratic Party (BNDP), March 16, 1993, 1, cited in Dhakal and Strawn, *Bhutan*, 115.

30. Hutt, *Unbecoming Citizens*, 32.

31. Hutt, *Unbecoming Citizens*, 39.

32. Charles A. Bell, "Report on Area in Bhutan West of the Ammo Chu. Confidential to the Chief Secretary to the Government of Bengal, Dated Gangtok, 21 July 1904," Oriental and India Office Collection L/P&S/12/2230, National Archives, London, 2.

33. Awadhesh Coomar Sinha, *Himalayan Kingdom Bhutan: Tradition, Transition, and Transformation* (New Delhi: Indus, 2001), 140, 220.

34. Sinha, *Himalayan Kingdom Bhutan*, 164.

35. Sinha, *Himalayan Kingdom Bhutan*, 239.

36. In later years, both before and during the country's democratic transition, members of the Dorji family became prime ministers.

37. It is also true that Kalimpong was within Bhutanese territory before the British annexed it.

38. Dhakal and Strawn, *Bhutan*, 122.

39. Dhakal and Strawn, *Bhutan*, 122.

40. Dhakal and Strawn, *Bhutan*, 131–32; Lok Raj Baral, *Regional Migrations, Ethnicity and Security: The South Asian Case* (New Delhi: Sterling, 1990).

41. Kanak Mani Dixit, "The Dragon Bites Its Tail," *Himal Southasian*, July–August 1992.

42. Dhakal and Strawn, *Bhutan*, 131. Of course, progovernment sources *did* assume significant migration, but the point here is that, had the migration been as high after 1958 as the government insisted, then the number of Bhutanese would have been much higher.

43. Mahmood Ansari, "Distress Migration and Individual Happiness in Bhutan," in *Development Challenges in Bhutan: Perspectives on Inequality and Gross National Happiness*, ed. J. D. Schmidt (Cham: Springer International, 2017), 90.

44. Awadhesh Coomar Sinha, *Dawn of Democracy in the Eastern Himalayan Kingdoms: The 20th Century* (London: Routledge India, 2018), chap. 7, Kindle.

45. Rizal, *Royal Semi-Authoritarian Democracy of Bhutan*, 25.

46. Parmanand, an apologist for the monarchy, admitted that, in the wake of the assassination of the country's first prime minister in 1964, the king never appointed a new one, and thus "showed that he would like to function as his own Prime Minister," in Parmanand, *Politics of Bhutan*, 85.

47. Dhakal and Strawn, *Bhutan*, 134–35.

48. Sinha, *Dawn of Democracy*, chap. 1.

49. Sinha, *Dawn of Democracy*, 154.

50. Dhakal and Strawn, *Bhutan*; Sinha, *Dawn of Democracy*; Hutt, *Unbecoming Citizens*.

51. Dhakal and Strawn, *Bhutan*, 576.

52. Hutt, *Unbecoming Citizens*, 56.

53. Dhakal and Strawn, *Bhutan*, 135.

54. Hutt, *Unbecoming Citizens*, 47.

55. Sinha, *Dawn of Democracy*, chap. 7.

56. Dhakal and Strawn, *Bhutan*, 136–37; Hutt, *Unbecoming Citizens*, 118.

57. Veena Das, *Critical Events: An Anthropological Perspective on Contemporary India* (New Delhi: Oxford University Press, 1996).

58. Martin Sökefeld, "Mobilizing in Transnational Space: A Social Movement Approach to the Formation of Diaspora," *Global Networks* 6, no. 3 (2006): 265–84.

59. Hutt notes that the origin of the slogan "Jai Gorkha"—which is well remembered among older Bhutanese Nepalis—is unclear. It may have been the name of a wing of an Indian revolutionary group or it may have been something the two *mandals* invented. Hutt, *Unbecoming Citizens*, 116–17.

60. Compare Sinha, *Dawn of Democracy*, which asserts that an Indian, Sahabir Rai, crossed into Bhutan to enroll members in and collect money for his pro-Nepali cause in India. There is no way to resolve whether Rai came to Bhutan or Bhutan came to Rai, and it hardly matters, considering how porous the borders were. What does matter is that the India-Bhutan border was historically stitched with social networks that could now be easily politicized.

61. Dhakal and Strawn, *Bhutan*, 135.

62. Bhutan News Service, "The Forgotten Story of 1950 Prison Escapee," *Bhutan News Service*, January 10, 2012.

63. Interview with D. N. S. Dhakal, March 2019, Birtamod.

64. Hutt, *Unbecoming Citizens*, 121; Sinha, *Himalayan Kingdom Bhutan*, 172; Dhakal and Strawn, *Bhutan*, 136–37.

65. Hutt, *Unbecoming Citizens*, 121.

66. *Times of India*, May 27, 1953, cited in Rose, *Politics of Bhutan*, 110.

67. "An Appeal to His Majesty's Government of Bhutan," as cited in Dhakal and Strawn, *Bhutan*, appendix C, 598–601.

68. Dhakal and Strawn, *Bhutan*, 138–39.

69. Dhakal and Strawn, *Bhutan*, 138–41.

70. "Appeal to His Majesty's Government of Bhutan," Dhakal and Strawn, *Bhutan*, 598–601.

71. Rose, *Politics of Bhutan*, 111.

72. Sinha, *Dawn of Democracy*, chap. 7.

73. Sinha, *Himalayan Kingdom Bhutan*, 171.

74. Dhakal and Strawn, *Bhutan*, 139.

75. Sinha, *Himalayan Kingdom Bhutan*, 168.

76. Sinha, *Dawn of Democracy*, chap. 7.

77. Dhakal and Strawn, *Bhutan*, 133–43.

78. Sinha, *Himalayan Kingdom Bhutan*, 173–74.

79. Kamal Sadiq, *Paper Citizens: How Illegal Immigrants Acquire Citizenship in Developing Countries* (Oxford: Oxford University Press, 2008), chap. 3.

80. Jawaharlal Nehru, *Selected Works of Jawaharlal Nehru*, series 2, vol. 25, ed. Ravinder Kumar and H. Y. Sharada Prasad (New Delhi: Jawaharlal Nehru Memorial Fund, 1992), 459.

81. Nehru, *Selected Works*, 25:465–66.

82. Nehru, *Selected Works*, 25:464.

83. Hutt, *Unbecoming Citizens,* 122–24.

84. B.D. Gurung, "Political Problems of Bhutan," *United Asia* 12, no. 4 (1960), 369.

85. Hutt, *Unbecoming Citizens*, 126.

86. Sinha, *Himalayan Kingdom Bhutan,* 174.

87. Dhakal and Strawn, *Bhutan*, 141.

88. Richard W. Whitecross, "Intimacy, Loyalty and State Formation: The Spectre of the 'Anti-National,'" in *Traitors: Suspicion, Intimacy and the Ethics of State-Building*, ed. Sharika Thiranagama and Tobias Kelly (Philadelphia: University of Pennsylvia Press, 2009), 68–88.

89. Dhakal and Strawn, *Bhutan*, 141.

90. Betts and Jones, *Mobilising the Diaspora*.

91. Dhakal and Strawn, *Bhutan*, 142.

92. Parmanand, *Politics of Bhutan,* 134.

93. Rosalind Evans, "The Perils of Being a Borderland People: On the Lhotshampas of Bhutan," *Contemporary South Asia* 18, no. 1 (2010): 30.

94. Sikkim state admin report, 1932–2 (IOR V/10/1980, British Library), as cited in Andrew Duff, *Sikkim: Requiem for a Himalayan Kingdom* (Edinburgh: Birlinn, 2015), 23.

95. Interview with Ben Schonveld, representative of the Office of the High Commissioner for Human Rights, August 2007, Kathmandu.

96. Sinha, *Dawn of Democracy*, chap. 8.

97. Sinha, *Himalayan Kingdom Bhutan*, 173. See also Evans, "Perils of Being a Borderland People," 28; Rose, *Politics of Bhutan*, 112; Hutt, *Unbecoming Citizens*, 125.

98. Sadiq, *Paper Citizens*, chap. 3.

3. THE PASSAGE OF PROTEST

Epigraph: Interview with R. P. Subba, January 2019, via email.

1. Interview with Y. P. Dhungel, January 2018, Sydney.

2. Elena Phoutrides, "'Like a Parrot Screaming in Its Cage': Activism and Empowerment in Nepal's Bhutanese Refugee Community," Independent Study Project (ISP) Collection, 311, 2006, 17.

3. Hutt, *Unbecoming Citizens*; Sinha, *Himalayan Kingdom Bhutan*; Rizal, *Royal Semi-Authoritarian Democracy of Bhutan*.

4. HRW, "Last Hope: The Need for Durable Solutions for Bhutanese Refugees in Nepal and India," Human Rights Watch, New York, May 16, 2007, https://www.hrw.org/report/2007/05/16/last-hope/need-durable-solutions-bhutanese-refugees-nepal-and-india; Amnesty International, "Bhutan: Crack-Down on 'Anti-Nationals' in the East," Amnesty International, January 12, 1998, ASA 14/002/1998, https://www.amnesty.org/en/documents/asa14/002/1998/en/.

5. Lutheran World Federation Nepal, "Annual Report 2004."

6. Tek Nath Rizal, *From Palace to Prison* (Kalikasthan, Kathmandu: Oxford International, 2009); Govinda Rizal, *A Pardesi in Paradise* (Kathmandu: Discourse, 2018); N. B. Giri, *Justice to Justice: Bhutan* (Kathmandu: Rosy Giri, Success Foundation, 2014).

7. Guarnizo, Portes, and Haller, "Assimilation and Transnationalism"; Portes, Guarnizo, and Landolt, "Commentary on the Study of Transnationalism"; Chaudhary and Moss, "Suppressing Transnationalism"; Adamson, "Non-State Authoritarianism and Diaspora Politics"; Betts and Jones, *Mobilising the Diaspora*; Quinsaat, "Migrant Mobilization for Homeland Politics"; Koinova, "Sending States and Diaspora Positionality"; Nicholas Van Hear and Robin Cohen, "Diasporas and Conflict: Distance, Contiguity and Spheres of Engagement," *Oxford Development Studies* 45, no. 2 (2017): 171–84.

8. Wahlbeck, "The Concept of Diaspora as an Analytical Tool in the Study of Refugee Communities," 223.

9. Sinha, *Bhutan*, 191; Hutt, *Unbecoming Citizens*, 146.

10. Hutt, *Unbecoming Citizens*, 146.

11. Hutt, "Introduction," 16.

12. Van Schendel, "Making the Most of 'Sensitive' Borders," 269.

13. Sankaran Krishna, "Cartographic Anxiety: Mapping the Body Politic in India," *Alternatives: Global, Local, Political* 19, no. 4 (1994): 507–21.

14. Van Schendel, "Making the Most of 'Sensitive' Borders," 269.

15. Gellner, *Borderland Lives*.

16. Van Schendel, "Making the Most of 'Sensitive' Borders," 269.

17. Rajesh S. Kharat, "Indo-Bhutan Relations: Strategic Perspectives," in *Himalayan Frontiers of India: Historical, Geo-Political and Strategic Perspectives*, ed. K. Warikoo (Abingdon: Routledge, 2009).

18. Embassy of India, "India–Bhutan Trade Relation," https://www.indembthimphu .gov.in/pages/MzI.

19. Mark Turner, Sonam Chuki, and Jit Tshering, "Democratization by Decree: The Case of Bhutan," *Democratization* 18, no. 1 (2011): 195.

20. Steven Lee Myers, "Squeezed by an India-China Standoff, Bhutan Holds Its Breath," *New York Times*, August 15, 2017.

21. Pradyumna P. Karan and William M. Jenkins, *The Himalayan Kingdoms: Bhutan, Sikkim, and Nepal* (Princeton: D. Van Nostrand, 1963), 6.

22. Ranjan Gupta, "Sikkim: The Merger with India," *Asian Survey* 15, no. 9 (1975): 786–98.

23. Julia Sable, "Reconciling Culture, Security and Development in Bhutan" (master's thesis, Tufts University, 2005), 22.

24. Duff, *Sikkim*, 155.

25. Duff, *Sikkim*, 153.

26. Hutt, *Unbecoming Citizens*, 197.

27. Sinha, *Himalayan Kingdom Bhutan*, 184.

28. Dhurba Rizal, "The Unknown Refugee Crisis: Expulsion of the Ethnic Lhotsampa from Bhutan." *Asian Ethnicity* 5, no. 2 (June 2004): 156.

29. Rizal, "The Unknown Refugee Crisis," 156.

30. Hutt, *Unbecoming Citizens*, 170.

31. Dhakal and Strawn also argue that Bhutanization led to religious oppression, because efforts to bring specific Hindu religious sites and practices in line with Buddhist ones were a form of cooptation. See Dhakal and Strawn, *Bhutan*, 206–7.

32. Hutt, *Unbecoming Citizens*; Richard W. Whitecross, "Law, 'Tradition' and Legitimacy: Contesting Driglam Namzha," in *Development Challenges in Bhutan*, ed. Johannes Dragsbaek Schmidt (Cham: Springer, 2017), 1–16. However, see below, chapter 6, where I point to work by Christensen that suggests that Driglam Namzha can, in fact, be a silencing force on the topic of ethnicity. Line Kikkenborg Christensen, "Driglam Namzha and Silenced Ethnicity in Bhutan's Monarchical Democracy," *Social Identities* 27, no. 6 (2021): 644–59.

33. See Hutt, *Unbecoming Citizens*, 173; Dhakal and Strawn, *Bhutan*, 205.

34. Dhakal and Strawn, *Bhutan*.

35. Human Rights Council of Bhutan (HRCB), "Bhutan: Political Crisis and Bhutanese Refugees," Report, HRCB, Kathmandu, 2003.

36. Hutt, *Unbecoming Citizens*, 176; Dhakal and Strawn, *Bhutan*, 206.

37. HRCB, "Bhutan," 9; Jamie Zeppa, *Beyond the Sky and the Earth: A Journey into Bhutan* (New York: Riverhead, 1999), chap. "The Movement Order," Kindle.

38. Zeppa, *Beyond the Sky and the Earth*, chap. "Peak of Higher Learning."

39. Sue Wright, *Community and Communication: The Role of Language in Nation State Building and European Integration* (Bristol: Multilingual Matters, 2000).

40. Hutt, *Unbecoming Citizens*, 186.

41. Hutt, *Unbecoming Citizens*, 185.

42. Jigmi Y. Thinley, "Bhutan: A Kingdom Besieged," in *Bhutan: Perspectives on Conflict*, ed. Michael Hutt (Gartmore: Kiscadale, 1994), 43–76.

43. Hutt, *Unbecoming Citizens*, 174.

44. Interview with Padam Kafley, June 2013, Sydney.

45. For a discussion about the juridical specifics of the 1977 and 1985 legislation, see Ben Saul, "Cultural Nationalism, Self-Determination and Human Rights in Bhutan," *International Journal of Refugee Law* 12, no. 3 (2000): 321–53; Tang Lay Lee, "Refugees from Bhutan: Nationality, Statelessness, and the Right to Return," 10, no. 1/2 (1998): 118–55.

46. Dhakal and Strawn, *Bhutan*, 192–93; Hutt, *Unbecoming Citizens*, 197–98.

47. Sinha, *Himalayan Kingdom Bhutan*, 184.

48. Hutt, *Unbecoming Citizens*, 153–54.

49. Tapan Kumar Bose, "Bhutan: Creating Statelessness—a Recipe for Regional Instability," in *Missing Boundaries: Refugees, Migrants, Stateless and Internally Displaced Persons in South Asia*, ed. P. R Chari, Mallika Joseph, and Suba Chandran (New Delhi: Manohar, 2003), 61–86; Hutt, *Unbecoming Citizens*, 154–55.

50. Hutt, *Unbecoming Citizens*, 152–59.

51. Dhakal and Strawn, *Bhutan*, 192.

52. Hutt, *Unbecoming Citizens*, chap. 14.

53. Lyonpo Om Pradhan, *Bhutan: The Roar of the Thunder Dragon* (Thimphu: K Media, 2012), 159.

54. National Assembly of Bhutan (NAB), "Proceedings and Resolutions of the 69th Session of the National Assembly of Bhutan" (1990), 25–26, annexure 1, "Green Belt Along the Indo-Bhutan Border."

55. Sinha, *Himalayan Kingdom Bhutan*, 229–30.

56. Bhakti Prasad Bandari, "Hostage in Thimphu," *Himal Southasian*, March 1, 2004.

57. Sinha, *Himalayan Kingdom Bhutan*, 230.

58. Sinha, *Himalayan Kingdom Bhutan*, 243.

59. Sinha, *Himalayan Kingdom Bhutan*, 220.

60. Dixit, "Dragon Bites Its Tail."

61. Ilcan, "Fleeing Syria."

62. Hari K. Chhetri, *Reminiscence: Petition and Politics* (Kathmandu: Sabi HADA, 2013).

63. The entire text of the petition can be found in appendix B of Dhakal and Strawn, *Bhutan*, 591–97.

64. Hutt, *Unbecoming Citizens*, 200; Dhakal and Strawn, *Bhutan*, 195.

65. Chhetri, *Reminiscence*, 12.

66. Chhetri, *Reminiscence*, 13.

67. Rizal, *From Palace to Prison*, 94. Tek Nath Rizal's autobiographical accounts of his time in prison include lengthy descriptions of how his captors engaged in mind control techniques to make him say and do certain things and how, on his release, he spent a great deal of energy trying to remedy the mind control. Few medical experts are willing to substantiate these assertions. The time that Tek Nath Rizal spent in solitary confinement in prison might explain a fragile sense of reality and a certain level of paranoia, manifesting in the erratic behavior for which he is now notorious. However, I feel compelled to note that in my three long-ranging interviews with Tek Nath Rizal, he was clearheaded and calm. He accepts, with some resignation, that few people believe that he was (and remains, he insists) a victim of mind control. He is still seeking a cure, he told me, for both his own ills and the problems of the population that he served.

68. Hutt, *Unbecoming Citizens*, 201.

69. Dhakal and Strawn, *Bhutan*, 196, 201.

70. Interview with Bishwanath Chhetri, January 2019, online interview.

71. Interview with R. P. Subba, January 2019, via email.

72. Dhakal and Strawn, *Bhutan*, 209; Sinha, *Himalayan Kingdom Bhutan*, 228.

73. Dhakal and Strawn, *Bhutan*, 143.

74. Sinha, *Himalayan Kingdom Bhutan*, 174.

75. Interview with Bishwanath Chhetri, January 2019, online interview.

76. Interview with Bishwanath Chhetri, January 2019, online interview.

77. Bhakti Prasad Bhandari is also sometimes referred to as Bhakti Sharma or with a differently spelled last name, Bandari. This is important to note because he is referred to differently in different advocacy documents. I will refer to him as Bhakti Bhandari.

78. To recall, the Sharchops are a significant ethnic minority group in southern Bhutan. There have also been calls for equal representation from a small number of Sharchops leaders. That story is told in chapter 4.

79. Interview with Bhakti Bhandari, July 2013, Houston, Texas.

80. Dhakal and Strawn, *Bhutan*, 210.

81. NAB, 68th Session (October 23, 1989–October 31, 1989), 9.

82. Hutt, *Unbecoming Citizens*, 200.

83. Amnesty International, "Bhutan: Appeal for the Release of Tek Nath Rizal: Prisoner of Conscience," Amnesty International, March 1, 1994, ASA 14/002/1994, https://www.amnesty.org/download/Documents/184000/asa140021994en.pdf.

84. Dhakal and Strawn, *Bhutan*, 211.

85. Rizal, *From Palace to Prison*, 125–49. Of the forty-five arrested, most were pardoned by the king and released in January 1990, but not all. In May 1990, Amnesty International adopted the following six as Prisoners of Conscience: Bishwanath Chhetri (released December 1991), Bhakti Bhandari (released December 1991), Ratan Gazmere (released December 1991), Jogen Gazmere (released January 1992), Sushil Pokhrel (released January 1992), and Tek Nath Rizal, who remained in prison far longer than the others, and was eventually pardoned in December 1999.

86. Interview with Bishwanath Chhetri, January 2019, online interview.

87. Hutt, *Unbecoming Citizens*, 203; Zeppa, *Beyond the Sky and the Earth*, chap. "Involvement."

88. Zeppa, *Beyond the Sky and the Earth*, chap. "Involvement."

89. Zeppa, *Beyond the Sky and the Earth*, chap. "Involvement."

90. Whitecross, "Intimacy, Loyalty and State Formation," 74.

91. Whitecross, "Intimacy, Loyalty and State Formation," 86.

92. Dhakal and Strawn, *Bhutan*, 213.

93. Hutt, *Unbecoming Citizens*, 205; Michael Hutt, "Ethnic Nationalism, Refugees and Bhutan," *Journal of Refugee Studies* 9, no. 4 (1996): 406.

94. Dhakal and Strawn, *Bhutan*, 213–15.

95. Hutt, *Unbecoming Citizens*, 209.

96. Interview with Hari Khanal, January 2019, online interview.

97. Evans, "Perils of Being a Borderland People, 34."

98. Interviews with: Balaram Poudel, March 2019, Kathmandu; Govinda Rizal, March 2019, Kathmandu; Bishwanath Chhetri, January 2019, online interview.

99. Pradhan, *Bhutan*, 174.

100. Whitecross, "Law, 'Tradition' and Legitimacy."

101. Interview with Birendra Dhakal, June 2018, Atlanta, Georgia.

102. Interview with Bishwanath Chhetri, January 2019, online interview.

103. Hutt, *Unbecoming Citizens*, 223–25.

104. Hutt, *Unbecoming Citizens*, 227.

105. Girija is a reference to the politician Girija Prasad Koirala, who, at that time, had just become Nepal's first prime minister following the end of absolute monarchical rule. Girija's active involvement in bringing down the traditional Panchayat system, his leadership in the Nepali Congress Party, and his time in prison and exile for challenging Nepal's traditional authority may also have been on the minds of those who goaded Narayan.

106. Interview with Narayan Sharma, January 2019, online interview.

107. Interview #69, name withheld, January 2019, online interview.

108. Susan Banki, "Refugee Mobilization in the Nepal-India Borderlands: The Production of Porosity," *Journal of Refugee Studies* (2023). Over time, eastern Nepal became the site of seven refugee camps for Bhutanese Nepalis.

109. National Assembly of Bhutan (NAB), "Translation of the Proceedings and Resolutions of the 76th Session of the National Assembly of Bhutan Held from the Fifth Day of the Fifth Month to the Seventh Day of the Sixth Month of the Male Earth Tiger Year (June 29–July 30, 1998), 158–59.

110. Bhim Subba's resignation letter as the director of the Ministry of Power on May 16, 1991, can be found here: http://www.oocities.org/bhutaneserefugees/resignation.htm. A word copy is also in the author's possession as this is an outdated website.

111. Interview with Y. P. Dhungel, January 2018, Sydney.

112. Interview with Y. P. Dhungel, January 2018, Sydney.

113. Sadiq, *Paper Citizens.*

4. THE POWER OF PROXIMITY

Epigraph: Interview with Mangala Sharma, January 2019, online interview.

1. Interview with Bhampa Rai, July 2013, Damak.

2. Interview with Bhampa Rai, July 2013, Damak.

3. Catherine Brun and Tariq Jazeel, eds., *Spatialising Politics: Culture and Geography in Postcolonial Sri Lanka* (New Delhi: SAGE, 2009).

4. Paul Virilio, *Polar Inertia* (London: SAGE, 2000), 76.

5. Susan Bibler Coutin, "Illegality, Borderlands, and the Space of Nonexistence," in *Globalization under Construction: Governmentality, Law, and Identity,* ed. Richard Warren Perry and Bill Maurer (Minneapolis: University of Minnesota Press, 2003), 171.

6. Amnesty International, "Bhutan: Crack-Down on 'Anti-Nationals' in the East."

7. HUROB, "Druk National Congress Launched: Profile," *Bhutan Review* 2, no. 7 (1994): 1.

8. Interview with Thinley Penjore, November 2007, Kathmandu. Like the larger movement, the DNC was not free from intragroup fragmentation. Thinley Penjore actually led a breakaway faction that claimed that it was the legitimate leader of the DNC, and splinter groups formed even from this. I cover this fragmentation in the following chapter.

9. Hutt and Sharkey, "Nepalese in Origin but Bhutanese First," 35.

10. Nicholas Van Hear, "Reconsidering Migration and Class," *International Migration Review* 48, no. 1 supplement (2014): 100–121.

11. HUROB, "Druk National Congress Launched."

12. HUROB, "A Time for Change," *Bhutan Review* 2, no. 10 (1994): 3.

13. HUROB, "The Enemy Within," *Bhutan Review* 3, no. 6 (1995): 2.

14. Interview #89; name, date, and place withheld.

15. Interviews #21 and #39 with Nepali journalists; names, dates, and places withheld.

16. See, for example, Dixit, "Dragon Bites Its Tail." This describes how government civil service nearly collapsed with the departure of 3,000 high-skilled workers.

17. *Japan Economic Review*, September 8, 1991, as cited in Minorities at Risk Project, "Chronology for Lhotshampas in Bhutan," Refworld, 2004, http://www.refworld.org/docid/469f386a1e.html.

18. Interview with Harka Jung Subba, July 2013, Kathmandu; translated by Kamal Sigdel and Mom Bishwakarma.

19. "UFD not supporting ULFA in Bhutan," *Hindustan Times*, November 22, 1997.

20. Amnesty International, "Bhutan: Crack-Down on 'Anti-Nationals' in the East."

21. These districts are Samdrup Jonkhar, Pemagatshel, Mongar, and Trashigang.

22. National Assembly of Bhutan (NAB), "Translation of the Proceedings and Reso-lutions of the 76th Session of the National Assembly of Bhutan Held from the Fifth Day of the Fifth Month to the Seventh Day of the Sixth Month of the Male Earth Tiger Year (June 29–July 30, 1998), 186.

23. Interview with Pema Tendzin, March 2019, Kathmandu.

24. Pradhan, *Bhutan*, 131.

25. Interview with Rinzin Dorji, March 2019, Beldangi refugee camp.

26. The *Kuensel* article, published October 25, 1997, is cited in Amnesty International, "Bhutan: Crack-Down on 'Anti-Nationals' in the East."

27. Interviews with Rinzin Dorji, March 2019, Beldangi refugee camp, and Thinley Penjore, November 2007, Kathmandu.

28. Also known as the Mai Khola or Kankai River (see map 3).

29. Interview with Narayan Sharma, January 2019, online interview.

30. Interview with Sushil Niroula, October 2014, Adelaide.

31. Interview with Niran Gautam, July 2013, Sydney.

32. Bhutanese Refugees Aiding the Victims of Violence (BRAVVE), "The Profile of Torture Victims in the Prisons of Bhutan," BRAVVE, Jhapa, Nepal, 2006.

33. Interview with Birendra Dhakal, June 2018, Atlanta, Georgia.

34. HUROB, "Photos Tell a Tale of Woe," *Bhutan Review*, 1, no. 11/12 (1993): 3.

35. Interview with Om Dhungel, January 2018, Sydney.

36. Interview with Om Dhungel, January 2018, Sydney.

37. HUROB, "73rd Session of the National Assembly," *Bhutan Review* 2, no. 10 (1994): 1.

38. HUROB, "Goodbye Dr. Shaw," *Bhutan Review* 1, no. 3 (1993): 1.

39. Association of Human Rights Activists (AHURA), "Bhutanese Refugees: Victims of Forced Eviction. A Report on the Problem and Resistance Efforts" (Association of Human Rights Activists, Jhapa, Nepal, 1999); Centre for Housing Rights and Evictions (COHRE), *Forced Evictions: Violations of Human Rights* (Geneva: COHRE, 1998), 16.

40. Interview with Ratan Gazmere, October 2014, Adelaide.

41. *Longyi* is a skirt-like garment worn by men in the region.

42. Interview with Bhakta Ghimire, June 2018, Harrisburg, Pennsylvania.

43. Interview with Ratan Gazmere, October 2014, Adelaide.

44. A. K. Biswas, "Paradox of Anti-Partition Agitation and Swadeshi Movement in Bengal (1905)," *Social Scientist* 23, no. 4/6 (1995): 38–57.

45. Interview with Ratan Gazmere, October 2014, Adelaide.

46. Interview with Ratan Gazmere, October 2014, Adelaide.

47. Rizal, *Pardesi in Paradise*, 291.

48. Susan Banki, Bhakta Ghimire, and Hari Khanal, "Displaced but Not Disempow-ered: Bhutanese Refugees and Grassroots Activism," *Fletcher Forum of World Affairs* 43, no. 2 (2019): 37–56.

49. Agence France-Presse, "Indian Police again Stop Bhutan Marchers from Entering India," *Agence France-Presse*, January 24, 1996; Agence France-Presse, "The Refugees Plan to Go to the Bhutanese Capital Thimpu to Appeal to the King," *Agence France-Presse*, January 24, 1996; BBC Monitoring Asia-Pacific, "Darjeeling Ghorkas Hold Strike for Re-lease of Bhutan Marchers," *BBC Monitoring Asia-Pacific*, January 22, 1996; BBC Monitor-ing Southasia, "Marchers Bound for Thimpu Arrested by Indian Police," *BBC Monitoring Southasia*, January 19, 1996; Binaya Guruacharya, "Refugees Begin March to Demand Right to Live in Bhutan," *Associated Press*, January 14, 1996; Japan Economic Newswire, "India Arrests Bhutanese Peace Marchers," *Japan Economic Newswire*, January 18, 1996.

50. Interview with D. N. S. Dhakal, March 2019, Birtamod.

51. Interview with Harka Jung Subba, July 2013, Kathmandu.

52. Interview with Ratan Gazmere, October 2014, Adelaide.

53. Dhakal and Strawn, *Bhutan*.

54. Interview with Y. P. Dhungel, January 2018, Sydney.

55. Interview with D. N. S. Dhakal, March 2019, Birtamod.

56. C. Wright Mills, *The Power Elite* (Oxford: Oxford University Press, 1956).

57. Roy Chowdhury, *Sunandan: Politics, Policy and Higher Education in India* (Singapore: Springer Singapore, 2017).

58. Giri, *Justice to Justice*.

59. Interview with N. B. Giri, March 2019, Kathmandu.

60. Interview with Bishwanath Chhetri, January 2019, online interview.

61. Bhampa Rai, *Bhutan and Its Agonised People* (Damak, Jhapa: Sumnima Offset Press, 2013), 40.

62. HUROB. "The Third Man," *Bhutan Review*, 1, no. 9 (1993): 2.

63. HUROB. "Third Man," 2

64. AHURA, "Bhutanese Refugees," 21.

65. See, for example, "Bhutan Refugee Repatriation Committee Says More Verification Teams Needed," *Kathmandu Post*, May 22, 2001.

66. Interview with Ratan Gazmere, October 2014, Adelaide.

67. Interview with Om Dhungel, January 2018, Sydney.

68. Interview with Bhampa Rai, July 2013, Damak.

69. Thomas M. Wilson and Hastings Donnan, eds., *Border Identities: Nation and State at International Frontiers* (Cambridge: Cambridge University Press, 1998).

70. Ratan Gazmere and Dilip Bishwo, "Bhutanese Refugees: Rights to Nationality, Return and Property," *Forced Migration Review* 7 (2000): 20–22.

71. Interview with Hari Khanal, January 2019, online interview.

72. Interview with Ramlal Acharya, November 2007, Damak. A copy of the database is also in the author's possession.

73. Fires in the refugee camps were not uncommon. When camp residents' huts burned, their documentation was lost as well.

74. Interview with Ratan Gazmere, October 2014, Adelaide.

75. Association of Human Rights Activists (AHURA), "Bhutan, a Shangri-La without Human Rights" (Association of Human Rights Activists, Jhapa, Nepal, 2000), 76–78.

76. Interviews with: Bhampa Rai, March 2019, Damak; N. B. Giri, March 2019, Kathmandu; Ratan Gazmere, October 2014, Adelaide.

77. Interview with Gopal Gartoula, July 2013, Damak.

78. Amanda Burrell, "The Forgotten Refugees," BBC with WFP and UNHCR, Rockhopper TV, September 2008.

79. Interview with Ratan Gazmere, October 2014, Adelaide.

80. Pradhan, *Bhutan*, 159.

81. Interview with Ratan Gazmere, October 2014, Adelaide.

82. Interview with Ratan Gazmere, October 2014, Adelaide. See also Aruni John, "Potential for Militancy among Bhutanese Refugee Youth," RCSS Policy Studies 15, Regional Center for Strategic Studies, Colombo, Sri Lanka, 2000.

83. S. Chandrasekharan, "Bhutan: Update No. 11—Is UNHCR Going for a Pro Active Role?" South Asia Analysis Group, 2000.

84. BRAVVE, "Report of Activities 1999," BRAVVE, Jhapa, Nepal, 2000, 16.

85. Michael Hutt, "The Bhutanese Refugees: Between Verification, Repatriation, and Royal Realpolitik," *Peace and Democracy in South Asia* 1, no. 1 (2005): 49.

86. For more information about the problems of the JVT process, see Susan Banki, "Resettlement of the Bhutanese from Nepal: The Durable Solution Discourse," in *Protracted Displacement in Asia: No Place to Call Home*, ed. Howard Adelman (London: Ash-

gate, 2008), 43; Hutt, "Bhutanese Refugees." For a perspective from inside the Nepal government, see R. S. Mahat, *In Defense of Democracy: Dynamics and Fault Lines of Nepal's Political Economy* (New Delhi: Adroit, 2005), 261.

87. Interview with N. B. Giri, July 2013, Kathmandu.

88. Interview with Bhampa Rai, March 2019, Damak.

89. Interview with Bhampa Rai, March 2019, Damak.

90. Adamson, "Spaces of Global Security: Beyond Methodological Nationalism," 22.

5. PRECARITY IN EXILE

Epigraph: Interview with D. N. S. Dhakal, March 2019, Jhapa.

1. Amy Murrell Taylor, *The Divided Family in Civil War America* (Chapel Hill: University of North Carolina Press, 2009); Tomi Kaizawa Knaefler, *Our House Divided: Seven Japanese American Families in World War II* (Honolulu: University of Hawai'i Press, 1991).

2. Banki, "Precarity of Place."

3. Ilcan, Rygiel, and Baban, "Ambiguous Architecture of Precarity."

4. Ilcan, Rygiel, and Baban, "Ambiguous Architecture of Precarity," 55.

5. Ilcan, Rygiel, and Baban, "Ambiguous Architecture of Precarity," 56.

6. Ilcan, Rygiel, and Baban, "Ambiguous Architecture of Precarity," 56.

7. Sondra L. Hausner and Jeevan R. Sharma, "On the Way to India: Nepali Rituals of Border Crossing," in *Borderland Lives in Northern South Asia*, ed. David N. Gellner (Durham, NC: Duke University Press, 2014), 99.

8. Hausner and Sharma, "On the Way to India." 102.

9. Dhakal and Strawn, *Bhutan*, 267–80.

10. Dhakal and Strawn, *Bhutan*, 273.

11. Interview with Birendra Dhakal, June 2018, Atlanta, Georgia.

12. Interview with Hari Khanal, January 2019, online interview.

13. Human Rights Watch, "Last Hope."

14. Interviews with Hari Khanal, January 2019, online interview; and Padam Kafley, July 2013, Sydney.

15. Gerrard Khan, "Citizenship and Statelessness in South Asia," Working paper no. 47, UNHCR, Geneva, 2001, 22.

16. Susan Banki and Hazel Lang, "Protracted Displacement on the Thai-Burmese Border: The Interrelated Search for Durable Solutions," in *Protracted Displacement in Asia: No Place to Call Home*, ed. Howard Adelman (London: Ashgate, 2008), 59–82.

17. Ellie Vasta, "Immigrants and the Paper Market: Borrowing, Renting and Buying Identities," *Ethnic and Racial Studies* 34, no. 2 (2011): 199.

18. Sadiq, *Paper Citizens*.

19. Interview with Gopal Gartoula, July 2013, Damak.

20. Banki, Ghimire, and Khanal, "Displaced but Not Disempowered," 43, 55n9.

21. Michael Hutt, "Bhutan in 1996: Continuing Stress," *Asian Survey* 37, no. 2 (1997): 155–59.

22. Interview with Bhakta Ghimire, March 2019, online interview. Govinda Rizal's book also pays attention to the death of Baburan Sengden, including the difficulty of getting the body released, having the autopsy conducted, and planning the funeral procession. See Rizal, *Pardesi in Paradise*, 257–77.

23. Interview with Y. P. Dhungel, January 2018, Sydney.

24. Interview with Y. P. Dhungel, January 2018, Sydney.

25. Interview with Padam Kafley, July 2013, Sydney.

26. Interview with R. P. Subba, January 2019, online interview.

27. Interview with Govinda Rizal, March 2019, Kathmandu.

28. Interview with Bishwanath Chhetri, January 2019, online interview.

29. Govinda Rizal offers a rich description of the intergroup frustrations and conflicts that formed during this time. See Rizal, *Pardesi in Paradise.*

30. Amnesty International, "Bhutan: Crack-Down on 'Anti-Nationals' in the East."

31. Narad Adhikari, "Late Dorji's Contributions in Retrospection," *AFPA News,* October 20, 2011, http://apfanews.com/rongthong-kunley-dorji.

32. Interview with Om Dhungel, January 2018, Sydney. See also Adhikari, "Late Dorji's Contributions in Retrospection."

33. Interview with Om Dhungel, January 2018, Sydney.

34. Kesang Lhendup, "Statement from His Party," *APFA News,* October 20, 2011.

35. Interview with Karma Dupthob, March 2019, Kathmandu.

36. Dixit, "Dragon Bites Its Tail."

37. Dixit, "Dragon Bites Its Tail."

38. John Quigley, "Bhutanese Refugees in Nepal: What Role Now for the European Union and the United Nations High Commission for Refugees?" *Contemporary South Asia* 13, no. 2 (2004): 187–200; Hutt, "Bhutanese Refugees," 51.

39. *Hindustan Times,* October 20, 1990, 6, as cited in Parmanand, *Politics of Bhutan,* 144.

40. Haifeng Huang, Serra Boranbay-Akan, and Ling Huang, "Media, Protest Diffusion, and Authoritarian Resilience," *Political Science Research and Methods* 7, no. 1 (2019): 23–42.

41. Adam Ramadan, "Spatialising the Refugee Camp," *Transactions of the Institute of British Geographers* 38, no. 1 (2013): 65–77.

42. Bhutanese Women and Youth Empowerment Program (BWYEP), "Bhutanese Women and Youth Empowerment Program Report," BWYEP, Birtamode, Nepal, no date, 22; in the possession of the author.

43. Interview with I. P. Adhikari, October 2014, Adelaide.

44. Interview with I. P. Adhikari, October 2014, Adelaide.

45. Interview with Hari Khanal, January 2019, by phone.

46. Interview with Suman Chettri, April 2013, Sydney.

47. Interviews with D. N. S Dhakal, March 2019, Jhapa; and Bhakta Ghimire, June 2018, Harrisburg, Pennsylvania.

48. Interview with Suman Chettri, April 2013, Sydney.

49. US Committee for Refugees and Immigrants (USCRI), *World Refugee Survey 2007,* ed. Merrill Smith (Washington, DC: US Committee for Refugees and Immigrants [USCRI], 2008).

50. Betts and Jones, *Mobilising the Diaspora.*

51. Interview with N. B. Giri, July 2013, Kathmandu.

52. Susan Banki, "Transnational Activism as Practised by Activists from Burma: Negotiating Precarity, Mobility and Resistance," in *Metamorphosis: Studies in Social and Political Change in Myanmar,* ed. Renaud Egreteau and François Robinne (Singapore: NUS Press, 2015), 234–59.

53. Interview with Hari Khanal, January 2019, online interview.

54. Vidhyapati Mishra, "Open Letter to Nepali Prime Minister Jhala Nath Khanal," *APFA News,* February 25, 2011.

55. "Yearning to Be Free," *Nepali Times,* August 7, 2009.

56. Interview with Tek Nath Rizal, July 2013, Kathmandu.

57. Mahat, *In Defense of Democracy.*

58. Interview with Ram Sharan Mahat, March 2019, Kathmandu.

59. Interviews #5, #6, and #9, names and locations withheld, November and December 2007.

60. S. Chandrasekharan "Bhutan: Distribution of Maoist Document in Refugee Camps: Should Be Cause for Concern. Update 30," South Asia Analysis Group, 2003.

61. Evans, "Perils of Being a Borderland People," 38.

62. Interviews #5, #6, and #9, names and locations withheld, November and December 2007.

63. Interview #33, name withheld, July 2013, Kathmandu.

64. Interview #44, name and location withheld, July 2013.

65. See, for example, Kathleen Gallagher Cunningham, *Inside the Politics of Self-Determination* (Oxford: Oxford University Press, 2014).

66. Deborah B. Balser, "The Impact of Environmental Factors on Factionalism and Schism in Social Movement Organizations," *Social Forces* 76, no. 1 (1997): 199–228.

67. Kenneth D. Bush, "Reading between the Lines: Intra-Group Heterogeneity and Conflict in Sri Lanka," *Refuge: Canada's Journal on Refugees* 13, no. 3 (1993): 15–22.

68. Cunningham, *Inside the Politics of Self-Determination*, 129–50.

69. Cunningham, *Inside the Politics of Self-Determination*, 129–50.

70. Dixit, "Dragon Bites Its Tail."

71. Interview #70, name, date, and place withheld.

72. Interview with Kanak Mani Dixit, December 2007, Kathmandu.

73. Hutt, "Bhutan in 1996," 158.

74. Sinha describes the difficult position of this population of Bhutanese Nepalis who remained in Bhutan when the majority left: "Those of the Lhotshampas, who are left behind in the villages, are invariably from broken families living under a sense of panic, fear, uncertainty and continuous harassment. . . . Worst of all, many of them are considered spies by both parties—the Drukpa establishment as well as the Nepalese in the camps." See Sinha, *Himalayan Kingdom Bhutan*, 243.

75. Interview #76, name and location withheld, March 2019.

76. Interview #76, name and location withheld, March 2019.

77. Interviews with: Bishwnath Chhetri, January 2019, online interview; Karma Thuptob, March 2019, Kathmandu; Govinda Rizal, March 2019, Kathmandu; Ratan Gazmere, October 2014, Adelaide.

78. Interview #26, a refugee leader, name withheld, December 2007, Kathmandu.

79. Bob, *Marketing of Rebellion*.

80. See, for example, Lewis et al., *Precarious Lives*.

81. Banki, Ghimire, and Khanal, "Displaced but Not Disempowered," 40.

82. Interview with Om Dhungel, January 2018, Sydney.

83. Interview with Bhampa Rai, March 2019, Kathmandu.

84. BBC Monitoring Southeast Asia, "Bhutanese Refugees in Dispute over Repatriation Process," *BBC Monitoring Southeast Asia*, August 10, 2005.

85. Interview with N. B. Giri, July 2013, Kathmandu.

86. Interview with N. B. Giri, July 2013, Kathmandu.

87. Susan Banki and Nicole Phillips, "Leaving in Droves from the Orange Groves: The Nepali-Bhutanese Refugee Experience and the Diminishing of Dignity," in *Human Dignity: Establishing Worth and Seeking Solutions*, ed. Edward Sieh and Judy McGregor (London: Palgrave Macmillan, 2017), 335–52.

88. Information about such difficulties came from nearly all my interview participants, but especially N. B. Giri, Y. P. Dhungel, and Ganga Dhungel.

6. EXPANSION OF THE ECOSYSTEM

Epigraph: Interview with Vidhyapati Mishra, June 2018, Charlotte, North Carolina.

1. Interview with Shankar Basnet, senior officer, Advocacy Forum, Eastern Regional Office, December 2007, Biratnagar.

2. Interview with N. B. Giri, March 2019, Kathmandu.

3. Data on refugee resettlement comes from UNHCR's Resettlement Data Finder. For information on 2008 data, see UNHCR, "Resettlement Data Finder," UNHCR, https://rsq.unhcr.org/en/#bE8r. For data on the total number of refugees globally in 2008, see "2008 Global Trends: Refugees, Asylum-Seekers, Returnees, Internally Displaced and Stateless Persons," UNHCR, Geneva, 2009, https://www.unhcr.org/us/media/2008-global-trends-refugees-asylum-seekers-returnees-internally-displaced-and-stateless.

4. US Committee for Refugees and Immigrants (USCRI), *World Refugee Survey 2009: Nepal*, (Washington, DC: US Commitee for Refugees and Immigrants (USCRI)), 2009, https://www.refworld.org/docid/4a40d2aec.html.

5. UNHCR, "Resettlement Data Finder." Data from UNHCR shows that of the remaining six countries where Bhutanese refugees were resettled, 6,723 were resettled in Canada, 862 in Denmark, 301 in the Netherlands, 1,302 in New Zealand, 539 in Norway, and 356 in the United Kingdom.

6. Banki, "Resettlement of the Bhutanese from Nepal."

7. Himali Dixit, "Repatriation or Resettlement: Resolving the Lhotshampa Dilemma," *Himal Southasian*, June 2007.

8. Interview #31, a diplomat working in Kathmandu, name, place and date withheld. Interview with Graeme Lade, Australian ambassador to Nepal, December 2007, Kathmandu.

9. Interview #3, a US State Department official, name and date withheld, Kathmandu.

10. Interview with Ratan Gazmere, October 2014, Adelaide.

11. Susan Banki and Hazel Lang, "Difficult to Remain: The Impact of Mass Resettlement," *Forced Migration Review* 30 (2008): 42–44.

12. Susan Banki, "Bhutanese Refugees in Nepal: Anticipating the Impact of Resettlement," Briefing paper, Austcare, Griffith University, Sydney, 2008.

13. Shiva K. Dhungana, "Third Country Resettlement and the Bhutanese Refugee Crisis: A Critical Reflection," *Refugee Watch* 35 (2010): 19.

14. Interview with Himali Dixit, November 2007, Kathmandu.

15. Interview with Bhampa Rai, July 2013, Damak. See also Dhungana, "Third Country Resettlement and the Bhutanese Refugee Crisis," 23–24.

16. Banki, "Anticipating the Impact of Resettlement," 6–7.

17. Evans, "Perils of Being a Borderland People," 34.

18. Interview #26, name withheld, December 2007, Kathmandu.

19. Interview with Mangala Sharma, January 2019, online interview.

20. Hasta Bhattarai, "Question of Defeating Miserable Life," *Bhutan Reporter*, August 2008, http://thebhutanreporter.blogspot.com/2008/08/opinion.html; Republished as "Question of Defeating Miserable Life," *Bhutan News Service*, http://www.bhutannewsservice.org/question-of-defeating-miserable-life-remembering-hasta-bhattarai/.

21. As well summarized in Guarnizo, Portes, and Haller, "Assimilation and Transnationalism."

22. Benedict Anderson, "Long-Distance Nationalism," in *The Spectre of Comparisons: Nationalism, Southeast Asia, and the World*, ed. Benedict Anderson (London: Verso, 1998), 58–74.

23. Adamson, "Spaces of Global Security."

24. Catherine Brun and Nicholas Van Hear, "Between the Local and the Diasporic: The Shifting Centre of Gravity in War-Torn Sri Lanka's Transnational Politics," *Contemporary South Asia* 20, no. 1 (2012): 61–75.

25. Bob, *Marketing of Rebellion*.

26. Guarnizo, Portes, and Haller, "Assimilation and Transnationalism"; Guarnizo, Chaudhary, and Sørensen, "Migrants' Transnational Political Engagement in Spain and Italy," 1217.

27. David N Gellner, "Introduction: The Nepali/Gorkhali Diaspora since the Nineteenth Century," in *Global Nepalis: Religion, Culture, and Community in a New and Old Diaspora*, ed. David N. Gellner and Sondra L. Hausner (Oxford: Oxford University Press, 2018), 23.

28. Turner, Chuki, and Tshering, "Democratization by Decree," 201.

29. Kinga, *Democratic Transition in Bhutan*, chap. 1.

30. Kinga, *Democratic Transition in Bhutan*, 21.

31. Kinga, *Democratic Transition in Bhutan*, 31.

32. Rizal, *Royal Semi-Authoritarian Democracy of Bhutan*, 29.

33. Kinga, *Democratic Transition in Bhutan*, 24.

34. Kinga, *Democratic Transition in Bhutan*, 22.

35. Kinga, *Democratic Transition in Bhutan*, 2.

36. Winnie Bothe, "The Monarch's Gift: Critical Notes on the Constitutional Process in Bhutan," *European Bulletin of Himalayan Research* 40 (2012): 27–58; Stephanie De-Gooyer, "Democracy, Give or Take?" *Humanity: An International Journal of Human Rights, Humanitarianism, and Development* 5, no. 1 (2014): 93–110.

37. Dhakal and Strawn, *Bhutan*; Dhurba Rizal, "The Unknown Refugee Crisis: Expulsion of the Ethnic Lhotsampa from Bhutan," *Asian Ethnicity* 5, no. 2 (2004): 151–77.

38. Kinga, *Democratic Transition in Bhutan*, 13–15.

39. Interview with R. P. Subba, January 2019, online interview.

40. Interview with R. P. Subba, January 2019, online interview.

41. Mark Turner and Jit Tshering, "Is Democracy Being Consolidated in Bhutan?," *Asian Politics and Policy* 6, no. 3 (2014): 413–31.

42. Stephan Sonnenberg, "Formalizing the Informal: Development and Its Impacts on Traditional Dispute Resolution," *Washington University Journal of Law and Policy* 63 (2020): 143–206.

43. Sonnenberg, "Formalizing the Informal," 179.

44. Economist Intelligence Unit, "Country Report: Bhutan," *The Economist*, accessed June 16, 2023, https://country.eiu.com/bhutan.

45. Turner and Tshering, "Is Democracy Being Consolidated in Bhutan?," 426.

46. Lisa Napoli, *Radio Shangri-La: What I Discovered on My Accidental Journey to the Happiest Kingdom on Earth* (New York: Crown, 2011), 226.

47. S. D. Muni, "Bhutan's Deferential Democracy," *Journal of Democracy* 25, no. 2 (2014): 158–63.

48. Muni, "Bhutan's Deferential Democracy," 160.

49. Muni, "Bhutan's Deferential Democracy," 160.

50. Thierry Mathou, "Bhutan in 2017: Preparing a New Cycle," *Asian Survey* 58, no. 1 (2018): 138–41.

51. Joseph C. Mathew, "Bhutan: 'Democracy' from Above," *Economic and Political Weekly* 43, no. 19 (2008): 29–31.

52. Mathew, "Bhutan," 29.

53. Line Kikkenborg Christensen, "Freedom of Speech and Silent Youth Protest in Bhutan: 'Plz Delete It from Your Inbox,'" *South Asia Research* 37, no. 1 (2017): 93–108.

54. Christensen, "Driglam Namzha and Silenced Ethnicity."

55. Line Kikkenborg Christensen, "Piecing together Past and Present in Bhutan: Narration, Silence and Forgetting in Conflict," *International Journal of Conflict and Violence* 12 (2018): 6, 10.

56. Susan Banki and Ram Karki, "Bhutan's Democratic Growing Pains," *Current History* 123, no. 852 (2024).

57. Bhutan Watch, "Rights under Shadow," Bhutan Watch, April 29, 2019, http://www.bhutanwatch.org/rights-under-shadow/. April 2019.

58. US State Department, "Country Reports on Human Rights Practices for 2018," United States Department of State, Bureau of Democracy, Human Rights and Labor, Washington, DC, 2018.

59. Human Rights Watch (HRW), "Bhutan: Free Long-Term Political Prisoners," March 13, 2023, https://www.hrw.org/news/2023/03/13/bhutan-free-long-term-political-prisoners.

60. Freedom House, "Freedom in the World, 2019: Bhutan," Freedom House, Washington DC, 2020, https://freedomhouse.org/country/bhutan/freedom-world/2019.

61. Proceedings and Resolutions of the 85th Session of the National Assembly of Bhutan, as cited in Human Rights Watch, "Last Hope."

62. "HM Grants Citizenship to 359 People," *Kuensel*, March 14, 2019.

63. Interview with Bishwanath Chhetri, January 2019, online interview.

64. Interview with Tikaram Rasaily, March 2019, Beldangi refugee camp.

65. Interview with Karma Dupthob, March 2019, Kathmandu.

66. An article about this media analysis is currently in the writing stages.

67. Interview with Tikaram Rasaily, March 2019, Beldangi refugee camp.

68. Interview with Harka Jung Subba, July 2013, Kathmandu, translated by Kamal Sigdel and Mom Bishwakarma. Here Harka Jung is using a common Nepali expression, "Hattiko Dekhaune Danta ra Chapaune Dant," referring to the way that leaders project one image publicly but then follow a set of actions that defy that image. This expression was also referred to in Aditya Adhikari, *The Bullet and the Ballot Box: The Story of Nepal's Maoist Revolution* (New Delhi: Verso Trade, 2014), 64–65. It is also captured in the title of a 2023 book about Bhutanese refugees by Alice Neikirk, *The Elephant Has Two Sets of Teeth: Bhutanese Refugees and Humanitarian Governance* (Edmonton: University of Alberta, 2023).

69. For example, interviews with Bhampa Rai, Balaram Poudel, and D. N. S. Dhakal. These events were also covered regularly in *Bhutan News Service*.

70. Interview with Tikaram Rasaily, March 2019, Beldangi refugee camp.

71. Interviews with Tek Nath Rizal, July 2013, Kathmandu; S. B. Subba, March 2019, Kakarbhitta; N. B. Giri, March 2019, Kathmandu; Govinda Rizal, March 2019, Kathmandu; and others who requested anonymity.

72. Interview #94, name withheld, March 2019, Beldangi refugee camp.

73. In possession of the author.

74. Interview with Bishwanath Chhetri, January 2019, online interview.

75. Dhruva Mishra, "The Tale of Political Discrimination," *Bhutan News Service*, March 27, 2011.

76. Bikash Regmi, "What Citizenship Means without a Country," TEDx Talks, May 25, 2017, YouTube video, 12:03, https://www.youtube.com/watch?v=6w5pOi0uJUI.

77. Brett Williamson, "After 17 Years in a Refugee Camp, Sushil Finally Has a Place to Call Home," *ABC Adelaide*, June 14, 2013.

78. Helena Oliviero, "Bhutanese Brothers Overcome Adversity," *Atlanta Journal-Constitution*, December 30, 2013.

79. Bhutan News Service, "BAF Europe Lobbies for Solidarity," *Bhutan News Service*, January 28, 2010; Bhutan News Network, "Bhutan Human Rights Issues Raised with EU Officials," *Bhutan News Network*, July 20, 2019.

80. Ram Karki arrived in the Netherlands prior to the process of mass resettlement, receiving asylum through an individualized application process.

81. Interview with Ram Karki, January 2020, online interview.

82. Interview with Ram Karki, January 2020, online interview.

83. Interview with Karma Dupthob, March 2019, Kathmandu.

84. See, for example, Bhutan News Service, "Journalist Freed, Appeals UNHCR for Reunion with Family," *Bhutan News Service*, September 1, 2014.

85. Interview with Durga Acharya, March 2019, Beldangi refugee camp.

86. Interview with Govinda Rizal, March 2019, Kathmandu.

87. Bhutan News Service, "Rights Activist Whereabouts Remains Mystery," *Bhutan News Service*, November 29, 2014.

88. Interview #60b, name withheld, June 2015, Sydney.

89. United Nations Human Rights Council, "Opinions Adopted by the Working Group on Arbitrary Detention at Its Seventy-Eighth Session, 19–28 April 2017," A/HRC/WGAD/2017/29, Human Rights Council, Geneva, 2017.

90. Bhutan News Network, "Campaign to Release Political Prisoners in Bhutan," *Bhutan News Network*, December 14, 2019.

91. R. B. Chhetri, "Signature Campaign to Release Political Prisoners in Bhutan," Petitions.net, https://www.petitions.net/stats.php?id=244951&s=65979626.

92. A video of Ram Karki's intervention was posted on the GCRPPB Facebook page: Ram Karki, "UN High Commissioner for Human Rights Madam Michelle Bachelet Responding to My Intervention on the Issue of Bhutanese Political Prisoners and Other Human Rights Issues," Facebook, June 6, 2020, https://www.facebook.com/chhetri3/videos/10163528727385099.

93. HRW, "Bhutan."

94. Bhutan News Service, "Bhutanese Orgs Submits Memorandum to Massachusetts Governor," *Bhutan News Service*, October 18, 2018.

95. Bhutan News Service, "New Hampshire Senate Hearing on Bhutanese Issue," *Bhutan News Service*, May 8, 2015.

96. New Hampshire State Senate, N.H. SCR 1, December 16, 2015.

97. Bhutan News Service, "New Hampshire Senate Hearing on Bhutanese Issue."

98. Interviews with: Deepesh Shrestha, UNHCR official, March 2019, Kathmandu, and Gopal Siwakoti, INHURED chair, March 2019, Kathmandu.

99. This phenomenon is explained in depth in Rizal, *Pardesi in Paradise*, 362.

100. Bhutan News Service, "15 Exiled Women Go on Fast-Unto-Death Demanding 'Refugee Status.'" *Bhutan News Service*, November 16, 2011.

101. Interview with Champa Singh Rai, Sanischare camp secretary, March 2019, Sanischare refugee camp.

102. Rana B. Khoury, "Aiding Activism? Humanitarianism's Impacts on Mobilized Syrian Refugees in Jordan," *Middle East Law and Governance* 9, no. 3 (2017): 267–81.

103. Susan Banki, "Urbanity, Precarity, and Homeland Activism: Burmese Migrants in Global Cities," *Moussons* 22, no. 2 (2013): 35–56.

104. Susan Banki and Nicole Phillips, "'We Are the Victims of the Separation': A Report on Bhutanese Refugees Remaining in Nepal," May 2014, https://ses.library.usyd.edu.au/bitstream/handle/2123/21075/Banki%20Phillips%20Victims%20of%20Separation%202014.pdf.

105. Interview with Ram Karki, January 2020, online interview.

106. Bhutan News Service, "Bhutanese Begin Drive to Support Quake Devastated Nepal," *Bhutan News Service*, April 26, 2015.

107. Elizabeth Jelin, *State Repression and the Labors of Memory*, trans. Marcial Godoy-Anativia and Judy Rein (Minneapolis: University of Minnesota Press, 2003).

108. Maria Mälksoo, "'Memory Must Be Defended': Beyond the Politics of Mnemonical Security," *Security Dialogue* 46, no. 3 (2015): 221–37.

109. Susan Banki and I. P. Adhikari, "Contesting Memories in and of Bhutan: Diaspora Radio as a Mnemonic Challenge," in *Defending Memory*, ed. Dovile Budryte (London: Routledge, forthcoming).

110. Bhutan News Service, "Forgotten Story of 1950 Prison Escapee."

111. Bhutan News Service, "Legendary Marriage of Mahasur Chhetri's Son," *Bhutan News Service*, January 10, 2011; "Moments of Transitioning History," *Bhutan News Service*, August 12, 2012.

112. Bhutan News Service, "Moments of Transitioning History."

113. From 2006 to 2008, *Bhutan News Service* operated without online coverage. My comprehensive analysis of all articles begins only with the 2008 online coverage.

114. Bhutan News Service, "BNS Shifts Course," *Bhutan News Service*, January 12, 2020.

115. R. P. Subba, "BNS Should Be Saved," *Bhutan News Service*, January 14, 2020.

116. Interview with D. N. S. Dhakal, March 2019, Birtamod.

117. Susan Banki, "Bhutanese Refugee Cultural Complex: An Outsider-Insider Perspective," *Bhutan Journal* 2, no. 1 (2021): 73–83.

118. Interview with D. N. S. Dhakal, March 2019, Birtamod.

119. Comment by Puran Thapa, November 2, 2009 at 4:20 p.m., about the article: Bhutan News Service, "Adhikari after Intricate Surgery Starts New Life," *Bhutan News Service*, October 31, 2009.

7. CONCLUSION

Epigraph: *Interview with Birendra Dhakal, June 2018, Atlanta, Georgia.*

1. Bob, *Marketing of Rebellion.*

2. Betts and Jones, *Mobilising the Diaspora.*

3. David Ley, "Transnational Spaces and Everyday Lives," *Transactions of the Institute of British Geographers* 29 (2004): 151–64; Yvonne Riaño, "Conceptualising Space in Transnational Migration Studies: A Critical Perspective," in *Border Transgression: Mobility and Mobilization in Crisis*, ed. Eva Youkhana (Bonn: Bonn University Press, 2017), 35–48.

4. Rainer BaubÖck and Thomas Faist, *Diaspora and Transnationalism: Concepts, Theories and Methods* (Amsterdam: Amsterdam University Press, 2010).

5. Michael Milshtein, "Memory 'from Below': Palestinian Society and the Nakba Memory," in *Palestinian Collective Memory and National Identity*, ed. Meir Litvak (New York: Palgrave Macmillan, 2009), 71–96.

6. Lee Ann Roripaugh, "Transplanting," in *Year of the Snake* (Carbondale: Southern Illinois University Press, 2004), 32.

7. Adam Zagajewski, "To Go to Lvov," trans. Renata Gorczynski, in *Without End: New and Selected Poems* (New York: Farrar, Straus & Giroux, 2002), 79.

8. Lefebvre, *Production of Space*; Massey, *Space, Place and Gender*; Soja, *Seeking Spatial Justice.*

9. Susan Banki, Elisabeth Valiente-Riedl, and Paul Duffill, "Teaching Human Rights at the Tertiary Level: Addressing the 'Knowing-Doing Gap' through a Role-Based Simulation Approach," *Journal of Human Rights Practice* 5, no. 2 (2013): 318–36.

10. Elizabeth Chacko and Marie Price, "(Un)Settled Sojourners in Cities: The Scalar and Temporal Dimensions of Migrant Precarity," *Journal of Ethnic and Migration Studies* 47, no. 20 (2020): 4597–614.

11. For a good discussion of remote-control protection of refugees, see FitzGerald, *Refuge beyond Reach.*

12. Maria Koinova, "Critical Junctures and Transformative Events in Diaspora Mobilisation for Kosovo and Palestinian Statehood," *Journal of Ethnic and Migration Studies* 44, no. 8 (2018): 1289–308.

13. Keane, *New Despotism*, 57.

14. Keane, *New Despotism*, 238.

15. Curato and Fossati, "Authoritarian Innovations."

16. Hannah Arendt, *The Origins of Totalitarianism* (New York: Harvest, 1979); Giorgio Agamben, *Homo Sacer: Sovereign Power and Bare Life*, trans. Daniel Heller-Roazen (Stanford, CA: Stanford University Press, 1998).

17. Laura Bingham and Natasha Arnpriester, "Unmaking Americans: Insecure Citizenship in the United States," Open Society Foundation, New York, September 2019, https://www.justiceinitiative.org/publications/unmaking-americans.

18. Sangeetha Pillai, "The Latest Citizenship-Stripping Plan Risks Statelessness, Indefinite Detention and Constitutional Challenge," *The Conversation*, November 24, 2018.

19. Bingham and Arnpriester, "Unmaking Americans."

20. BBC News, "Citizenship Amendment Bill: India's New 'Anti-Muslim' Law Explained," *BBC News*, December 11, 2019.

21. Susan Banki, "The Paradoxical Power of Precarity: Refugees and Homeland Activism," *Refugee Review* 1, no. 1 (2013): 1–19.

22. There are exceptions, most notably in South America, where countries have in the first instance offered a range of rights to displaced populations. In general, however, and certainly over time, proximate host governments have grown more rather than less restrictive in residence and work rights.

23. See, for example, Phil Orchard, *The Right to Flee* (Cambridge: Cambridge University Press, 2014).

24. Virtual participation of refugees and migrants at humanitarian and human rights conferences has increased considerably in the context of COVID-19. Familiarity with the technology and ways of doing business online may encourage a virtual path to proximate mobilization, but this is not a foregone conclusion. Further, it is not clear whether online conferences are being attended by proximate homeland activists or those further afield. Facilitating the inclusion of proximate actors in online meetings may require additional support, such as targeted training and technologies.

25. Christensen, "Piecing together Past and Present in Bhutan."

Bibliography

Adamson, Fiona B. "Non-State Authoritarianism and Diaspora Politics." *Global Networks* 20, no. 1 (2020): 150–69.

Adamson, Fiona B. "Spaces of Global Security: Beyond Methodological Nationalism." *Journal of Global Security Studies* 1, no. 1 (2016): 19–35.

Adhikari, Aditya. *The Bullet and the Ballot Box: The Story of Nepal's Maoist Revolution.* New Delhi: Verso Trade, 2014.

Adhikari, Narad. "Late Dorji's Contributions in Retrospection." *APFA News*, October 20, 2011. http://apfanews.com/rongthong-kunley-dorji.

Agamben, Giorgio. *Homo Sacer: Sovereign Power and Bare Life.* Translated by Daniel Heller-Roazen. Stanford, CA: Stanford University Press, 1998.

Agence France-Presse. "Indian Police again Stop Bhutan Marchers from Entering India." *Agence France-Presse*, January 24, 1996.

Agence France-Presse. "The Refugees Plan to Go to the Bhutanese Capital Thimpu to Appeal to the King . . . ," *Agence France-Presse*, January 24, 1996.

Amnesty International. "Bhutan: Appeal for the Release of Tek Nath Rizal: Prisoner of Conscience." Amnesty International, March 1, 1994. ASA 14/002/1994. https://www.amnesty.org/download/Documents/184000/asa140021994en.pdf.

Amnesty International. "Bhutan: Crack-Down on 'Anti-Nationals' in the East." Amnesty International, January 12, 1998. ASA 14/002/1998. https://www.amnesty.org/en/documents/asa14/002/1998/en/.

Amnesty International. "Bhutan: Human Rights Violations against the Nepali-Speaking Population in the South." Amnesty International, December 1, 1992. ASA 14/004/1992. https://www.amnesty.org/en/documents/asa14/004/1992/en/.

Anderson, Benedict. "Long-Distance Nationalism." In *The Spectre of Comparisons: Nationalism, Southeast Asia, and the World*, edited by Benedict Anderson, 58–74. London: Verso, 1998.

Ansari, Mahmood. "Distress Migration and Individual Happiness in Bhutan." In *Development Challenges in Bhutan: Perspectives on Inequality and Gross National Happiness*, edited by J. D. Schmidt, 61–91. Cham: Springer International, 2017.

Arendt, Hannah. *The Origins of Totalitarianism.* New York: Harvest, 1979.

Aris, Michael. *Bhutan, the Early History of a Himalayan Kingdom.* Aris and Phillips Central Asian Studies. Warminster: Aris & Phillips, 1979.

Association of Human Rights Activists (AHURA). "Bhutan, a Shangri-La without Human Rights." Association of Human Rights Activists, Jhapa, Nepal, 2000.

Association of Human Rights Activists (AHURA). "Bhutanese Refugees: Victims of Forced Eviction. A Report on the Problem and Resistance Efforts." Association of Human Rights Activists, Jhapa, Nepal, 1999.

Balser, Deborah B. "The Impact of Environmental Factors on Factionalism and Schism in Social Movement Organizations." *Social Forces* 76, no. 1 (1997): 199–228.

Bandari, Bhakti Prasad. "Hostage in Thimphu." *Himal Southasian*, March 1, 2004.

Banki, Susan. "Bhutanese Refugee Cultural Complex: An Outsider-Insider Perspective." *Bhutan Journal* 2, no. 1 (2021): 73–83.

Banki, Susan. "Bhutanese Refugees in Nepal: Anticipating the Impact of Resettlement." Briefing paper. Austcare, Griffith University, Sydney, 2008.

Banki, Susan. "The Paradoxical Power of Precarity: Refugees and Homeland Activism." *Refugee Review* 1, no. 1 (2013): 1–19.

Banki, Susan. "Precarity of Place: A Complement to the Growing Precariat Literature." *Global Discourse* 3, no. 3–4 (2013): 450–63.

Banki, Susan. "Refugee Mobilization in the Nepal-India Borderlands: The Production of Porosity." *Journal of Refugee Studies* (2023): fead053. https://academic.oup.com /jrs/advance-article/doi/10.1093/jrs/fead053/7238803#413141748.

Banki, Susan. "Resettlement of the Bhutanese from Nepal: The Durable Solution Discourse." In *Protracted Displacement in Asia: No Place to Call Home*, edited by Howard Adelman, 27–56. London: Ashgate, 2008.

Banki, Susan. "Transnational Activism as Practised by Activists from Burma: Negotiating Precarity, Mobility and Resistance." In *Metamorphosis: Studies in Social and Political Change in Myanmar*, edited by Renaud Egreteau and François Robinne, 234–59. Singapore: NUS Press, 2015.

Banki, Susan. "Urbanity, Precarity, and Homeland Activism: Burmese Migrants in Global Cities." *Moussons* 22, no. 2 (2013): 35–56.

Banki, Susan, and I. P. Adhikari. "Contesting Memories in and of Bhutan: Diaspora Radio as a Mnemonic Challenge." In *Defending Memory*, edited by Dovile Budryte. London: Routledge, forthcoming.

Banki, Susan, Bhakta Ghimire, and Hari Khanal. "Displaced but Not Disempowered: Bhutanese Refugees and Grassroots Activism." *Fletcher Forum of World Affairs* 43, no. 2 (2019): 37–56.

Banki, Susan, and Ram Karki. "Bhutan's Democratic Growing Pains." *Current History* 123, no. 852 (2024).

Banki, Susan, and Hazel Lang. "Difficult to Remain: The Impact of Mass Resettlement." *Forced Migration Review* 30 (2008): 42–44.

Banki, Susan, and Hazel Lang. "Protracted Displacement on the Thai-Burmese Border: The Interrelated Search for Durable Solutions." In *Protracted Displacement in Asia: No Place to Call Home*, edited by Howard Adelman, 59–82. Abingdon: Ashgate, 2008.

Banki, Susan, and Nicole Phillips. "Leaving in Droves from the Orange Groves: The Nepali-Bhutanese Refugee Experience and the Diminishing of Dignity." In *Human Dignity: Establishing Worth and Seeking Solutions*, edited by Edward Sieh and Judy McGregor, 335–52. London: Palgrave Macmillan, 2017.

Banki, Susan, and Nicole Phillips. "'We Are the Victims of the Separation': A Report on Bhutanese Refugees Remaining in Nepal." 2014. https://ses.library.usyd.edu.au /bitstream/handle/2123/21075/Banki%20Phillips%20Victims%20of%20Separation%202014.pdf.

Banki, Susan, Elisabeth Valiente-Riedl, and Paul Duffill. "Teaching Human Rights at the Tertiary Level: Addressing the 'Knowing-Doing Gap' through a Role-Based Simulation Approach." *Journal of Human Rights Practice* 5, no. 2 (2013): 318–36.

Bauböck, Rainer, and Thomas Faist. *Diaspora and Transnationalism: Concepts, Theories and Methods*. Amsterdam: Amsterdam University Press, 2010.

BBC Monitoring Asia-Pacific. "Darjeeling Ghorkas Hold Strike for Release of Bhutan Marchers." *BBC Monitoring Asia-Pacific*, January 22, 1996.

BBC Monitoring Southasia. "Marchers Bound for Thimpu Arrested by Indian Police." *BBC Monitoring Southasia*, January 19, 1996.

BBC Monitoring Southeast Asia. "Bhutanese Refugees in Dispute over Repatriation Process." *BBC Monitoring Southeast Asia*, August 10, 2005.

BBC News. "Citizenship Amendment Bill: India's New 'Anti-Muslim' Law Explained." *BBC News*, December 11, 2019.

Bell, Charles A. "Report on Area in Bhutan West of the Ammo Chu. Confidential to the Chief Secretary to the Government of Bengal, Dated Gangtok, 21 July 1904." Oriental and India Office Collection L/P&S/12/2230, National Archives, London.

Bergen, Nicole. "Narrative Depictions of Working with Language Interpreters in Cross-Language Qualitative Research." *International Journal of Qualitative Methods* 17, no. 1 (2018): 1–11.

Betts, Alexander, and Will Jones. *Mobilising the Diaspora: How Refugees Challenge Authoritarianism.* Cambridge: Cambridge University Press, 2016.

Bhattarai, Hasta. "Question of Defeating Miserable Life." *Bhutan Reporter*, August 2008. http://thebhutanreporter.blogspot.com/2008/08/opinion.html.

Bhutanese Refugees Aiding the Victims of Violence (BRAVVE). "Report of Activities 1999." BRAVVE, Jhapa, Nepal, 2000.

Bhutanese Refugees Aiding the Victims of Violence (BRAVVE). "The Profile of Torture Victims in the Prisons of Bhutan." BRAVVE, Jhapa, Nepal, 2006.

Bhutanese Women and Youth Empowerment Program (BWYEP). "Bhutanese Women and Youth Empowerment Program Report." BWYEP, Birtamode, Nepal, no date.

Bhutan News Network. "Bhutan Human Rights Issues Raised with EU Officials." *Bhutan News Network*, July 20, 2019.

Bhutan News Network. "Campaign to Release Political Prisoners in Bhutan." *Bhutan News Network*, December 14, 2019.

Bhutan News Service. "15 Exiled Women Go on Fast-Unto-Death Demanding 'Refugee Status.'" *Bhutan News Service*, November 16, 2011.

Bhutan News Service. "Adhikari after Intricate Surgery Starts New Life." *Bhutan News Service*, October 31, 2009.

Bhutan News Service. "BAF Europe Lobbies for Solidarity." *Bhutan News Service*, January 28, 2010.

Bhutan News Service. "Bhutanese Begin Drive to Support Quake Devastated Nepal." *Bhutan News Service*, April 26, 2015.

Bhutan News Service. "Bhutanese Orgs Submits Memorandum to Massachusetts Governor." *Bhutan News Service*, October 18, 2018.

Bhutan News Service. "BNS Shifts Course." *Bhutan News Service*, January 12, 2020.

Bhutan News Service. "The Forgotten Story of 1950 Prison Escapee." *Bhutan News Service*, January 10, 2012.

Bhutan News Service. "Journalist Freed, Appeals UNHCR for Reunion with Family." *Bhutan News Service*, September 1, 2014.

Bhutan News Service. "Legendary Marriage of Mahasur Chhetri's Son." *Bhutan News Service*, January 10, 2011.

Bhutan News Service. "Moments of Transitioning History . . ." *Bhutan News Service*, August 12, 2012.

Bhutan News Service. "New Hampshire Senate Hearing on Bhutanese Issue." *Bhutan News Service*, May 8, 2015.

Bhutan News Service. "Rights Activist Whereabouts Remains Mystery." *Bhutan News Service*, November 29, 2014.

"Bhutan Refugee Repatriation Committee Says More Verification Teams Needed." *Kathmandu Post*, May 22, 2001.

Bhutan Watch. "Rights under Shadow." *Bhutan Watch*, April 29, 2019. http://www.bhutanwatch.org/rights-under-shadow/.

Bingham, Laura, and Natasha Arnpriester. "Unmaking Americans: Insecure Citizenship in the United States." Open Society Foundation, New York, September 2019. https://www.justiceinitiative.org/publications/unmaking-americans.

Biswas, A. K. "Paradox of Anti-Partition Agitation and Swadeshi Movement in Bengal (1905)." *Social Scientist* 23, no. 4/6 (1995): 38–57.

Bob, Clifford. *The Marketing of Rebellion: Insurgents, Media and International Activism.* Cambridge: Cambridge University Press, 2005.

Bose, Tapan Kumar. "Bhutan: Creating Statelessness—a Recipe for Regional Instability." In *Missing Boundaries: Refugees, Migrants, Stateless and Internally Displaced Persons in South Asia*, edited by P. R. Chari, Mallika Joseph, and Suba Chandran, 61–86. New Delhi: Manohar, 2003.

Bothe, Winnie. "The Monarch's Gift: Critical Notes on the Constitutional Process in Bhutan." *European Bulletin of Himalayan Research* 40 (2012): 27–58.

Brigden, Noelle Kateri. *The Migrant Passage: Clandestine Journeys from Central America.* Ithaca, NY: Cornell University Press, 2018.

Brinson, Charmian. *The Strange Case of Dora Fabian and Mathilde Wurm: A Study of German Political Exiles in London during the 1930's.* Berne: Peter Lang, 1996.

Brun, Catherine, and Nicholas Van Hear. "Between the Local and the Diasporic: The Shifting Centre of Gravity in War-Torn Sri Lanka's Transnational Politics." *Contemporary South Asia* 20, no. 1 (2012): 61–75.

Brun, Catherine, and Tariq Jazeel, eds. *Spatialising Politics: Culture and Geography in Postcolonial Sri Lanka.* New Delhi: SAGE, 2009.

Burrell, Amanda. "The Forgotten Refugees." BBC with WFP and UNHCR, RockhopperTV, September 2008.

Bush, Kenneth D. "Reading between the Lines: Intra-Group Heterogeneity and Conflict in Sri Lanka." *Refuge: Canada's Journal on Refugees* 13, no. 3 (1993): 15–22.

Central Intelligence Agency (CIA). "Bhutan." https://www.cia.gov/the-world-factbook /countries/bhutan/.

Centre for Housing Rights and Evictions (COHRE). *Forced Evictions: Violations of Human Rights.* Geneva: COHRE, 1998.

Chacko, Elizabeth, and Marie Price. "(Un)Settled Sojourners in Cities: The Scalar and Temporal Dimensions of Migrant Precarity." *Journal of Ethnic and Migration Studies* 47, no. 20 (2020): 4597–614.

Chandrasekharan, S. "Bhutan: Distribution of Maoist Document in Refugee Camps: Should Be Cause for Concern. Update 30." South Asia Analysis Group, 2003.

Chandrasekharan, S. "Bhutan: Update No. 11: Is UNHCR Going for a Pro Active Role?" South Asia Analysis Group, 2000.

Chaudhary, Ali R., and Dana M. Moss. "Suppressing Transnationalism: Bringing Constraints into the Study of Transnational Political Action." *Comparative Migration Studies* 7, no. 1 (2019): 1–9.

Chhetri, Hari K. *Reminiscence: Petition and Politics.* Kathmandu: Sabi HADA, 2013.

Chhetri, R. B. "Signature Campaign to Release Political Prisoners in Bhutan." Petitions .net. https://www.petitions.net/stats.php?id=244951&s=65979626.

Chowdhury, Roy. *Sunandan: Politics, Policy and Higher Education in India.* Singapore: Springer Singapore, 2017.

Christensen, Line Kikkenborg. "Driglam Namzha and Silenced Ethnicity in Bhutan's Monarchical Democracy." *Social Identities* 27, no. 6 (2021): 644–59.

Christensen, Line Kikkenborg. "Freedom of Speech and Silent Youth Protest in Bhutan: 'Plz Delete It from Your Inbox.'" *South Asia Research* 37, no. 1 (2017): 93–108.

Christensen, Line Kikkenborg. "Piecing together Past and Present in Bhutan: Narration, Silence and Forgetting in Conflict." *International Journal of Conflict and Violence* 12 (2018): 1–11.

Coutin, Susan Bibler. "Illegality, Borderlands, and the Space of Nonexistence." In *Globalization under Construction: Governmentality, Law, and Identity*, edited by Richard Warren Perry and Bill Maurer, 171–202. Minneapolis: University of Minnesota Press, 2003.

Cunningham, Kathleen Gallagher. *Inside the Politics of Self-Determination*. Oxford: Oxford University Press, 2014.

Curato, Nicole, and Diego Fossati. "Authoritarian Innovations: Crafting Support for a Less Democratic Southeast Asia." *Democratization* 27, no. 6 (2020): 1006–20.

Curtis, Bruce. *The Politics of Population: State Formation, Statistics, and the Census of Canada, 1840–1875*. Toronto: University of Toronto Press, 2001.

Das, Veena. *Critical Events: An Anthropological Perspective on Contemporary India*. New Delhi: Oxford University Press, 1996.

Davis, Jeffrey. *Justice across Borders: The Struggle for Human Rights in US Courts*. Cambridge: Cambridge University Press, 2008.

DeGooyer, Stephanie. "Democracy, Give or Take?" *Humanity: An International Journal of Human Rights, Humanitarianism, and Development* 5, no. 1 (2014): 93–110.

Dhakal, D. N. S., and Christopher Strawn. *Bhutan: A Movement in Exile*. Jaipur: Nirala, 1994.

Dhungana, Shiva K. "Third Country Resettlement and the Bhutanese Refugee Crisis: A Critical Reflection." *Refugee Watch* 35 (2010): 14–36.

Dixit, Himali. "Repatriation or Resettlement: Resolving the Lhotshampa Dilemma." *Himal Southasian*, June 2007.

Dixit, Kanak Mani. "The Dragon Bites Its Tail." *Himal Southasian*, July–August 1992. https://www.himalmag.com/politics/the-dragon-bites-its-tail-part-i-bhutan-nepal-lhotshampa-kanak-dixit-1992.

Donà, Giorgia, Cigdem Esin, and Aura Lounasmaa. "Qualitative Research in Refugee Studies." In *Research Methods Foundations*, edited by Paul Atkinson, Sara Delamont, Alexandru Cernat, Joseph W. Sakshaug and Richard A. Williams. London: Sage, 2019.

Dorji, Kinley. "Bhutan's Current Crisis: A View from Thimphu." In *Bhutan: Perspectives on Conflict and Dissent*, edited by Michael Hutt, 77–96. Gartmore: Kiscadale, 1994.

Duff, Andrew. *Sikkim: Requiem for a Himalayan Kingdom*. Edinburgh: Birlinn, 2015.

Eberle, Meghan L., and Ian Holliday. "Precarity and Political Immobilisation: Migrants from Burma in Chiang Mai, Thailand." *Journal of Contemporary Asia* 41, no. 3 (2011): 371–92.

Economist Intelligence Unit. "Country Report: Bhutan." *The Economist*. Accessed June 16, 2023, https://country.eiu.com/bhutan.

Embassy of India. "India–Bhutan Trade Relation." https://www.indembthimphu.gov.in/pages/MzI.

Esposito, Roberto. *Communitas: The Origin and Destiny of Community Cultural Memory in the Present*. Stanford, CA: Stanford University Press, 2010.

Esposito, Roberto. "Immunization and Violence." In *Terms of the Political: Community, Immunity, Biopolitics*, edited by Rhiannon Noel Welch and Timothy Campbell, 59–60. New York: Commonalities, 2013.

Evans, Rosalind. "The Perils of Being a Borderland People: On the Lhotshampas of Bhutan." *Contemporary South Asia* 18, no. 1 (2010): 25–42.

Faist, Thomas. "Toward a Transnational Methodology: Methods to Address Methodological Nationalism, Essentialism, and Positionality." *Revue Européenne des Migrations Internationales* 28, no. 1 (2012): 51–70.

Fiddian-Qasmiyeh, Elena. "*Repress*entations of Displacement from the Middle East and North Africa." *Public Culture* 28, no. 3 (2016): 457–73.

FitzGerald, David Scott. *Refuge beyond Reach: How Rich Democracies Repel Asylum Seekers.* Oxford: Oxford University Press, 2019.

Freedom House. "Freedom in the World, 2019: Bhutan." Freedom House, Washington, DC, 2020. https://freedomhouse.org/country/bhutan/freedom-world/2019.

Gazmere, Ratan, and Dilip Bishwo. "Bhutanese Refugees: Rights to Nationality, Return and Property." *Forced Migration Review* 7 (2000): 20–22.

Gellner, David N. *Borderland Lives in Northern South Asia.* Durham, NC: Duke University Press, 2013.

Gellner, David N. "Introduction: The Nepali/Gorkhali Diaspora since the Nineteenth Century." In *Global Nepalis: Religion, Culture, and Community in a New and Old Diaspora*, edited by David N. Gellner and Sondra L. Hausner, 1–26. Oxford: Oxford University Press, 2018.

Giri, N. B. *Justice to Justice: Bhutan.* Kathmandu: Rosy Giri, Success Foundation, 2014.

Goldring, Luin, Carolina Berinstein, and Judith K. Bernhard. "Institutionalizing Precarious Migratory Status in Canada." *Citizenship Studies* 13, no. 3 (2009): 239–65.

Goldring, Luin, and Patricia Landolt. "Caught in the Work-Citizenship Matrix: The Lasting Effects of Precarious Legal Status on Work for Toronto Immigrants." *Globalizations* 8, no. 3 (2011): 325–41.

Guarnizo, Luis Eduardo, Ali Chaudhary, and Ninna Nyberg Sørensen. "Migrants' Transnational Political Engagement in Spain and Italy." *Migration Studies* 7, no. 3 (2017): 281–322.

Guarnizo, Luis Eduardo, Alejandro Portes, and William Haller. "Assimilation and Transnationalism: Determinants of Transnational Political Action among Contemporary Migrants." *American Journal of Sociology* 108, no. 6 (2003): 1211–48.

Gupta, Ranjan. "Sikkim: The Merger with India." *Asian Survey* 15, no. 9 (1975): 786–98.

Guruacharya, Binaya. "Refugees Begin March to Demand Right to Live in Bhutan." *Associated Press*, January 14, 1996.

Gurung, B. D. "Political Problems of Bhutan." *United Asia* 12, no. 4 (1960): 368–69.

Harrell-Bond, Barbara. *Imposing Aid: Emergency Assistance to Refugees.* Oxford: Oxford University Press, 1986.

Hausner, Sondra, and Jeevan R. Sharma. "On the Way to India: Nepali Rituals of Border Crossing." In *Borderland Lives in Northern South Asia*, edited by David N. Gellner, 94–116. Durham, NC: Duke University Press, 2014.

"HM Grants Citizenship to 359 People." *Kuensel*, March 14, 2019.

Huang, Haifeng, Serra Boranbay-Akan, and Ling Huang. "Media, Protest Diffusion, and Authoritarian Resilience." *Political Science Research and Methods* 7, no. 1 (2019): 23–42.

Human Rights Council of Bhutan (HRCB). "Bhutan: Political Crisis and Bhutanese Refugees." Report, HRCB, Kathmandu, 2003.

Human Rights Organization of Bhutan (HUROB). "73rd Session of the National Assembly." *Bhutan Review* 2, no. 10 (1994): 1–4.

Human Rights Organization of Bhutan (HUROB). "Druk National Congress Launched: Profile." *Bhutan Review* 2, no. 7 (1994): 1–4.

Human Rights Organization of Bhutan (HUROB). "The Enemy Within." *Bhutan Review* 3, no. 6 (1995): 1–4.

Human Rights Organization of Bhutan (HUROB). "Goodbye Dr. Shaw." *Bhutan Review* 1, no. 3 (1993): 1–4.

Human Rights Organization of Bhutan (HUROB). "Media Scan." *Bhutan Review* 1, no. 1 (1993):1–4.

Human Rights Organization of Bhutan (HUROB). "Photos Tell a Tale of Woe." *Bhutan Review* 1, no. 11/12 (1993): 1–8.

Human Rights Organization of Bhutan (HUROB). "A Time for Change." *Bhutan Review* 2, no. 10 (1994): 1–4.

Human Rights Organization of Bhutan (HUROB). "The Third Man." *Bhutan Review*, 1, no. 9 (1993): 1–4.

Human Rights Watch (HRW). "Bhutan: Free Long-Term Political Prisoners." March 13, 2003. https://www.hrw.org/news/2023/03/13/bhutan-free-long-term-political-prisoners.

Human Rights Watch (HRW). "Last Hope: The Need for Durable Solutions for Bhutanese Refugees in Nepal and India." Human Rights Watch, New York, May 16, 2007. https://www.hrw.org/report/2007/05/16/last-hope/need-durable-solutions-bhutanese-refugees-nepal-and-india.

Human Rights Watch (HRW). "Nepal: Bhutanese Refugee Tensions Erupt into Violence." Human Rights Watch, New York, May 31, 2007. https://www.hrw.org/news/2007/05/31/nepal-bhutanese-refugee-tensions-erupt-violence.

Human Rights Watch (HRW). "'We Don't Want to Be Refugees Again': A Human Rights Watch Briefing Paper for the Fourteenth Ministerial Joint Committee of Bhutan and Nepal." Human Rights Watch, New York, May 19, 2003. https://www.hrw.org/sites/default/files/media_2021/08/202108asia_bhutan_refugees.pdf.

Hutt, Michael, ed. *Bhutan: Perspectives on Conflict and Dissent.* Gartmore: Kiscadale, 1994.

Hutt, Michael. "The Bhutanese Refugees: Between Verification, Repatriation, and Royal Realpolitik." *Peace and Democracy in South Asia* 1, no. 1 (2005): 44–56.

Hutt, Michael. "Bhutan in 1996: Continuing Stress." *Asian Survey* 37, no. 2 (1997): 155–59.

Hutt, Michael. "Ethnic Nationalism, Refugees and Bhutan." *Journal of Refugee Studies* 9, no. 4 (1996): 397–420.

Hutt, Michael. "Introduction." In *Bhutan: Perspectives on Conflict and Dissent*, edited by Michael Hutt, 5–20. Gartmore: Kiscadale, 1994.

Hutt, Michael. "Sociocultural and Political Change in Bhutan since the 1980s: Reflections from a Distance." In *Development Challenges in Bhutan: Perspectives on Inequality and Gross National Happiness*, edited by Johannes Dragsbaek Schmidt, 19–27. Cham: Springer, 2017.

Hutt, Michael. *Unbecoming Citizens: Culture, Nationhood, and the Flight of Refugees from Bhutan.* Oxford: Oxford University Press, 2003.

Hutt, Michael, and Gregory Sharkey. "'Nepalese in Origin but Bhutanese First': A Conversation with Bhim Subba and Om Dhungel (Human Rights Organization of Bhutan)." *European Bulletin of Himalayan Research* 9, no. 4 (1995): 32–42.

Hyndman, Jennifer. *Managing Displacement: Refugees and the Politics of Humanitarianism.* Minneapolis: University of Minnesota Press, 2000.

Ilcan, Suzan. "Fleeing Syria: Border Crossing and Struggles for Migrant Justice." In *Mobilities, Mobility Justice, and Social Justice*, edited by Nancy Cook and David Butz, 54–66. London: Routledge, 2018.

Ilcan, Suzan, Kim Rygiel, and Feyzi Baban. "The Ambiguous Architecture of Precarity: Temporary Protection, Everyday Living, and Migrant Journeys of Syrian Refugees." *International Journal of Migration and Borders* 4, no. 1/2 (2018): 51–70.

Japan Economic Newswire. "India Arrests Bhutanese Peace Marchers." *Japan Economic Newswire*, January 18, 1996.

Jelin, Elizabeth. *State Repression and the Labors of Memory*. Translated by Marcial Godoy-Anativia and Judy Rein. Minneapolis: University of Minnesota Press, 2003.

Jit Hasrat, Bikrama. *History of Bhutan: Land of the Peaceful Dragon*. Bhutan: Education Department, 1980.

John, Aruni. "Potential for Militancy among Bhutanese Refugee Youth." RCSS Policy Studies 15. Regional Center for Strategic Studies, Colombo, Sri Lanka, 2000.

Johnson, Heather. "Moments of Solidarity, Migrant Activism and (Non) Citizens at Global Borders." In *Citizenship, Migrant Activism and the Politics of Movement*, edited by Peter Nyers and Kim Rygiel, 109–28. New York: Routledge, 2012.

Jones, Martin. "Protecting Human Rights Defenders at Risk: Asylum and Temporary International Relocation." *International Journal of Human Rights* 19, no. 7 (2015): 935–60.

Karan, Pradyumna P., and William M. Jenkins. *The Himalayan Kingdoms: Bhutan, Sikkim, and Nepal*. Princeton, NJ: D. Van Nostrand, 1963.

Keane, John. *The New Despotism*. Cambridge, MA: Harvard University Press, 2020.

Keck, Margaret, and Kathryn Sikkink. *Activists beyond Borders: Advocacy Networks in International Politics*. Ithaca, NY: Cornell University Press, 1998.

Khan, Gerrard. "Citizenship and Statelessness in South Asia." Working paper no. 47. UNHCR, Geneva, 2001.

Kharat, Rajesh S. "Indo-Bhutan Relations: Strategic Perspectives." In *Himalayan Frontiers of India: Historical, Geo-Political and Strategic Perspectives*, edited by K. Warikoo, 137–66. Abingdon: Routledge, 2009.

Khoury, Rana B. "Aiding Activism? Humanitarianism's Impacts on Mobilized Syrian Refugees in Jordan." *Middle East Law and Governance* 9, no. 3 (2017): 267–81.

Kibreab, Gaim. "Myth of Dependency among Camp Refugees in Somalia, 1979–1989." *Journal of Refugee Studies* 6, no. 4 (1993): 321–49.

Kinga, Sonam. *Democratic Transition in Bhutan: Political Contests as Moral Battles*. London: Routledge, 2020.

Knaefler, Tomi Kaizawa. *Our House Divided: Seven Japanese American Families in World War II*. Honolulu: University of Hawai'i Press, 1991.

Koinova, Maria. "Beyond Statist Paradigms: Sociospatial Positionality and Diaspora Mobilization in International Relations." *International Studies Review* 19, no. 4 (2017): 597–621.

Koinova, Maria. "Can Conflict-Generated Diasporas Be Moderate Actors during Episodes of Contested Sovereignty? Lebanese and Albanian Diasporas Compared." *Review of International Studies* 37, no. 1 (2011): 437–62.

Koinova, Maria. "Critical Junctures and Transformative Events in Diaspora Mobilisation for Kosovo and Palestinian Statehood." *Journal of Ethnic and Migration Studies* 44, no. 8 (2018): 1289–308.

Koinova, Maria. *Diaspora Entrepreneurs and Contested States*. Oxford: Oxford University Press, 2021.

Koinova, Maria. "Diasporas and Secessionist Conflicts: The Mobilization of the Armenian, Albanian and Chechen Diasporas." *Ethnic and Racial Studies* 34, no. 2 (2011): 333–56.

Koinova, Maria. "Sending States and Diaspora Positionality in International Relations." *International Political Sociology* 12, no. 2 (2018): 190–210.

Krishna, Sankaran. "Cartographic Anxiety: Mapping the Body Politic in India." *Alternatives: Global, Local, Political* 19, no. 4 (1994): 507–21.

Laird, Thomas. "Going Nowhere." *Asia Week*, November 30, 2000.

Lecadet, Clara. "Refugee Politics: Self-Organized 'Government' and Protests in the Agamé Refugee Camp (2005–13)." *Journal of Refugee Studies* 29, no. 2 (2016): 187–207.

Lee, Tang Lay. "Refugees from Bhutan: Nationality, Statelessness, and the Right to Return." *International Journal of Refugee Law* 10, no. 1/2 (1998): 118–55.

Lefebvre, Henri. *The Production of Space*. Translated by Donald Nicholson-Smith. Oxford: Blackwell, 1991.

Levitsky, Steven, and Lucan A. Way. *Competitive Authoritarianism: Hybrid Regimes after the Cold War*. Cambridge: Cambridge University Press, 2010.

Lewis, Hannah, Peter Dwyer, Stuart Hodkinson, and Louise Waite. *Precarious Lives: Forced Labour, Exploitation and Asylum*. Bristol: Policy Press, 2015.

Ley, David. "Transnational Spaces and Everyday Lives." *Transactions of the Institute of British Geographers* 29 (2004): 151–64.

Lhendup, Kesang. "Statement from His Party." *APFA News*, October 20, 2011.

Lok Raj Baral. *Regional Migrations, Ethnicity and Security: The South Asian Case*. New Delhi: Sterling, 1990.

Luchner, Carmen Delgado, and Leïla Kherbiche. "Without Fear or Favour? The Positionality of ICRC and UNHCR Interpreters in the Humanitarian Field." *Target: International Journal of Translation Studies* 30, no. 3 (2018): 408–29.

Lutheran World Federation Nepal. "Annual Report 2004." 1–44. Kathmandu, Nepal: Lutheran World Federation-Nepal, 2004.

Lyons, Terrence, and Peter G. Mandaville, eds. *Politics from Afar: Transnational Diasporas and Networks*. London: Hurst, 2012.

Mahat, R. S. *In Defense of Democracy: Dynamics and Fault Lines of Nepal's Political Economy*. New Delhi: Adroit, 2005.

Mälksoo, Maria. "'Memory Must Be Defended': Beyond the Politics of Mnemonical Security." *Security Dialogue* 46, no. 3 (2015): 221–37.

Massey, Doreen. *Space, Place and Gender*. Minneapolis: University of Minnesota Press, 1994.

Mathew, Joseph C. "Bhutan: 'Democracy' from Above." *Economic and Political Weekly* 43, no. 19 (2008): 29–31.

Mathou, Thierry. "Bhutan in 2017: Preparing a New Cycle." *Asian Survey* 58, no. 1 (2018): 138–41.

McNevin, Anne. *Contesting Citizenship: Irregular Migrants and New Frontiers of the Political*. New York: Columbia University Press, 2011.

Mills, C. Wright. *The Power Elite*. Oxford: Oxford University Press, 1956.

Milshtein, Michael. "Memory 'from Below': Palestinian Society and the Nakba Memory." In *Palestinian Collective Memory and National Identity*, edited by Meir Litvak, 71–96. New York: Palgrave Macmillan, 2009.

Minorities at Risk Project. "Chronology for Lhotshampas in Bhutan." Refworld, 2004. https://www.refworld.org/docid/469f386a1e.html.

Mishra, Dhruva. "The Tale of Political Discrimination." *Bhutan News Service*, March 27, 2011.

Mishra, Vidhyapati. "Open Letter to Nepali Prime Minister Jhala Nath Khanal." *APFA News*, February 25, 2011.

Muni, S. D. "Bhutan's Deferential Democracy." *Journal of Democracy* 25, no. 2 (2014): 158–63.

Myers, Steven Lee. "Squeezed by an India-China Standoff, Bhutan Holds Its Breath." *New York Times*, August 15, 2017.

Napoli, Lisa. *Radio Shangri-La: What I Discovered on My Accidental Journey to the Happiest Kingdom on Earth*. New York: Crown, 2011.

National Assembly of Bhutan (NAB). "Proceedings and Resolutions of the 69th Session of the National Assembly of Bhutan." National Assembly of Bhutan, 1990.

National Assemby of Bhutan (NAB). 68th Session. October 23, 1989–October 31, 1989. National Assembly of Bhutan, 1989.

National Assembly of Bhutan (NAB). "Translation of the Proceedings and Resolutions of the 76th Session of the National Assembly of Bhutan Held from the Fifth Day of the Fifth Month to the Seventh Day of the Sixth Month of the Male Earth Tiger Year (June 29–July 30, 1998). " NAB, 2014.

National Statistics Bureau of Bhutan. "2017 Population and Housing Census of Bhutan." Edited by Kuenga Wangmo. Thimphu, Bhutan: National Statistics Bureau, Royal Government of Bhutan, 2018. https://www.nsb.gov.bt/wp-content/uploads/dlm _uploads/2020/07/PHCB2017_wp.pdf.

Nehru, Jawaharlal. Selected Works of Jawaharlal Nehru. Series 2, vol. 25. Edited by Ravinder Kumar and H. Y. Sharada Prasad. New Delhi: Jawaharlal Nehru Memorial Fund, 1992.

Neikirk, Alice. The Elephant Has Two Sets of Teeth: Bhutanese Refugees and Humanitarian Governance. Edmonton: University of Alberta, 2023.

Nelson, Andrew, and Kathryn Stam. "Bhutanese or Nepali? The Politics of Ethnonym Ambiguity." South Asia: Journal of South Asian Studies 44, no. 4 (2021): 772–89.

Odugbesan, Abimbola, and Helge Schwiertz. ""We Are Here to Stay": Refugee Struggles in Germany between Unity and Division." In Protest Movements in Asylum and Deportation, edited by Sieglinde Rosenberger, Verena Stern, and Nina Merhaut, 185–203. Cham: Springer, 2018.

Oliviero, Helena. "Bhutanese Brothers Overcome Adversity." Atlanta Journal-Constitution, December 30, 2013.

Orchard, Phil. The Right to Flee. Cambridge: Cambridge University Press, 2014.

Parmanand, Parashar. The Politics of Bhutan: Retrospect and Prospect. New Delhi: Pragati, 1998.

Peil, Michael. "Semi-Colonialism and International Legal History: The View from Bhutan." Völkerrechtsblog 28 (2019). https://voelkerrechtsblog.org/de/semi-colonialism -and-international-legal-history-the-view-from-bhutan/.

Penjore, Thinley. The Quest for Democracy: Against All Odds. Bhutan: A. K. Books and Educational Enterprises, 2010.

Phoutrides, Elena. "'Like a Parrot Screaming in Its Cage': Activism and Empowerment in Nepal's Bhutanese Refugee Community." Independent Study Project (ISP) Collection, 311, 2006. https://digitalcollections.sit.edu/isp_collection/311.

Pillai, Sangeetha. "The Latest Citizenship-Stripping Plan Risks Statelessness, Indefinite Detention and Constitutional Challenge." The Conversation, November 24, 2018.

Portes, Alejandro, Eduardo Guarnizo, and Patricia Landolt. "Commentary on the Study of Transnationalism: Pitfalls and Promise of an Emergent Research Field." Ethnic and Racial Studies 40, no. 9 (2017): 1486–91.

Pradhan, Lyonpo Om. Bhutan: The Roar of the Thunder Dragon. Thimphu: K Media, 2012.

Quigley, John. "Bhutanese Refugees in Nepal: What Role Now for the European Union and the United Nations High Commission for Refugees?" Contemporary South Asia 13, no. 2 (2004): 187–200.

Quinsaat, Sharon Madriaga. "Diaspora Activism in a Non-Traditional Country of Destination: The Case of Filipinos in the Netherlands." Ethnic and Racial Studies 39, no. 6 (2016): 1014–33.

Quinsaat, Sharon Madriaga. "Migrant Mobilization for Homeland Politics: A Social Movement Approach." Sociology Compass 7, no. 11 (2013): 952–64.

Quinsaat, Sharon Madriaga. "Transnational Contention, Domestic Integration: Assimilating into the Hostland Polity through Homeland Activism." *Journal of Ethnic and Migration Studies* 45, no. 3 (2019): 419–36.

Rai, Bhampa. *Bhutan and Its Agonised People.* Damak, Jhapa: Sumnima Offset Press, 2013.

Ramadan, Adam. "Spatialising the Refugee Camp." *Transactions of the Institute of British Geographers* 38, no. 1 (2013): 65–77.

Regmi, Bikash. "What Citizenship Means without a Country." TEDx Talks, May 25, 2017. YouTube video, 12:03. https://www.youtube.com/watch?v=6w5pOi0uJUI.

Rennie, David Field. *Bhotan and the Story of the Doar War.* New Delhi: Manjusri, 1970.

Riaño, Yvonne. "Conceptulising Space in Transnational Migration Studies: A Critical Perspective." In *Border Transgression: Mobility and Mobilization in Crisis*, edited by Eva Youkhana, 35–48. Bonn: Bonn University Press, 2017.

Rizal, Dhurba. *The Royal Semi-Authoritarian Democracy of Bhutan.* Lanham, MD: Lexington, 2015.

Rizal, Dhurba. "The Unknown Refugee Crisis: Expulsion of the Ethnic Lhotsampa from Bhutan." *Asian Ethnicity* 5, no. 2 (2004): 151–77.

Rizal, Govinda. *A Pardesi in Paradise.* Kathmandu: Discourse, 2018.

Rizal, Tek Nath. *Ethnic Cleansing and Political Repression in Bhutan: The Other Side of the Shangri-La.* Kathmandu: Human Rights Council of Bhutan, 2004.

Rizal, Tek Nath. *From Palace to Prison.* Kalikasthan, Kathmandu: Oxford International, 2009.

Robertson, Shanthi. "The Temporalities of International Migration: Implications for Ethnographic Research." In *Social Transformation and Migration: National and Local Experiences in South Korea, Turkey, Mexico and Australia*, edited by Stephen Castles, Derya Ozkul, and Magdalena Arias Cubas, 45–60. Basingstoke: Palgrave Macmillan, 2015.

Rodgers, Graeme. "'Hanging out' with Forced Migrants: Methodological and Ethical Challenges." *Forced Migration Review* 21 (2004).

Roripaugh, Lee Ann. *Year of the Snake.* Carbondale: Southern Illinois University Press, 2004.

Rose, Leo E. *The Politics of Bhutan.* Ithaca, NY: Cornell University Press, 1977.

Sable, Julia. "Reconciling Culture, Security and Development in Bhutan." Masters thesis, Tufts University, 2005.

Sadiq, Kamal. *Paper Citizens: How Illegal Immigrants Acquire Citizenship in Developing Countries.* Oxford: Oxford University Press, 2008.

Salehyan, Idean. *Rebels without Borders: Transnational Insurgencies in World Politics.* Ithaca, NY: Cornell University Press, 2009.

Saul, Ben. "Cultural Nationalism, Self-Determination and Human Rights in Bhutan." *International Journal of Refugee Law* 12, no. 3 (2000): 321–53.

Sinha, Awadhesh Coomar. *Bhutan: Ethnic Identity and National Dilemma.* New Delhi: Reliance, 1991.

Sinha, Awadhesh Coomar. *Dawn of Democracy in the Eastern Himalayan Kingdoms: The 20th Century.* London: Routledge India, 2018. Kindle.

Sinha, Awadhesh Coomar. *Himalayan Kingdom Bhutan: Tradition, Transition, and Transformation.* New Delhi: Indus, 2001.

Soja, Edward. *Seeking Spatial Justice.* Minneapolis: University of Minnesota Press, 2010.

Sökefeld, Martin. "Mobilizing in Transnational Space: A Social Movement Approach to the Formation of Diaspora." *Global Networks* 6, no. 3 (2006): 265–84.

Sonnenberg, Stephan. "Formalizing the Informal: Development and Its Impacts on Traditional Dispute Resolution in Bhutan." *Washington University Journal of Law and Policy* 63 (2020): 143–206.

Standing, Guy. *The Precariat: The New Dangerous Class*. London: Bloomsbury Academic, 2011.

Subba, R. P. "BNS Should Be Saved." *Bhutan News Service*, January 14, 2020.

Taylor, Amy Murrell. *The Divided Family in Civil War America*. Chapel Hill: University of North Carolina Press, 2009.

Thinley, Jigmi Y. "Bhutan: A Kingdom Besieged." In *Bhutan: Perspectives on Conflict*, edited by Michael Hutt, 43–76. Gartmore: Kiscadale, 1994.

Thrift, Nigel. "Space: The Fundamental Stuff of Geography." In *Key Concepts in Geography*, edited by Sarah L. Holloway, Stephen P. Rice, and Gill Valentine, 95–107. London: Sage, 2003.

Turner, Mark, Sonam Chuki, and Jit Tshering. "Democratization by Decree: The Case of Bhutan." *Democratization* 18, no. 1 (2011): 184–210.

Turner, Mark, and Jit Tshering. "Is Democracy Being Consolidated in Bhutan?" *Asian Politics and Policy* 6, no. 3 (2014): 413–31.

"UFD Not Supporting ULFA in Bhutan." *Hindustan Times*, November 22, 1997.

United Nations High Commissioner for Refugees (UNHCR). "2008 Global Trends: Refugees, Asylum-Seekers, Returnees, Internally Displaced and Stateless Persons." UNHCR, Geneva, 2009. https://www.unhcr.org/us/media/2008-global-trends-refugees-asylum-seekers-returnees-internally-displaced-and-stateless.

United Nations High Commissioner for Refugees (UNHCR). "Resettlement Data Finder." https://rsq.unhcr.org/en/#bE8r.

United Nations Human Rights Council. "Opinions Adopted by the Working Group on Arbitrary Detention at Its Seventy-Eighth Session, 19–28 April 2017." A/HRC/WGAD/2017/29. Human Rights Council, Geneva, 2017.

US Committee for Refugees and Immigrants (USCRI). *World Refugee Survey 2007*. Edited by Merrill Smith. Washington, DC: US Committee for Refugees and Immigrants (USCRI), 2008.

US Committee for Refugees and Immigrants (USCRI). *World Refugee Survey 2009: Nepal*. Washington, DC: US Commitee for Refugees and Immigrants (USCRI), 2009. https://www.refworld.org/docid/4a40d2aec.html.

US State Department. "Country Reports on Human Rights Practices for 2018." United States Department of State, Bureau of Democracy, Human Rights and Labor, Washington, DC, 2018.

Van Hear, Nicholas. "Reconsidering Migration and Class." *International Migration Review* 48, no. 1 supplement (2014): 100–21.

Van Hear, Nicholas, and Robin Cohen. "Diasporas and Conflict: Distance, Contiguity and Spheres of Engagement." *Oxford Development Studies* 45, no. 2 (2017): 171–84.

Van Schendel, Willem. "Making the Most of 'Sensitive' Borders." In *Borderland Lives in Northern South Asia*, edited by David N. Gellner, 266–71. Durham, NC: Duke University Press, 2013.

Vasta, Ellie. "Immigrants and the Paper Market: Borrowing, Renting and Buying Identities." *Ethnic and Racial Studies* 34, no. 2 (2011): 187–206.

Verdirame, Guglielmo, and Barbara E. Harrell-Bond. *Rights in Exile: Janus-Faced Humanitarianism*. New York: Berghahn, 2005.

Virilio, Paul. *Polar Inertia*. London: SAGE, 2000.

Wahlbeck, Osten. "The Concept of Diaspora as an Analytical Tool in the Study of Refugee Communities." *Journal of Ethnic and Migration Studies* 28, no. 2 (2002): 221–39.

Waite, Louise. "A Place and Space for a Critical Geography of Precarity?" *Geography Compass* 3, no. 1 (2009): 412–33.

Whitecross, Richard W. "Intimacy, Loyalty and State Formation: The Spectre of the 'Anti-National.'" In *Traitors: Suspicion, Intimacy and the Ethics of State-Building*, edited by Sharika Thiranagama and Tobias Kelly, 68–88. Philadelphia: University of Pennsylvia Press, 2009.

Whitecross, Richard W. "Law, 'Tradition' and Legitimacy: Contesting Driglam Namzha." In *Development Challenges in Bhutan: Perspectives on Inequality and Gross National Happiness*, edited by Johannes Dragsbaek Schmidt, 1–16. Cham: Springer, 2017.

Williamson, Brett. "After 17 Years in a Refugee Camp, Sushil Finally Has a Place to Call Home." *ABC Adelaide*, June 14, 2013.

Wilson, Thomas M., and Hastings Donnan, eds. *Border Identities: Nation and State at International Frontiers*. Cambridge: Cambridge University Press, 1998.

Wright, Sue. *Community and Communication: The Role of Language in Nation State Building and European Integration*. Bristol: Multilingual Matters, 2000.

"Yearning to Be Free." *Nepali Times*, August 7, 2009.

Zagajewski, Adam. *Without End: New and Selected Poems*. New York: Farrar, Straus & Giroux, 2002.

Zeppa, Jamie. *Beyond the Sky and the Earth: A Journey into Bhutan*. New York: Riverhead, 1999. Kindle.

Index

Note: Pages in *italics* refer to illustrative matter.

Acharya, Lok Nath, 106
Acharya, Shantiram, 105
activism. *See* homeland activism; student activism; transnational activism
Adhikari, Indra Prasad (I. P. Adhikari), 81–82, 106, 109
Adhikari, Narad, 79
Adhikari, Pashupati, 25–26
Advani, Lal Krishna, 78
AHURA (Association of Human Rights Activists), 1, 61–62, 68–69, 83, 88
AMCC (Appeal Movement Coordinating Council), 63–65
Amnesty International, 45, 55, 104, 135n85
anti-nationals (ngolops), 34, 47–49, 71–72

Banaras Hindu University, 30, 78
Bastola, Chakra Prasad, 66
Beldangi Camp, *xiv*, 69, 102–3, 106
Bhandari, Bhakti (Prasad), 45, 135n77, 135n85
Bhandari, Bidyapati, 42
Bhattarai, Hasta, 96
Bhutan: Bhutanization policies, 38–41, 44–45, 133n31; demographics of, 19–24, 101, 130n42; human rights violations and, 15, 47, 55, 57, 59–60; maps of, *xi–xii*; political dissent in, 24–28, 130n46; political history of, 4, 17–20, 31; regional politics of, 35–38, 65. *See also* southern Bhutan
Bhutan News Service, 13, 26, 102, 105, 109, 113, 146n113
Bhutan Reporter, 96
Bhutan Review, 61
Bhutan Revolutionary Free Students' Force, 88
Bhutan Watch, 103
Bhutan: We Want Justice (Gazmere), 44–45
"Bhutan: Where Are Our Human Rights?" (pamphlet), 45
Bhutanese Nepalis: Bhutanization policies and, 38–41, 44–45, 133n31; demographics of, 20–24, 129n22; exodus of, 1–2, 34, 42, 49,

130n42; representation in government, 26, 34, 50–52, 58; resettlement map, *xv*; residence in India and Nepal, 75–76; student activism of, 30, 43–49, 77–78
Bhutanese Refugee Cultural Complex, 110–12
Bhutanese Woman and Youth Empowerment Program (BWYEP), 81
Bhutanization, 38–41, 44–45, 133n31
BNDP (Bhutan National Democratic Party), 56–57, 65, 79, 85–86
BPP (Bhutan People's Party), 14, 47–49, 56–57, 85–86, 103
BRAVVE (Bhutanese Refugees Aiding the Victims of Violence), 60–61, 81
BRRRC (Bhutanese Refugee Representative Repatriation Committee), 53–54, 63, 67–68, 103
BSC (Bhutan State Congress), 26–32, 34–35, 44–46, 99
Budathoki, R. K., 88
Buddhism, 17–18, 55, 58, 102

census (1988), 20, 40–43, 69, 101
Centre for Housing Rights and Evictions (COHRE), 61–62
Chhetri, Bishwanath, 44, 46, 49, 135n85
Chhetri, Hari, 42–43
Chhetri, Man Bahadur, 45–47, 59
Chhetri, Masur, 25–26, 60, 109, 111
Chhetri, Ranjit, 110
China–Bhutan relations, 36, 80, 85
citizenship: Bhutan State Congress and, 29, 31; census (1988) and, 20–23, 40, 42, 69; despotism and, 119–20; documentation and, 52–53; ecosystem of exile politics and, 101–2; homeland activism and, 114; Marriage Act (1980) and, 39; precarity and, 75–76, 93–94; proximity and, 63–71
Citizenship Act (1985), 42
"Clear Mirror of Bhutan, The ("Druk [Gi] Selwai Melong"), 57
colonialism, 18–19, 22, 35
critical events, 26, 39

Dagana, *xii*, 47–49
Dahal, Kailash, 46–47
Darjee, Sita Mothe, 39, 48
Darjeeling, *xiii*, 24–25
database, digital, 1–3, 62, 68–69, 83–84, 88, 94
democracy: Bhutan and, 19, 97–102, 112–13; despotism and, 119; India and Bhutanese, 80; powerholders and, 24; pro-democracy movements and, 37, 47, 58–59; proximity and, 56–60
despotism, 119–20
Deuba, Sher Bahadur, 66
Dhakal, Birendra, 60
Dhakal, Deo Narayan Sharma (D. N. S.), 23–30, 40, 65, 110, 133n31
Dhungel, Ganga, 51
Dhungel, Om, 61, 67, 79
Dhungel, Yadu (Y. P.), 33–35, 49–52, 121–22
diaspora: demographics and, 20–21; dissident organizations of, 83; distant, 12, 92, 96, 103–113; ecosystem of exile politics and, 116; life cycle of, 7, 30, 116; physical space and, 6–8, 117–19; refugee narratives and, 104; resettlement and, 95–96, 113. *See also* exodus of Bhutanese Nepalis
diaspora death, 7, 30, 116
Diaspora Entrepreneurs and Contested States (Koinova), 7–8
disappearances, 72, 73, 105–106
dissent, political, 24–28, 44, 59, 65, 119, 130n46. *See also* homeland activism
Dixit, Kanak Mani, 41, 57, 85–86
DNC (Druk National Congress), 55–59, 89, 102–3, 105, 136n8 (ch. 4)
DNC-D (Druk National Congress-Democratic), 89, 102
Dorji family, 23, 25, 57, 130n36
Dorji, Rinzin, 59, 153n25, 153n27
Dorji, Rongthong Kunley (R. K.), 55–56, 78–79, 84, 87, 89 (ch. 4)
Driglam Namzha (code of etiquette and dress), 38, 40
Drukpa (peoples), 18, 20–23, 31, 37–39, 47, 61, 122
Drukpa Kagyu tradition of Buddhism, 18, 20, 55
Dupthob, Karma, 79–80, 102, 105
Dzongkha language, x, 18, 20, 33, 38–39, 51, 67. *See also* Nepali language

Economist Intelligence Unit, 99–100
ecosystem of exile politics: as compared to physical ecosystems, 3, 5–6, 30–31, 115, 118–119; complexity of, 83–84; diversity of,
61; dormancy of, 30–31; growth of, 19, 25, 34; introduction to, 5–6; proximity and, 3–4, 71, 74; reconciliation and, 123; resettlement and, 92–97, 112–13, 118–19; state power and, 8–10; transnational activism and, 105–6, 115–16. *See also* precarity; proximity
exodus of Bhutanese Nepalis, 41, 49–52, 60, 114. *See also* Bhutanese Nepalis

Fernandes, George, 66, 79
Fourth World Conference on Women (Beijing), 3
fragmentation, organizational, 56–57, 85–89, 95, 115, 136n8 (ch. 4)
From Palace to Prison (Rizal), 135n85

Garganda, 45, 47
Gazmere, Ratan: *Bhutan: We Want Justice*, 44; refugee camp activism and, 62–65; refugee database and, 1, 3, 68–69, 83–84, 138n73; resettlement, on, 94
GCRPPB (Global Campaign for the Release of Political Prisoners in Bhutan), 106–7
Ghimire, Bhakta, 2, 62, 139n22 (ch. 5)
Giri, Balaram, 46–47
Giri, Nar Bahadur (N. B.), 66, 89–90
Global Forum on Refugees, 104
Goldhap Camp, *xiv*
Gorkhaland National Liberation Front (GNLF), 35, 37
Great Britain, colonial, 18–19, 22
Greater Nepal narrative, 35–37, 42, 80
Green Belt Proposal, 40–41
Gurung, Bikh Bahadur (B. B.), 26, 109
Gurung, Dal Bahadur (D. B.), 26–27
Gurung, Garjaman, 25–26

Himal Southasian (publication), 57, 85–86
Hindu festivals, 12, 38
Hindu religion, 12, 20, 38, 47, 133n31
Hindustan Times, 80
homeland activism: activities overview, 114–15; Bhutan, inside and outside, 41–49, 54–56; despotism and, 119–20; introduction to, 1–3; as lobbying powerholders, 65–67, 77–79; in midcentury Bhutan, 26–32; organizational fragmentation and, 88–89; physical space and, 6–8, 116–19; protection and, 121; proximity and, 53–65; refugee narratives and, 60; resettlement and, 94, 96–97; post-2008 activities, 102–13; student activism, 30, 43–49, 77–78; transnational

activism, 83, 116. *See also* Bhutanese Nepalis; political dissent; precarity; proximity
Human Rights Defenders, 12, 121
Human Rights Organization of Bhutan (HUROB), 13, 61, 72, 79
human rights violations, 15, 44–45, 47, 55, 57, 59–60
Human Rights Watch, 76, 101, 107

immunitary politics: in Bhutan, 31, 130n42; border porosity and, 32; ecosystem of exile politics and, 25; *immunitary dispositif*, 8–9, 19, 21, 24; violence and, 27–28
India:—Bhutan relations, 26–29, 35–37; Bhutanese Nepali exodus and, 41–42; British colonialism and, 18–19, 22; precarity and, 75–80; refugee marches and, 2, 64; support of activists, 66
India-Nepal Treaty of Peace and Friendship (1950), 75, 79
Indian National Congress, 27, 90
International Committee of the Red Cross, 105–6
International Organization for Migration (IOM), 12, 110

Jaigaon, *xiii*, 51, 64
Jai Gorkha, 26, 109, 131n59–60
Joint Ministerial Committee (JMC), 66–67, 70
Joint Verification Team (JVT), 69–71

Kakarbhitta, *xiii, xiv*, 44, 50, 64, 72, 73
Karki, Ram, 104, 106
Karma, Gomchen, 58–59
Kathmandu, 61, 65, 67, 82
Katwal, Nandalal, 87
Khanal, Hari, 68, 83
Khundunabari Camp, *xiv*, 70
Kinga, Sonam, 97–99
King of Bhutan, 2, 20, 24, 38, 41, 48–49, 52, 66, 130n46
Koirala, Girija Prasad, 27, 49, 135n105
Koirala, Matrika Prasad (M. P.), 25, 28
Kuensel (newspaper), 47, 59, 101

legal precarity, 74–76. *See also* precarity
Lhotshampa, as term, x, 20, 39. *See also* Bhutanese Nepalis
lobbying, 65–67, 77–79, 103–4, 108, 114–15. *See also* homeland activism

Mahat, Ram Sharan, 66, 84
Maidhar Camp, *xiv*, 75

marches, refugee, 2, 27–29, 47–49, 63–65, 72, 77
Marriage Act (1980), 39
Mechi Bridge, *xiii, xiv*, 65, 73, 77
migration, 4–5, 19–23
mobilization, 6, 10, 31–32, 96, 115, 116–17

Namgyal, Chogyal Palden Thondup, 36
narratives, refugee, 60, 97–99, 104, 109, 123
Nationality Law (1958), 21, 31
National Assembly of Bhutan, 29, 42, 45, 58, 97–99, 101
National Council for Social and Cultural Promotion (NCSCP), 34–35
National Refugee Coordination Unit (NUCRA), 83, 108
Nehru, Jawaharlal, 27–29
Nepal: Bhutanese Nepali exodus and, 41–42; Bhutanese Refugee Cultural Complex in, 110–12; border porosity and, 27, 32; democratization of, 56; Greater Nepal narrative and, 35–37; homeland, as adopted, 112–13, 117; immigration and, 23; lobbying of powerholders in, 114–15; maps of, *xi, xiii, xiv*; precarity and, 75–77, 80–85; refugee crisis and, 66–67; resettlement and, 93–94, 108–9
Nepali Congress, 27, 56, 135n105
Nepali language, 20, 38–39. *See also* Dzongkha language
Nepalis. *See* Bhutanese Nepalis
Ngalong (peoples), 20–21
Ngawang Namgyal (monk), 18, 20
ngolops (anti-nationals), 34, 47–49, 71–72
NIE (National Institute of Education), 44–45
nonviolence, 27–29, 64–65
Nyingmapa tradition of Buddhism, 55, 58, 102

Ogata, Sadako, 69
One Nation, One Policy, 38–39

Panchayat political system, 56, 80
Paper Citizens (Sadiq), 48–49
Penjore, Thinley, 56, 136n8 (ch. 4)
People's Forum on Human Rights (PFHR), 43–49, 88
Phuntsholing, *xii, xiii*, 50, 64, 75
physical space, 3, 5–6, 30–31, 115, 116–119
Pokhrel, Sushil, 46, 135n85
political dissent, 24–28, 44, 59, 65, 119, 130n46. *See also* homeland activism
political precarity, 77–78. *See also* precarity

porosity of borders: Greater Nepal narrative and, 35; Green Belt Proposal and, 40–41; precarity and, 74–75; proximity and, 31–32, 118; transnational activism and, 15, 45, 57; tripartite, 62, 72

Poudel, Balaram, 13–14, 48, 84

powerholders: activist access to, 90; Bhutanese Nepali political dissent and, 27–28; colonialism and, 18–19; corrupt government and, 57; democracy and, 24; distrust and, 52; ecosystem of exile politics and, 8–10; ethnic issues and, 55; human rights violations of, 59–60; lobbying of, 65–67, 77, 112; physical space and, 6–7; precarity and, 115; refugee database and, 83; resettlement and, 104; statistical knowledge and, 20. *See also* Bhutan; India; Nepal

Pradhan, Om, 40, 42, 48, 59

Pradhan, S. K., 88

precarity: Bhutan State Congress and, 31; in early India, 28–29; Joint Verification Team and, 71; legal, 74–76; mitigation of, 30; physical space and, 117–18; of place; 10, 74; political, 77–85; political dissent and, 25; proximity, relation to, 46, 74, 84, 120–21; refugee experience of, 9–10, 115; resettlement and, 93–97; social, 85–91. *See also* homeland activism; proximity

prisons and prisoners: in Bhutan, 43, 46, 55, 60, 87, 105–107, 122, 134n67, 135n85; in India, 2, 77

"Profile of the Torture Victims in the Prisons of Bhutan" (BRAVVE), 60

protection, 120–21, 147n22, 147n24

protest, public, 8–9, 28, 58–59, 63–65, 77, 102

proximity: border porosity and, 31–32, 62; citizenship and, 67–71; distrust and, 85–90; ecosystem of exile politics and, 3–4; homeland activism and, 53–65, 115; human rights and, 61–63, 69; physical space and, 117–18; precarity, relationship to, 46, 74, 84, 118, 120–21; public protest and, 63–66; resettlement and, 103, 105. *See also* precarity

Radio Pahichan, 109

Rai, Bhampa, 53–54, 67–68, 70, 88

Rai, Sahabir, 131n60

Raye, Dalamarden, 28

reconciliation, 121–22

Red Cross, 79, 105–6

refugee camps: Beldangi Camp, 69, 102–3, 106; governance of, 81, 84–85, 94; Khundunabari Camp, 70; Maidhar Camp, 75; map of, *xiv*; public protest at, 65; purpose in, collective, 60; refugee database and, 1; resource for protests, as, 67; Sanischare Camp, 145

Refugee Convention Relating to the Status of Refugees (1951), 21, 50, 129n28

refugee narratives, 60, 97–99, 104, 109, 123

Regmi, Bikash, 104

repatriation, 95–96

resettlement: ecosystem of exile politics, 93–97, 118–19; homeland activism and, 115; idea of homeland and, 108–9, 112–13; map of, *xv*; paradoxes of, 94–95, 110; proximity and, 102–5; reconciliation and, 122–23

Rights under Shadow (Bhutan Watch), 103

Rizal, Dhurba, 98

Rizal, Govinda, 64, 78, 106

Rizal, Tek Nath, 42–44, 46, 80–81, 84, 134n67, 135n85

Robinson, Mary, 69

routes, refugee, 8–9, 50–52

Royal Bhutan Army (RBA), 34, 36, 48, 66

Royal Semi-Authoritarian Democracy of Bhutan, The (Rizal), 98

SAARC (South Asian Association for Regional Cooperation), 58, 118

Sadiq, Kamal, 28, 48–49, 76

Samtse, x, *xiii*, 2, 22–23, 47–49

Sanischare Camp, *xiv*, 106

Sarpang, *xii*, 33, 47

satyagraha, 27–29, 65

Sengden, Baburam, 77

Sharchops (peoples), 20–21, 45, 55, 59, 135n78

Sharma, Ganesh Prasad (G. P.), 26–30

Sharma, Mangala, 2–3, 60, 96

Sharma, Narayan, 49

Sherubtse College, 33, 38, 44, 100

Sikkim (kingdom), *xiii*, 23, 25, 35–37

Sikkim: Requiem for a Himalayan Kingdom (Duff), 37

"The Silent Suffering in Bhutan" (DNC), 57

Singh, Hari Kishore, 80

Sinha, Awadhesh Coomar (A. C.), 19–20, 24–26, 31, 37, 40–41, 141n74

sites of homeland activism: in Australia, 2, 104, 106, 109, 122; in Europe, 3, 68–69, 83, 88, 104–106; in India, 4, 24–30, 43–47, 72, 77–81, 90–91, 106 (ch. 4); in Nepal, 27, 80–85, 88–91, 103, 106 (ch. 4); in South

Africa, 88; in the United States, 2, 65, 89, 96, 104–108, 122

social precarity, 85–91. *See also* precarity

sociospatial positionality, 7, 13–14

South Asia Analysis Group, 13

southern Bhutan, 35, 37–38, 40–43, 47–48, 62, 86. *See also* Bhutan

student activism, 30, 43–49, 77–78

Students Union of Bhutan (SUB), 44, 46–49

Subba, Bhim, 50

Subba, Harka Jung, 103, 144n68

Subba, R. P., 99

Subba, Suk Bahadur (S. B.), 72–73

Tendzin, Pema, 58

Timai Camp, *xiv*

transnational activism, 34, 45–46, 52, 105–7, 116–17. *See also* homeland activism

Tsirang, *xii*, 25, 33, 47, 49

UFD (United Front for Democracy), 78–79, 87–88

Unbecoming Citizens (Hutt), 10

UNHCR (United Nations High Commissioner for Refugees), 3, 65, 84–85, 93–94, 101–2, 115

United Nations High Commissioner for Human Rights, 106

United Nations Human Rights Council, 104

United Nations Working Group on Arbitrary Detention, 106

Voluntary Migration Forms (VMF), 67

Wangchuck, Jigme Dorji, 28–29

Wangchuck, Jigme Singye, 19, 97–99

Wangchuck, Ugyen, 19

women and children, 3, 43–44, 47, 60, 69–71, 81

www.ingramcontent.com/pod-product-compliance
Lightning Source LLC
Chambersburg PA
CBHW030846270326
41928CB00007B/1246